"William Hand's enthusiasm for food, life, and humor shine through the writing and keep readers engaged. This is a mouth-watering cookbook, inviting readers to join in and partake of the wide variety of dishes and in humor.... Hand in the Kitchen is a highly entertaining cookbook, full of stories and commentary with an emphasis on humor and a true gusto for food. The recipes cover a wide range, from old-fashioned American dishes using prepared foods such as canned onion rings and mushroom soup to more sophisticated and contemporary dishes using surprising combinations of fresh ingredients, as well as a variety of international cuisines."

Publishers Review

"It is obvious much care has gone into the presentation of this collection. It has the feel of one of those heirloom treasuries published from the past ... There are wonderful and tasty recipes, yes, but this is ultimately a collection of short stories that shares secrets from a delicious and remarkable life."

Shane Riggs
Author, Song of the Red Sparrow

Hand
•in the
Kitchen

A Collection of Culinary Columns, Concoctions, and Confections From California to the Classroom to the Kitchen

WILLIAM M. HAND

HAND IN THE KITCHEN
A COLLECTION OF CULINARY COLUMNS, CONCOCTIONS, AND CONFECTIONS FROM CALIFORNIA TO THE CLASSROOM TO THE KITCHEN

Cover Illustration by Drew Clark/ Drew by Design

Author Photo by Karen Morgan/Karen Morgan Photography

iUniverse books may be ordered through booksellers or by contacting:

iUniverse
1663 Liberty Drive
Bloomington, IN 47403
www.iuniverse.com
844-349-9409

ISBN: 978-1-6632-1463-8 (sc)
ISBN: 978-1-6632-1464-5 (hc)
ISBN: 978-1-6632-1462-1 (e)

Library of Congress Control Number: 2020924612

Print information available on the last page.

iUniverse rev. date: 12/22/2020

For Esther and Virginia

Introduction

Over my career as a writer, educator and editor, I have been asked to write letters of reference more times than I care to count. It's a perk of the profession. And I suppose it's always a big compliment when someone asks me to "put in a good word" or speak a kind word or 500 on his or her behalf.

This introduction to this fine cookbook and collection of culinary columns is by far the favorite "reference" I have ever given.

I have known the author of this cookbook for two decades. Very personally. But that is a story for another book and one that maybe I will author in the near future.

In February of 2001, shortly after Valentine's Day that year, I was working as the managing editor of a newspaper in North Canton, Ohio – right in the heartland of America. I was conducting one of our regular staff meetings and per usual we were – as it is called in the publishing world – brainstorming ideas for new stories and features that could appear in the publication. The newspaper already had a strong and lively "senior lifestyles" columnist and we had a passionate health and fitness columnist (who later went on to model for American Greetings – but again, that's a story for another book). We bounced some ideas off one another for other changes at the newspaper and then deferred a decision on what sort of column to add and what kind of person we should hire. We had all just returned from the Ohio Newspaper Association Awards in Columbus, where we'd swept most of the categories that year—including column writing—and so we all knew that any addition to the writing team would have to be someone who would be a great fit.

We kept the idea for a new column open as far as the subject matter was concerned and over the course of the next week or so, we introduced other plans and ideas we had for making the product not only a better looking paper but a more "user friendly" one too.

The following week – the new column – as a lucky twist of fate would have it – was picked for us. Our executive editor at that time came into the staff meeting and said that a reader survey we had been conducting online indicated the column the readers wanted most was one that would contain cooking tips and recipes. And then the editor turned to me and said "so, can you find us someone who can write that for us by the end of the week?"

I found someone by the end of the day. And I didn't have to look far. I left that staff meeting and that evening asked William Hand – who everyone calls Bill (or Billy, Mack or Buddy – but again, a story for another book) if he would be interested in coming on board and providing weekly tips and recipes. We decided to make it a bit easier to inspire what he could write about by inviting readers to submit culinary questions. And the readers responded.

That weekly column inspired three cookbooks inside of three years – two of which have become collectible Christmas items. I was then so impressed with Bill's work that I asked him to start writing the local restaurant reviews for us. And it wasn't long before his face – like those of other reporters at the now defunct Sun Journal newspaper – became recognized. He would be spotted out at events and people would stop him to ask questions or to tell him they tried his recipes. His boss at the restaurant where he worked at the time (the 356th Fighter Group near the Akron Canton Airport) cashed in on Bill's newfound notoriety and started putting Bill in his television commercials. A star was born.

But Bill had been fascinating long before newspaper readers discovered his column. He had worked in Hawaii, Hollywood, Ohio, and Maryland. He has made burgers for Madonna, catered parties for Wes Craven, exchanged recipes and rabbit ears with Donny Osmond, trained in Los Angeles, worked in the mess hall of a Navy Destroyer, has taught hundreds of college students, and has mentored countless others.

After a move to Maryland, I later founded Allegany Magazine in Cumberland and I again asked Bill if he would write for me. By now, Bill had moved into what would be a 15-year teaching position.

In addition to the magazine, Bill's columns now appear in more than a dozen publications nationally. He's gone from a humble Mom and Pop shop to a chain.

This cookbook marks an anniversary. As of February 2021, Chef Hand has now been a food writer and culinary columnist for two decades. And it's about time he put the best of his columns and recipes into one collection. And this is the collection you are holding in your … well…. Hand (excuse the pun).

Organized by month, week, and even occasion, this is a fun first-'hand' collection of columns featuring the wit, wisdom advice, humor and recipes from 20 years as a celebrated culinary contributor. This is not your typical cookbook. It does not have that "spiral" bound "fundraiser" look to it. It is obvious much care has gone into the presentation of this collection. Instead, this book has the classy presentation of one of those heirloom treasuries published from the past. This is also a deeply personal autobiography of a chef who has worked in some of the best places in the country, in the cities and small towns, for the rich and famous and those who direct soup kitchens and food banks. There are wonderful and tasty recipes, yes, but this is ultimately a collection of short stories that share secrets from a delicious and remarkable life.

Chef Hand does not have a show on the Food Network. He does not have a program produced by Oprah. At least not yet. But that actually works to his advantage. It keeps him approachable and personable. His life and his stories are ones that will surely inspire young culinary hopefuls. Not everyone is going to be the next Guy Fieri or Rachael Ray – most chefs will (like him) make their mark in local diners and fine establishments with strong loyal followings. And – if they get really lucky – they will enjoy a career as varied, as colorful, and as inspiring as Chef William Hand. I am excited to see what amazing chapter awaits him next!

Shane Riggs
Editor/Playwright/Journalist and Author
(Song of the Red Sparrow)

Preface

The strangest thing happened to me in 2020.

I was sitting on my couch, watching a show on Netflix – you know the one – about the wealthy people forced to go live in a small town motel. It was early summer. My dog was at my feet and my cat was in my lap. And I felt a weird twitch in my face. It was almost like a spasm, like my face had tightened below my nose and above my chin.

And for a moment I was a little freaked out and then I figured out what it was – it was a smile.

I realized then that I had been unhappy for quite some time. I mean, think about that – I had not genuinely or authentically smiled in so long that when I did, it caught me off guard and I thought I was suffering from a sudden medical condition.

Earlier in 2020 and before the pandemic, my kitchen at home was remodeled (thanks, Jared, Eric and Dylan). A wall between the kitchen and dining room was removed and the floor plan rearranged that made the space feel a lot more open. I remember standing in that newly remodeled kitchen and something felt incomplete. And for a chef to stand in a new kitchen and feel unfulfilled – well, let's just say that's not a good thing. And then I knew what that incomplete thing was – it was me.

And so during the COVID inspired lockdown, I started doing some real soul searching. Who was I, where was I, and where did I want life to next take me? And why did standing in a new kitchen make me feel unsettled?

After a very enriching and rewarding career in education for 15 years – with the classrooms now shuttered – I knew this was the time of change. If ever there was a time to hit the reset button, the year 2020 was it. Don't you think? And so I returned to my first and true love – cooking. I've always considered myself more of a laborer. "Just tell me what to do and I will do it." And so to get back into a restaurant kitchen as "just the chef" who is preparing meals to make hungry people happy was something I really had a desire to do. I simply went "home" – and for me, I am at home when I'm working in a restaurant's kitchen.

And once I made that move, I felt like the old Bill again – one I had somehow lost years earlier. And that's when I felt that smile.

Out of that experience, I was also approached about publishing my own cookbook – this cookbook you are holding in your hot little hands right now – a collection of 20 years' worth of columns and stories written for several publications over the last two decades and so I decided to accept that offer and here we are. And I am looking forward to seeing many of you out on a (at least for a while socially distanced) book tour I am supposed to start soon.

As I enter this reboot and this exciting my scary second chapter, welcome to the next few chapters of this new book. I do hope you enjoy it. It's full of memories, menus, and me. And like the subtitle says – it's a collection of culinary columns, concoctions, and confections

2020 certainly was the year it promised to be. It brought much into focus and made everything a lot clearer. It was also the year that we all had to find ways to turn lemons into lemonade – or in this case – lemon cheesecake cookies!

Enjoy!

William Hand
December, 2020

Bill's Lemon Cheesecake Cookies

1 cup butter, softened
3 ounces cream cheese, softened
1 cup sugar
1 egg
1 tsp grated lemon peel
1 tbs lemon juice
1 ½ cups flour
1 tsp baking powder

Cream butter, cheese and sugar until fluffy. Blend in remaining ingredients. Cover and chill for one hour. Preheat oven to 375 degrees. Fill cookie press with ¼ of dough at aa time. Form desired shapes on ungreased cookie sheet. Bake for 8-10 minutes or until edges are slightly browned.

Hand in the Kitchen
Let's Get Cooking!

Menu

JANUARY

Quiche me once,
Quiche me twice

An egg-sellent reason to celebrate

The very first culinary column I ever wrote – ever – was twenty years ago – for the Sun Journal newspaper in North Canton, Ohio. I had no idea how to start writing a column so I asked the editor if he could allow readers of the newspaper to submit questions that I could answer. I thought maybe that would help guide me in ideas for stories and columns every month

And to my surprise, in February 2001, this became a gig I was asked to continue on a regular basis. And by some twist of fate, it has continued now for two decades.

My anonymity was all over all that point. People started to recognize me when I was around town. Local restaurants thought I was there to review them or to steal from their menus. In some places it got me star and special treatment while in others, it caused some anxiety in the wait staff. I remember once a waiter asked if someone else could take my table because he was too worried about messing up and making his employer look bad.

"Hey Bill," people I didn't know would shout at me. "How about a column next month on soup! Or recipes with only five ingredients!"

I didn't need to receive emails through the newspaper or the editor. I started getting them at work. I was approached then and I get approached now when I dine out locally. It's not odd for the owner or a manager of a restaurant to walk over to my table and say "It's pretty intimidating to know when a food writer is in the building." But, hey, I'm just there to eat like everyone else. Most times.

And I remember the time I did get a letter from a lady who said "your column last month included a recipe for chocolate walnut cake. I made the cake like you said but realized no where in the directions did you tell me when to add the nuts. I realized this after the cake was in the oven. The cup of nuts was still on the countertop. So I just ate the walnuts while I waited for the cake to bake and it turned out fine without them."

I learned then to double check and triple check my directions.

I really didn't see myself becoming the Carrie Bradshaw of the culinary world – but my first column ever was aptly titled – *Eggs in the City*. Hey, what can I say? Remember, my very first cooking column first appeared in 2001? And to my credit, the show was the big thing on television that year so it made sense.

And so, all these years later, as I sit at my laptop and look out my window I can't help but wonder, does the advice from 20 years ago still hold up? Or is the yolk on me?

Let's find out with a repeat of that first ever "egg-sellent" question.

"Without looking at the expiration date, how can you tell if an egg has gone bad?"

Over Easy

Here are ten "hard boiled" facts about the "incredible edible" egg that won't leave you scrambled!

- To tell if an egg is raw or hard-cooked, spin it! If the egg spins easily, it is hard-cooked but if it wobbles, it is raw.
- Egg yolks are one of the few foods that are a naturally good source of Vitamin D.
- If an egg is accidentally dropped on the floor, sprinkle it heavily with salt for easy clean up.
- The "brightness of the yellow" of the yolk depends on the diet of the hen.

- Eggs age more in one day at room temperature than in one week in the refrigerator.
- Hens don't need a rooster to lay eggs. They need the rooster to fertilize the egg.
- Egg protein has just the right mix of essential amino acids needed by humans to build tissues. It is second only to mother's milk for human nutrition.
- An average hen lays 300 to 325 eggs a year.
- As a hen grows older she produces larger eggs.
- The fastest omelet maker in the world – Howard Helmer – made 427 two-egg omelets in 30 minutes. Mr. Helmer holds three Guinness World Records for omelet making.

Oh..and the answer to "how do you know if an egg has gone bad?" If you put the egg in a mug of cold water and it sinks, it's still good. If it floats to the top, throw it away. What spoils an egg, you see, is air. When air develops between the shell and the "meat" the egg rots. When enough air gets inside the egg, the egg becomes buoyant. Bouyant = bad.

Pizza Quiche

1 9" pie crust
3 cups shredded mozzarella cheese
2 cups shredded cheddar cheese
1/2 cup sliced pepperoni pieces
4 ounces mushrooms, drained
1/2 cup finely chopped onion
2 cloves, garlic, minced
1 tbs. olive oil
3/4 cups milk
2 eggs
1 tsp. dried Italian seasoning

Preheat oven to 400 degrees. Sprinkle cheeses in bottom of pie crust. Top with pepperoni and mushrooms. In a heavy skillet, cook onion and garlic in olive oil until crisp and tender. Sprinkle over mushrooms. Beat together milk, eggs, Italian seasoning and garlic in medium bowl and pour over mushrooms. Bake at 400 degrees for 40-45 minutes or until knife inserted near center of pie comes out clean. Let stand 15 minutes before cutting.

Crab Quiche

1 9" pie crust
1/2 cup mayonnaise
2 tablespoons of all purpose flour
2 eggs, beaten
1/2 cup of milk
2 cans (6 ounces each) flaked crabmeat, drained
1/3 cup of chopped green onions
1 tablespoon finely chopped parsley
2 cups shredded swiss cheese

In a mixing bowl, combine mayo, four, eggs and milk. Stir in crab, onion, parsley and cheese. Spoon into the pie shell. Bake at 350 degrees for one hour.

BACON AND EGGS BREAKFAST QUICHE

1 9" refrigerated pie crust, softened
1 cup half-and-half or milk
4 eggs, slightly beaten
1/4 teaspoon salt
1/4 teaspoon pepper
8 slices bacon, crisply cooked, crumbled
1 cup shredded Swiss or Cheddar cheese
1/4 cup grated Parmesan cheese
1 tablespoon chopped onion, if desired

Heat oven to 350 degrees. In medium bowl, mix half-and-half, eggs, salt and pepper; set aside. Layer bacon, cheeses and onion in crust-lined plate. Pour egg mixture over top. Bake 40 to 50 minutes or until knife inserted in center comes out clean. Let stand 5 minutes; cut into wedges.

INDIVIDUAL TOMATO AND CHEESE QUICHE

Nonstick cooking spray
1/2 teaspoon olive oil
1 leek, cleaned and finely chopped
1 cup shredded reduced-fat Cheddar cheese, divided
1 cup milk
1 egg
1/3 cup sun-dried tomatoes, plus additional for garnish
1/2 teaspoon fresh or dried thyme

Preheat oven to 350 degrees. Lightly spray a 12-cup muffin pan with the cooking spray. Heat oil in a small skillet over medium heat. Cook leeks until softened, stirring frequently, about 5 minutes. Divide leeks among muffin cups and top with 2/3 cup of Cheddar cheese. Blend milk, egg, sun-dried tomatoes and thyme in a blender or food processor for about 20 seconds or until tomato is minced. Pour mixture over cheese in muffin cups and top each with remaining cheese. Bake 30 minutes or until tops and edges are browned. Cool in pan for 3 minutes; serve warm or cold. Top with additional pieces of sun-dried tomato, if desired.

QUICHE LORRAINE

1 9" pie crust
8 slices bacon, crisply cooked, crumbled
1 cup shredded Swiss or Cheddar cheese
1/3 cup finely chopped onion
4 large eggs
2 cups whipping cream or half-and-half
1/4 teaspoon salt
1/4 teaspoon pepper
1/8 teaspoon ground red pepper

Sprinkle bacon, cheese and onion in pie crust. In medium bowl, beat eggs slightly; beat in remaining filling ingredients. Pour into quiche dish. Bake 45 to 50 minutes.

The Pasta-bilities of
New Beginnings

Using your Noodle in a New Year

Remember as a kid when a bowl of pasta came from a can with a chef on it? Or your Mom whipped up some mac and cheese from that blue box?

As you have grown up, so – I hope – have your taste buds. If your appetite, however, has not graduated beyond SpaghettiOs, than this chapter is for you. (But I will admit, now and again I do still crave the Spaghetti-Os – it's the alphabet pasta I think!)

Pasta literally comes in hundreds of shapes and sizes. Examples include spaghetti (thin rods), maccheroni (tubes or cylinders), fusilli (swirls), and lasagna (sheets). Gnocchi and spätzle are sometimes considered pasta. Pasta is categorized in two basic styles: dried and fresh. Dried pasta is generally made without egg and can be stored for up to two years, Fresh pasta will keep for a few days under refrigeration. Most pasta is cooked by boiling and then drained in a strainer.

The word "pasta" comes from the Italian for "pastry cake." Pasta…pastry… see the connection there? And here is the difference – doughy pastries are usually fried and sprinkled with sugar. But, get this – that same dough can be cut and shaped into noodles, boiled and salted. If you can make a basic dough, you can learn to make fresh pasta.

Pasta is usually cooked to what is called "al dente" (to the bite) so that each bite of pasta should be firm to the bite and not too soft.

While many different cultures ate some sort noodle-like food, composed mostly of grain, the key characteristics of pasta are durum wheat semolina, with high gluten content. Pasta is also made in a way that allows dough to be highly "malleable," (that's a fancy culinary term for "can be shaped into many things).

The familiar legend of Marco Polo importing pasta from China originated with the Macaroni Journal, published by an association of food industries with the goal of promoting the use of pasta in the United States. But did you know "pasta" may have originated by Arabic nations during their conquest of Sicily in the late 7th century? And one of the first notations of eating pasta may go as far back as 1BC when philosopher Horace writes of eating "fine sheets of dough" and in that same century, Athenaeus of Naucratis provides a recipe that became the ancestor of a popular dish still served today.

Anthenaeus used lemon juice, lettuce, and olive oil between layered sheets of pasta and then baked it in a deep dish. By the 15th century, the dish is finally named "lasagna" for the first time.

HOMEMADE PASTA

2 Cups flour
2 Eggs
1 Tbsp. olive oil
4 Tbsp. water

Add all ingredients in food processor. Process until mixture starts to form a ball. Wrap ball in plastic wrap and let rest for about an hour. Then make your pasta using a pasta machine or rolling out by hand.

SPAGHETTI ALLA CARBONARA

4 tbsp. extra-virgin olive oil
4 oz. thinly sliced guanciale or pancetta cut into 1/2" pieces
2 tsp. freshly cracked black pepper
1 3/4 cups finely grated Parmesan
1 egg plus 3 yolks
Salt to taste
1 lb. spaghetti

Heat oil in a skillet over medium heat. Add guanciale and cook, stirring occasionally, until lightly browned, 6–8 minutes. Add pepper and cook, stirring occasionally, until fragrant, 2 minutes more. Transfer guanciale mixture to a large bowl and let cool slightly; stir in 1 1/2 cups Parmesan and egg and yolks and stir to combine; set aside. Meanwhile, bring a 6-qt. pot of salted water to a boil. Add pasta; cook until al dente, 8–10 minutes. Reserve 3/4 cup water; drain pasta and transfer it to guanciale mixture. Toss, adding pasta water a little at a time to make a creamy sauce. Season with salt and pepper; serve with remaining Parmesan.

Pasta Di Pollo Al Suga Bianco

1/2 stick butter
1/2 cup red onions, diced
1/2 cup pancetta (Italian smoked bacon), drained and chopped
1 tbsp. garlic, chopped
3/4 cup green onion, tops only
3/4 lb. sliced grilled chicken
2 lb. bow-tie pasta, cooked
8 oz. heavy whipping cream
1 tbsp. chopped parsley

Sauté red onion in butter for a few seconds then add pancetta and garlic. Add chicken, green onions and pasta. Deglaze the pan with the cream. Add asiago sauce (see Sauce recipes).

Gamberetti E Noci Di Pino

24 jumbo shrimp peeled, deveined
3 cups washed, 1/4"-thick-sliced mushrooms
1 1/2 tablespoons roasted pine nuts
6 handfuls fresh spinach leaves
6 cups cooked vermicelli pasta
4 tablespoons butter
2 tablespoons minced fresh garlic

Preheat oven to 350 degrees. Wash spinach and remove stems before drying leaves between paper towels. Set aside. Spread pine nuts over bottom of sheet pan and place pan in oven on top rack. Roast until golden brown, approximately 2 to 4 minutes. Remove from oven and set aside. Peel and devein shrimp. Set aside. Wash and slice fresh mushrooms. Set aside. Boil pasta in large pot of water to al dente stage according to directions on package. Set aside.

Cacio e Pepe Pasta

2 pounds dried spaghetti
3 1/2 cups Pecorino Romano cheese, finely grated.
6 tablespoons unsalted butter 3/4 stick, cut into tablespoon-size pieces
2 teaspoons coarsely ground black pepper

Bring a large pot of heavily salted water to a boil over high heat. Add pasta and cook according to package directions. Drain pasta, reserving 2 cups of the cooking water. Return pasta and cooking water to the pot and place over low heat. Add remaining ingredients and stir until cheese and butter have melted and formed a creamy sauce, about 5 minutes. Season with salt, and serve with additional cheese if desired.

Hitting the Sauce

Basic Tomato Sauce with Onion and Butter Recipe

One 28-ounce can whole plum tomatoes
5 tablespoons salted butter
1 medium yellow onion, peeled and halved

Heat a heavy, medium saucepan over medium heat. Add all of the ingredients and bring to a simmer. Turn the heat to low to keep a steady simmer. Cook for 45 minutes, or until droplets of fat float free of the tomatoes. Stir occasionally. Discard the onion. Serve over cooked pasta. Just about anything can be added to this sauce to create your own signature pasta dish. For example, add cooked shrimp or chicken. Toss in lightly pre-cooked vegetables such as broccoli, asparagus, peas, carrots, mushrooms, add in spices like oregano, thyme and even rosemary – whatever your taste buds would like.

Alfredo sauce

1 cup butter
1 ¾ cup heavy cream
2 cups parmesan cheese grated
½ tsp. salt
Dash pepper

Heat butter and cream in a saucepan until butter is melted. Remove from heat. Add 1 ¾ cup parmesan, salt and pepper and stir until sauce is blended and fairly smooth. Add to drained cooked pasta and toss until noodles are well coated. Sprinkle pasta with remaining parmesan.

Asiago sauce

4 cups heavy whipping cream
1/8 tsp. paste or dried chicken base
1 1/4 cup asiago cheese
1 tbsp. cornstarch
2 oz water

Heat cream to very hot and just bubbly (but not a boil). Add chicken base and cheese. Stir constantly with a wire whisk and bring temperature back to just bubbly. Dissolve cornstarch in the cold water and add to sauce. Bring to a slow simmer to cook out starch. Transfer sauce to a container, cover and refrigerate until needed.

Pasta al Pesto

2 cups fresh basil leaves
2 cloves garlic
¼ cup pine nuts or walnuts
1 tbsp. olive oil
½ -3/4 cups grated parmesan cheese

Place ingredients in a food processor or blender. Process until smooth, using a rubber spatula to push down the sides occasionally. Use the sauce soon as it will darken in color over time.

3 Pasta Tips

1. Toast your black pepper: Crush whole black peppercorns in a mortar and pestle or grind them on the coarsest setting in a spice grinder. Then "toast" the cracked pepper by frying it in the olive oil you'll be using for the pasta sauce, heating it until it smells very fragrant.
2. Finish your pasta in the sauce: Here's a case where undercooking is the right thing to do. Boil your pasta until it's just short of al dente, then finish cooking it in the hot pan or skillet containing your sauce, tossing the pasta and the sauce together vigorously. This technique will cause the sauce to coat the pasta more thoroughly.
3. Reserve some of your pasta water: Adding a ¼ cup of salty, starchy pasta water to the pasta and the sauce as you toss them together will moisten your sauce and add an additional layer of flavor and body to the final dish

The Five Healthiest Winter Foods You Should Be Eating

Stay healthy and happy in the New Year with ingredients that are in season for a reason!

The first month of the year doesn't need to be a month where you stress over meal time preparation. There's a reason why your favorite restaurant offers soup and salad combinations. They are easy. But they also contain key ingredients in the winter time designed to keep your system in check and to keep you healthy and happy until spring. This is the time of year when root vegetables are in season – things like sweet potatoes, parsnips, carrots and radishes. And other ingredients like butter beans, black beans, black eyed peas, chickpeas, onions and cabbage are hearty choices. And citrus like blood oranges and grapefruits can be found. Want to start your brand new year off with a healthy balance and some quick and satisfying dishes? Here are the five healthiest winter foods you should be eating… starting now!

1) Pomegranates

Chances are you've already tasted pomegranate juice. And there's science behind it. Pomegranate juice is rich in antioxidants (more so than other fruit juices)—just a cup daily might help keep free radicals from oxidizing. Drinking pomegranate juice might also improve blood flow to the heart.

2) Dark Leafy Greens

Dark leafy greens, such as kale, chard and collards, thrive in the chill of winter. In fact, a frost can take away a lot of kale's bitterness. Dark leafy greens are rich in vitamins A, C and K.

3) Citrus

Citrus fruits, including lemons, limes, oranges and grapefruit, are at their best this time of year and can actually add some nice color to a winter plate. Citrus fruits are loaded with vitamin C—one medium orange delivers more than 100 percent of your daily dose. And when you're fighting off cold and flu season, that's a good thing.

4) Potatoes

Potatoes can sometimes get lumped (pun intended) in with starches like white rice or white bread and some health nuts will say if you want to stick to your "diet" resolution, lay off white starches. But potatoes are a whole food that contain several beneficial nutrients. They are an excellent source of two immunity boosters—vitamins C and B6. And they are a great source of fiber. Look for purple potatoes this time of year (yes, they exist) – they're rich in an antioxidant that has been reported to lower cancer and heart disease risk.

5) Winter Squash

One cup of cooked winter squash has few calories but is high in both vitamins A and C, as well as being a good source of vitamins B6 and K, potassium and folate.

Just for the Health of It

NATURAL HEALING FOODS

Here are some reported or widely held believed foods that help provide relief and in some cases purported cures for the ailments listed. As always check with your doctor before adding any natural supplements or foods to your regular diet.

Acne/Pimples: Cucumber Juice (apply on face), Lime, Lemon
Arthritis: Apple, Banana, Mango, Cucumber, Garlic
Asthma: Garlic
Cancer: Carrot, Garlic, Lime, Lemon. Flaxseeds
Cholera: Bitter Gourd (Karela),Coconut water, Cucumber, Onions
Cold and Cough: Garlic, Ginger, Lime, Lemon
Constipation: Almonds, Cabbage, Carrot, Cucumber, Lime, Lettuce, Banana
Heart Disease: Cabbage, Carrot, Honey, Apple, Asparagus, Oranges, Grapes, Grapefruit
Hemorrhoids: Figs, Onions, Radish, Lime
High Blood Pressure: Apple, Banana, Garlic, Lime, lemon, oats, Onions,
High Cholesterol: Apple, Garlic, Grapefruit, Lime, Lemon, Oats, Sunflower seeds
Impotency: Almonds, Black gram (Urad Dal)
Kidney Stones: Apple, Cranberry, Tomatoes
Peptic Ulcer: Lime
Prostate Health: Broccoli, Green Tea, Pomegranate, Turmeric

Winter Salad with Kale and Pomegranate

10-12 big leaves of kale
1 pomegranate
2 apples
3/4 cup almonds
2 Tbsp. red wine balsamic
1 tbsp. honey
For the dressing:
3 tbsp. red wine balsamic or a cherry vinegar
3 tbsp. olive oil
1 tsp honey
1 tsp Dijon mustard
Salt and pepper to taste

Heat a pan and dry roast the almonds for 1-2 minutes. Add the balsamic and as soon as it is gone add the honey and stir for 1 minute. Transfer almonds to a baking sheet and let them cool. Afterwards chop them coarsely. Wash and dry the kale. Remove the stems and use a food processor or mini chopper to chop the kale into a very fine texture. You can use a sharp knife. Prepare the pomegranate and cut the apple into thin slices and mix all of it with the kale. Make the dressing by stirring everything thoroughly together and season to taste. Stir everything together and serve.

Warm Mushroom Salad with Bacon Vinaigrette

1/2 cup extra-virgin olive oil
1/2 cup vegetable oil
1 head of garlic, cloves crushed but not peeled
1 pound mixed wild mushrooms.
Salt and freshly ground pepper
3/4 cup pecans
1/2 pound thickly sliced bacon, cut crosswise into 1/4-inch strips
1 leek, white and tender green parts, thinly sliced
1/2 cup cider vinegar
1 teaspoon molasses
1 teaspoon fresh lemon juice

6 ounces sturdy dark greens
3 ounces cold fresh goat cheese, crumbled

Preheat the oven to 425. In a saucepan, bring both oils to a simmer with the garlic. Cook over low heat for about 15 minutes. Strain the oil and discard the garlic. In a large bowl, toss the mushrooms with 6 tablespoons of the garlic oil and season with salt and pepper. (Reserve the remaining garlic oil for later use.) Spread the mushrooms in a baking pan and roast for 35 minutes, stirring once or twice, until crisp and golden. Spread the pecans in a pie plate and toast for 7 minutes, until fragrant. Let cool. In a large skillet, cook the bacon over moderately low heat, stirring frequently, until crisp, about 8 minutes. Using a slotted spoon, transfer the bacon to a paper towel–lined plate. Strain the fat into a heatproof bowl and return half of it to the skillet. Add the leek to the skillet and cook over moderately low heat until softened, about 6 minutes. Add the vinegar and simmer until reduced to 3 tablespoons, about 5 minutes. Remove from the heat and whisk in the molasses, lemon juice and the remaining bacon fat. In a large bowl, toss the greens with the vinaigrette, mushrooms and pecans. Season with salt and pepper and toss again. Sprinkle with the bacon and goat cheese and serve.

BEET SALAD WITH MISO AND BLACK SESAME

6 small beets, scrubbed and divided
3 tablespoons olive oil, divided
Salt and freshly ground black pepper
¼ cup white miso
2 tablespoons rice wine vinegar
1 bunch watercress, trimmed
1 teaspoon black sesame seeds or toasted white sesame seeds

Preheat oven to 400°. Place 4 beets on a large piece of foil and rub with 1 tbsp. oil; season with salt and pepper and close up foil around beets. Place on a rimmed baking sheet and roast until tender, 30–40 minutes. Unwrap beets and let cool slightly. Peel and cut into ½" wedges. Meanwhile, whisk miso, vinegar, remaining 2 tbsp. oil, and 3 tbsp. water in a small bowl. Set dressing aside. Thinly slice remaining 2 raw beets. Arrange watercress and roasted and raw beets on a platter and drizzle with reserved dressing; top with sesame seeds.

HERBED CARROT SOUP

2 lbs. carrots
1 medium potato
1 tbsp olive oil
1 medium yellow onion
1 clove garlic
2 tbsp fresh basil
1 tbsp fresh oregano
1 tbsp fresh thyme
Juice of 1/2 lemon (1-2 tablespoons)
Salt and pepper to taste

Peel and chop the carrots and potato into 1-inch chunks and place into a pot with 5-6 cups water. Bring to a boil over high heat, then reduce the heat to medium, cover and simmer for 20 or so minutes, until vegetables are tender and easily pierced with a fork. Remove from heat and set aside. In a small saucepan, heat up the olive oil over medium heat and add onions. Sauté for a few minutes, until soft and translucent. Add garlic and fresh herbs and continue cooking for another minute or so, stirring frequently, until garlic is fragrant and herbs are wilted. Combine the vegetables and cooking liquid, plus the onion mixture, plus the lemon juice, in a blender or food processor and blend until smooth. Season to taste with salt and pepper and return to the pot to reheat, stirring frequently, over medium heat. Serve hot.

LEEK AND GARLIC SOUP

2 leeks
2 whole garlic bulbs
1 cup of chicken stock
4 medium sized potatoes
½ cup sour cream, plus more to garnish
1 tbsp butter
Olive oil
Salt

Pre-heat oven to 200. Remove the 'tops' of the bulbs of garlic to expose the clove inside. Drizzle with olive oil, wrap in aluminum foil and place in the oven for 30 minutes. Remove, allow to cool and, with a firm hold of the base of the bulb, squeeze the soft, caramelized garlic into a small bowl. Remove the darkest green leaves from the leeks. Slice the stalks in half and wash well and then finely chop into small pieces. Peel potatoes and roughly chop into cubes. Heat butter and a drizzle of olive oil in a large pot. Add chopped leeks and stir until softened. Add the chicken stock, potatoes, garlic and a teaspoon of salt. Combine, bring to the boil then reduce heat to medium. Cover and allow to simmer for 30 minutes or until the vegetables have softened significantly. In batches, pour the soup into a blender and process until smooth. Return to the pot on low heat and add cream. Add a dollop of sour cream when serving

Organic Santa Barbara Greens Salad With a Hazelnut Vinaigrette dressing

1/2 cup Champagne vinegar
1 tablespoon Dijon mustard
1 shallot, minced
2 cloves garlic, minced
1 cup hazelnut oil
Salt
Pepper

For the salad:

12 ounces mixed field greens
1 bunch green asparagus, grilled then diced into 1-inch long pieces
1 sweet white onion, sliced thin
1 cup crushed hazelnuts

For the dressing:

Whisk all ingredients except hazelnut oil together. While whisking, slowly drizzle in hazelnut oil. Season with salt and pepper, to taste. Set aside until ready to serve salad.

Prepare the salad: When ready to serve toss greens, asparagus and vinaigrette together, seasoning with salt and pepper. Place a generous handful on each salad plate, top greens with onions and sprinkle with hazelnuts.

OATMEAL COOKIE PANCAKES

1 cup old fashioned oats
1 cup all-purpose flour
1/2 cup brown sugar
2 tsp baking powder
1/2 tsp baking soda
1 tsp ground cinnamon
2 ounces, 1/4 cup, chopped walnuts
3/4 cup sour cream
3/4 cup whole milk
2 large eggs
1 tsp vanilla extract
2 really ripe bananas, mashed up
3/4 cup raisins
1/2 stick butter, 1/4 cup, melted, plus additional for buttering skillet
Honey, for drizzling

Mix the dry ingredients in a bowl. In a another bowl, mix the wet ingredients. Whisk the wet ingredients into the dry until just combined, then fold in the mashed up bananas and the raisins. Stir in the melted butter. Heat a griddle over medium heat and brush with additional melted butter. Cook pancakes, each about 1/3 cup, until bubbles form on the top, then turn. Cakes will cook in about 2 minutes on each side. Serve with drizzled honey over the top.

LEMON BERRY SWIRL

4 cups oats (not quick-cook or instant)
1 1/2 cups whole almonds, shelled, but skin still on
1/2 cup flax seeds

1/2 cup light brown sugar
1/2 tsp salt
1/2 tsp ground cinnamon
1/4 cup neutral cooking oil (canola)
1/4 cup honey
1 tsp vanilla extract
1 1/2 cups raisins or dried cranberries
1 cup diced dried apricots
1/2 cup dried banana slices

Preheat oven to 300 degrees F. Mix oats, almonds, flax seeds, brown sugar, salt and cinnamon in a bowl. In a saucepan warm the oil and honey. Whisk in the vanilla extract. Pour the honey, oil, vanilla mixture over the oat mixture and mix gently, but well. Mix with spatula and eventually your hands. Spread out onto a sheet pan and bake for 40 minutes (stir after the first 20). Cool and break up any clumps. Mix in dried fruit.

Yogurt Parfait

3 cups mixed berries (any combination, strawberries, blueberries, raspberries, blackberries) frozen
1/4 cup confectioners' sugar
1 lemon, juiced
1 1/2 cups low-fat vanilla yogurt
1/2 tsp lemon zest
1 tbsp lemon juice

Add berries, lemon juice and confectioners' sugar in a pan over medium heat. Cook until the berries break down and mixture becomes syrupy, 10 to 12 minutes. Set aside to cool.

Combine the yogurt, zest and juice in a mixing bowl and stir. To serve, set up glasses and layer with granola, yogurt and berries

Cooking on a Budget 101

Start the New Year with New Menus…all under $10 each.

I know, I know…when you watch those cooking shows on weekends – or even explore cookbooks in the local bookstores – all those fancy meals and ga-gillion recipes can make cooking seem a bit overwhelming. And when you venture out into the grocery store to actually buy the items you saw on those shows to recreate those culinary masterpieces, it can get costly and confusing.

But let me tell you a little secret – making dinner in your own kitchen should not be expensive. The reason you cook at home is to save money, right? Eating at a restaurant is still a special occasion but eating at home can be too.

Family dinners are making a comeback. And there is a reason for this – not only are families gathering more around the evening meal, it has become a time to put down the cell phones, unplug, pull away from the TV or the computer and reconnect. If 2020 taught us anything, it coaxed us back into being creative in the kitchen – on a dime.

Eating at home is also a great way to watch your money. Think about this – if you only dine out once a week, dinner for just two can easily cost $50. That adds up to $200 a month. Just for two people. Now add two or three more family members to that budget and you get the idea.

But think how much further your dollar will go on groceries! I'm not saying never go to a restaurant. You should. I work at one and how else will I see you in person? Knowing this is the month where you are probably catching up on holiday bills and making a resolution to be more thrifty, it's also a good reminder that your meals at home don't have to suffer from a skinny wallet.

All of the meals in this chapter can be made at home for less than $10 – a meal. For a family of four, that's $2.50 per person – before tip – and yes, tip. Please remember to tip. But more on that later in this book.

Southwest Chicken

1 tbsp vegetable oil
4 skinless, boneless chicken breast halves
1 (10 ounce) can diced tomatoes with green Chile peppers
1 (15 ounce) can black beans, rinsed and drained
1 (8.75 ounce) can whole kernel corn, drained
1 pinch ground cumin

In a large skillet, heat oil over medium high heat. Brown chicken breasts on both sides. Add tomatoes with green Chile peppers, beans and corn. Reduce heat and let simmer for 25 to 30 minutes or until chicken is cooked through and juices run clear. Add a dash of cumin and serve.

Grilled Sausage with Potatoes and Green Beans

3/4 pound fresh green beans, trimmed and halved
1/2 pound red potatoes, quartered
1 large onion, sliced
1 pound smoked sausage, cut into 1 inch pieces
1 tsp salt
1 tsp ground black pepper
1 tsp vegetable oil
1 tsp butter
1/3 cup water

Preheat an outdoor grill for high heat. On a large sheet of foil, place the green beans, red potatoes, onion, and sausage. Season with salt and pepper, sprinkle with oil, and top with butter. Tightly seal foil around the ingredients, leaving only a small opening. Pour water into the opening, and seal. Place foil packet on the prepared grill. Cook 20 to 30 minutes, turning once, until sausage is browned and vegetables are tender.

BAKED ZITI

1 (16 ounce) package ziti pasta
24 ounces ricotta cheese
1 pound shredded mozzarella cheese
1 egg, beaten
1 (32 ounce) jar spaghetti sauce
1/4 cup grated Parmesan cheese

Bring a large pot of lightly salted water to a boil. Add ziti and cook for 8 to 10 minutes or until al dente; drain and rinse. In a medium bowl, mix ziti, ricotta cheese, mozzarella cheese, egg and 1 1/2 cups spaghetti sauce. Preheat oven to 375 degrees. Lightly grease a 9x13 inch baking dish and spoon in ziti mixture. Top with remaining spaghetti sauce, followed by Parmesan cheese. Bake in preheated oven for 30 minutes; let stand for 15 minutes before serving.

CHINESE CHICKEN FRIED RICE

1 egg
1 tbsp on water
1 tbsp butter
1 tbsp vegetable oil
1 onion, chopped
2 cups cooked white rice, cold
2 tbsp soy sauce
1 tsp ground black pepper
1 cup cooked, chopped chicken meat

In a small bowl, beat egg with water. Melt butter in a large skillet over medium low heat. Add egg and leave flat for 1 to 2 minutes. Remove from skillet and cut into shreds. Heat oil in same skillet; add onion and sauté until soft. Then add rice, soy sauce, pepper and chicken. Stir fry together for about 5 minutes, then stir in egg. Serve hot.

Penne Pasta with Spinach and Bacon

1 (12 ounce) package penne pasta
2 tablespoons olive oil, divided
6 slices bacon, chopped
2 tablespoons minced garlic
1 (14.5 ounce) can diced tomatoes
1 bunch fresh spinach, rinsed and torn into bite-size pieces

Bring a large pot of lightly salted water to a boil. Add the penne pasta, and cook until tender, 8 to 10 minutes. Meanwhile, heat 1 tablespoon of olive oil in a skillet over medium heat. Place bacon in the skillet, and cook until browned and crisp. Add garlic, and cook for about 1 minute. Stir in the tomatoes, and cook until heated through. Place the spinach into a colander, and drain the hot pasta over it so it is wilted. Transfer to a large serving bowl, and toss with the remaining olive oil, and the bacon and tomato mixture.

Easy Garlic Broiled Chicken

1/2 cup butter
3 tbsp minced garlic
3 tbsp soy sauce
1/4 tsp black pepper
1 tbsp dried parsley
6 boneless chicken thighs, with skin
Dried parsley, to taste

Preheat the oven broiler. Lightly grease a baking pan. In a microwave safe bowl, mix the butter, garlic, soy sauce, pepper, and parsley. Cook 2 minutes on High in the microwave, or until butter is melted. Arrange chicken on the baking pan, and coat with the butter mixture, reserving some of the mixture for basting. Broil chicken 20 minutes in the preheated oven, until juices run clear, turning occasionally and basting with remaining butter mixture. Sprinkle with parsley to serve.

Sicilian-Style Broccoli Rabe

1 bunch broccoli rabe, ends trimmed
2 tbsp olive oil, divided
1 clove garlic, very thinly sliced
1/4 tsp red pepper flakes
3 tbsp water
1/4 tsp salt

Cut thick, lower stems off broccoli rabe and peel. Reserve florets and leaves. Heat a large skillet over medium-high heat. Add 1 tablespoon olive oil, garlic, and red pepper flakes; sauté until fragrant, about 45 seconds. Add stems; sauté until coated with oil, about 45 seconds. Pour in water; continue cooking until stems are mostly tender, 3 to 4 minutes. Stir in florets, leaves, and salt. Cover skillet and cook until tender, about 5 minutes. Transfer broccoli rabe and its juices to a serving bowl. Top with remaining 1 tablespoon olive oil.

Skillet Chili 'N Eggs

2 (15 ounce) cans chili with beans
1 (7 ounce) can whole-kernel corn, drained
4 eggs, room temperature
3 slices American cheese, cut diagonally into halves

Stir chili with beans and corn together in a large skillet over medium heat; cook until heated through, about 5 minutes. Break eggs onto chili mixture and top eggs with American cheese. Cover skillet and cook until eggs are set and cheese is melted, about 10 minutes.

Barbecued Beef

This recipe comes from my own Mom's kitchen!

1 pound ground beef
1 large onion chopped and browned
2 tbsp brown sugar
2 tbsp mustard
1 tbsp vinegar
¼ to ½ tsp ground cloves
1 bottle of ketchup
1/3 green pepper – chopped

Brown the ground beef and chopped onions. Add the other ingredients to the beef mixture and simmer on low heat for ½ hour. Serve on warmed buns. This is also a dish that an served the next day. The recipe can easily be doubled or tripled.

Dijon Pecan Chicken

This recipe is award winning… just ask the Canton (Ohio) Repository.

8 tbsp. Dijon mustard
6 tbsp butter
1 cup chopped pecans
¾ cup sour cream
2 boneless skinless chicken breasts

Melt mustard and butter in a skillet. Place chicken between waxed paper and pound thin. Then dip chicken in mustard mixture and roll around in the chopped pecans. Place in oiled baking dish and bake at 400 degrees for 20 minutes. Just before you are ready to serve, melt the remaining mustard and blend in with sour cream to make a sauce to pour over the chicken.

Set your timers, turn on your burners

January is National Popcorn Month
Ready, set....pop

It's not just for the movies anymore. Well, it is for the movies – but you don't have to just eat it at the movies. Popcorn can be as healthy or as messy or as buttery or as plain as you want it. Whether you are making it over a stove or in a microwave, popcorn has its place in the culinary world. In fact, it has its own "appreciation" month – this one. It is reported that more people consume popcorn in January than in any other month of the year. Who knows why. Popcorn is in fact the world's most popular snack food. And it is also the most profitable. It costs pennies to harvest but a jar of uncooked "gourmet" kernels can actually cost $5 – and how much was that jumbo tub the last time you saw a film? No wonder Orville Redenbacher is smiling on that box.

Evidence of popcorn consumption dates back to 3600 BC in Mexico and can be traced in some records back to 4700 BC – that means Moses probably had popcorn at least once in those 40 years he was in the desert. Right?

And did you know that six locations in the United States alone claim to be the "Popcorn Capital of the World?" They are Ridgway, Illinois; Valparaiso, Indiana; Van Buren, Indiana; Schaller, Iowa; Marion, Ohio; and North Loup, Nebraska.

But at home, you can be the Popcorn King or Queen by following some of these super easy popcorn recipes this month. Butter and salt is just the beginning. Your popcorn palette is in for a treat!

Bacon-Chive

Cook 6 slices chopped bacon until crisp; drain on paper towels, reserving the drippings. Drizzle 2 tablespoons each reserved bacon drippings and melted butter over 16 cups hot popcorn. Toss with the bacon, 1/2 cup chopped chives and 1/2 teaspoon cayenne. Season with salt.

Barbecue

Melt 4 tablespoons butter with 1 teaspoon each cumin, paprika, granulated garlic, chili powder and barbecue sauce, and a pinch of cayenne; toss with 12 cups hot popcorn and 4 cups lightly crushed barbecue potato chips. Season with salt.

Buffalo Ranch

Place 16 cups popped popcorn in a large bowl. In a small bowl, combine ⅓ cup buffalo wing sauce, 2 tablespoons melted butter and ⅛ cayenne pepper; drizzle over popcorn and toss to coat. Sprinkle with 1 tablespoon ranch salad dressing mix and additional cayenne to taste; toss to coat.

Caramel-Coated

In a large saucepan, melt 1½ cups butter. Add 2⅔ cups brown sugar and 1 cup golden syrup, stirring to dissolve brown sugar. Bring to a full rolling boil. Boil and stir 1 minute. Remove from heat and quickly stir in 1 teaspoon vanilla. Pour caramel mixture over 24 cups popped popcorn, stirring lightly. Cool on waxed paper then break it up.

Cookies and Cream

Warm 1/4 cup sweetened condensed milk in a saucepan over medium heat; drizzle over 12 cups hot popcorn. Toss with 4 cups lightly crushed chocolate sandwich cookies (such as Oreos).

Crab Boil

Melt 4 tablespoons butter with 2 tablespoons Old Bay Seasoning in a small skillet over medium heat; drizzle over 12 cups hot popcorn and toss with 4 cups oyster crackers.

Everything Bagel

Toss 12 cups hot popcorn with 4 cups broken bagel chips, 6 tablespoons melted butter, 2 tablespoons each white and black sesame seeds, 1 tablespoon each caraway seeds, granulated onion and granulated garlic, and 1 1/2 teaspoons kosher salt.

Garlic-Herb

Melt 4 tablespoons butter in a saucepan; add 4 grated garlic cloves and 1 teaspoon each finely chopped fresh rosemary, sage and thyme and cook 1 minute. Drizzle over 16 cups hot popcorn and toss with 2 teaspoons kosher salt.

Island Breeze

Combine ⅓ cup softened butter, 2 teaspoons curry powder and 1 teaspoon sugar. Pop it in the microwave to melt the butter. Drizzle over 3½ quarts popped popcorn and toss. Sprinkle with toasted coconut, almonds, raisins and salt.

Italian Cheese

Mix 6 tablespoons grated Romano cheese, 2¼ teaspoons Italian seasoning and ¾ teaspoon garlic salt. Melt 1/3 cup butter; drizzle it over 3½ quarts popcorn and toss. Sprinkle on the Romano cheese mixture and toss.

Kettle Corn

Mix 1/2 cup confectioners' sugar, 2 tablespoons granulated sugar and 1 teaspoon kosher salt in a small bowl; set aside. Heat a few popcorn kernels in 1/4 cup vegetable oil in a large pot over medium-high heat until one pops. Add 3/4 cup popcorn kernels and cover. Cook, shaking the pot occasionally, until the popcorn starts rapidly popping. Crack the lid open and pour in the sugar mixture. Cover and cook, shaking the pot, until the popping subsides.

Marshmallow-Peanut

In a large bowl, combine 15 cups popped popcorn, 2 cups miniature marshmallows, 1 cup salted peanuts and 1 cup broken pretzel sticks. In a small saucepan, combine ⅔ cups sugar, ½ cup butter and ¼ cup corn syrup. Bring to a boil; cook and stir 2 minutes. Pour over popcorn mixture; toss to coat. Cool on waxed paper then break it up.

Movie Theater

Melt 1 stick butter in a small saucepan over low heat, skimming off the foam and solids; drizzle over 16 cups hot popcorn and toss with 2 teaspoons kosher salt.

Mustard-Pretzel

Whisk 4 tablespoons melted butter with 2 tablespoons Dijon mustard, 1 teaspoon sugar and 1/2 teaspoon kosher salt; drizzle over 12 cups hot popcorn and toss with 4 cups mini pretzels.

Parmesan Ranch

Mix ¼ cup grated Parmesan, 2 tablespoons rand salad dressing mix, 1 teaspoon dried parsley and ¼ teaspoon onion powder. Melt ⅓ cup butter; drizzle over 3½ quarts popped popcorn. Toss with the Parmesan cheese blend.

Parmesan-Rosemary

Toss 16 cups hot popcorn with 1/2 cup grated parmesan, 3 tablespoons olive oil, 1 tablespoon finely chopped fresh rosemary and 2 teaspoons kosher salt.

Pepperoni Pizza

Cook 1 cup chopped pepperoni in 1 tablespoon vegetable oil in a large pot until crisp; drain on paper towels, reserving the drippings. Pop 3/4 cup popcorn kernels in the drippings; toss with the pepperoni, 1 cup shredded mozzarella, 1/2 cup grated parmesan, 2 tablespoons olive oil and 1 teaspoon each granulated garlic and dried oregano. Season with salt.

Tex-Mex

In a Dutch oven over medium heat, cook ½ cup popcorn kernels, 3 tablespoons canola oil and ½ teaspoon cumin seeds until oil begins to sizzle. Cover and shake for 2-3 minutes or until popcorn stops popping. Transfer to a large bowl; spritz with butter-flavored spray. Add ¼ cup minced cilantro, 1 teaspoon salt, 1 teaspoon chili powder, ½ teaspoon garlic powder and ⅛ teaspoon smoked paprika. Toss; continue spritzing and tossing until popcorn is coated.

Truffle

Toss 16 cups hot popcorn with 6 tablespoons melted butter, 1 1/2 tablespoons truffle oil, 1/4 cup grated parmesan, 1 teaspoon kosher salt and 1/2 teaspoon pepper.

Veggie

Pulse 2 cups each mixed veggie chips and dehydrated snap peas in a food processor until powdery; toss with 8 cups hot popcorn and 2 cups each veggie chips and dehydrated snap peas. Season with salt.

FEBRUARY

Cabin Fever?

How to Eat Your Way Through the Winter Blues

The diet is over. You tried. You did your best. For a whole month, you were good. You gave up all those comfort foods and snacked on seaweed and kale and ice chips. You worked out. You used that "monthly food" service that brings the diet treats to your door. And now reality is settling in – you're craving comfort. We are still a little under two months away from spring and that big bulky sweater you got for the holidays will come in handy.

You know what causes a muffin top? Muffins! So have one. I always think of that scene from *Eat Pray Love* with Julia Roberts when she is convincing her friend to eat the pizza. If you have seen it, you know what I am talking about. If you haven't, I can't explain it in a family friendly cookbook. Trust me, it's totally different from that scene in *August: Osage County* when the same Ms. Roberts is trying to convince Meryl to eat the fish. Way different.

Anyway, it's February. And the good news is – you still have a few more months to get beach body ready – for right now, your winter weight is calling. And so is that macaroni and cheese and meatloaf.

And while I am not advocating stress eating, I am promoting stress cooking and baking – and since I don't believe in being wasteful – or waist full – to beat the last month of cabin fever, call some people up for a game night and find "comfort" in the plates of others.

Roasted Vegetable Mac and Cheese

1 large red bell pepper, cored and diced
1 medium sweet potato, peeled and diced
1 yellow squash, de-stemmed and diced
1 small head of broccoli florets, chopped into bite-sized pieces
1 (8-ounce) package button or baby portabella mushrooms, quartered
1 small white onion, peeled and diced
2 tbsp olive oil
1 head garlic, cloves peeled
1 (12-ounce) can 2% evaporated milk
1 large egg
1/2 tsp salt
1/4 tsp ground black pepper
1/2 tsp smoked paprika
Pinch of cayenne
12 ounces elbow macaroni (or any shape of pasta)
1 tbsp butter
8 ounces freshly-grated smoked or sharp white cheddar cheese (do not use pre-grated cheese)
1/4 cup freshly-grated Parmesan cheese, plus extra for garnish

Preheat oven to 400°F. Prepare a large baking sheet with parchment paper or aluminum foil. In a large bowl, toss diced vegetables with olive oil. Season with a few generous pinches of salt and pepper. Spread the vegetables out in an even layer on the baking sheet(s). Place the garlic cloves in the center of a sheet of aluminum foil, then wrap the foil around them to form a sealed packet and place the packet in the center of the baking sheet. Bake for 30-40 minutes, or until vegetables are soft and have begun to brown a bit around the edges, giving them a stir halfway through and checking on the garlic to be sure that it doesn't burn. While the vegetables are roasting, bring a large pot of generously-salted water to a boil, and cook the pasta until al dente (remember, we talked about what that term means?) Drain the pasta, and then return the pasta to the pot and toss with butter over medium-high heat until melted. Meanwhile, in a separate bowl, whisk together the evaporated milk, egg, salt, pepper, smoked paprika and cayenne until combined. As soon as the butter is melted with the macaroni, pour in the evaporated milk mixture and stir until combined.

Continue cooking over medium-high heat, stirring occasionally, for about 2-4 minutes, or until the sauce comes to a simmer. Remove pan from heat and stir in the grated cheddar and Parmesan until melted. Then gently stir in the roasted vegetables and roasted garlic cloves until combined. Serve immediately, topped with extra Parmesan cheese if desired.

Easy Quinoa Pizza Bowls

1 cup (dry) quinoa
2 cups chicken or vegetable stock
2 (14-ounce) jars pizza sauce
2 cups shredded Mozzarella cheese
2-3 cups of your favorite pizza toppings

Preheat oven to 425°F. Cook quinoa in the chicken or vegetable stock according to package instructions. When the quinoa has finished cooking, fluff the quinoa with a fork. Then stir about 1/2 cup pizza sauce into the quinoa until evenly combined. Set aside. Lightly spray 6 large (10-ounce) oven-safe ramekins with cooking spray. Place the ramekins on a large baking tray. Spread about 2 tablespoons of pizza sauce evenly over the bottom of each ramekin. Layer each with about 1/4 cup of quinoa, and spread with a spoon to flatten. Layer each evenly with pinch of shredded Mozzarella. Layer each with a single layer of pizza toppings. Repeat by layering each with another layer of sauce, quinoa, Mozzarella, pizza toppings, followed by a final layer of Mozzarella. The ramekins should be full but not overflowing. Transfer the baking sheet full of ramekins to the oven, and bake for 20 minutes, or until the cheese is melted and the ingredients are heated through. At this point, you can either remove the pizza bowls from the oven. Or if you'd like to get the cheese extra golden on top, you can turn the oven to "broil". Then — keeping a close eye on the cheese so that it does not burn — broil the pizza bowls until the cheese is golden on top. Remove and sprinkle each pizza bowl with a pinch of Parmesan cheese and crushed red peppers, if desired. Serve immediately.

Spaghetti Pie

Butter for greasing springform
1/2 pound broccoli rabe, toughest stems saved for another use, chopped into few-inch segments (optional)
1 pound dried spaghetti
1 1/2 cups milk
3 large eggs, lightly beaten
2 to 3 tsp ground black pepper
2 tsp coarse or kosher salt
8 ounces aged pecorino cheese, finely grated, divided
8 ounces fontina cheese, grated, divided

Heat oven to 425 degrees. Butter a 9-inch springform pan and this is very important, wrap the outside of the springform, focusing on the places where the ring meets the base, tightly in aluminum foil. Set aside. Bring a large pot of well-salted water to a boil. If using broccoli rabe, add it to the pot and boil for 1 to 2 minutes, until it has some give. Fish it out with a large slotted spoon and drain it well. Set aside. Add spaghetti to boiling water and cook until very al dente, as the spaghetti will continue cooking in the oven. Drain well and let cool slightly. If using broccoli rabe, wring all extra moisture out of it and blot greens on paper towels to be extra careful. Mince rabe into very small bits. You'll have about 1 cup total. In a large bowl, whisk eggs and milk together with salt and pepper. Stir in all but 1/2 cup of each cheese and chopped rabe, if using. Add spaghetti and toss to coat. Pour into prepared springform and sprinkle remaining cheese on top. Bake for 35 to 40 minutes (without greens) and up to 15 minutes more (with greens, as they add moisture too), until the cheese is melted and bubbling and a knife inserted into the center of the pie and turned slightly will not release any loose egg batter into the center. If the top of your pie browns too quickly before the center is set, cover it with foil for the remaining cooking time. Turn on your oven's broiler. Broil the pie a few inches from the heat for 2 to 3 minutes, until browned on top. Cut along springform ring to loosen, then remove ring. Run a spatula underneath the pie to loosen the base and slide onto a serving plate. Cut into wedges.

BEEF AND BACON MEATLOAF

1 tbsp olive oil
1 onion, grated on large holes of a box grater
1 garlic clove, finely chopped
¾ cup ketchup
¼ cup apple cider vinegar
3 tbsp dark brown sugar
¼ tsp cayenne pepper
¾ cup low-sodium chicken broth
½ cup chopped fresh parsley
2 large eggs
⅔ cup fine breadcrumbs
½ cup finely grated Parmesan
1 tbsp kosher salt
¼ tsp freshly ground black pepper
2 pounds ground beef chuck
6 thin strips bacon

Preheat oven to 350°. Line a rimmed baking sheet with foil, then parchment paper. Heat oil over medium in a small skillet. Cook onion and garlic, stirring occasionally, until very soft, about 4 minutes. Transfer to a large bowl. Meanwhile, bring ketchup, vinegar, brown sugar, and cayenne to a boil in a small saucepan, reduce heat, and simmer, stirring occasionally, until slightly reduced and syrupy, about 5 minutes. Transfer 2 tablespoons ketchup mixture to a blender; add broth and parsley and blend until smooth. Set remaining ketchup mixture aside. Add broth mixture, eggs, breadcrumbs, Parmesan, salt, and pepper to onion and garlic; mix to combine. Add beef and mix well with your hands to combine. Transfer meatloaf mixture to prepared pan and form into a long log (about 12"x5"), smoothing surface. Spread reserved ketchup mixture over top and drape bacon in a crisscross pattern over loaf, tucking underneath. Bake until an instant-read thermometer inserted into the center registers 165° and bacon is crisp, 70–80 minutes. Let rest 10 minutes before slicing.

Vegetarian Swedish Meatballs

3 cups cooked lentils
1/4 cup sautéed mushrooms
1/4 cup onion, finely diced
1 garlic clove, minced
1/4 cup finely chopped fresh parsley
2 tsp finely chopped fresh thyme
1 tsp finely chopped fresh sage
1/2 tsp whole fennel seeds
1/2 tsp crushed red pepper flakes
1/2 tsp salt and 1/2 teaspoon fresh cracked black pepper.
1 cup panko breadcrumbs
2 large eggs
1 cup part-skim ricotta
1 tbsp vegetarian Worcestershire sauce
1 tsp Dijon mustard
olive oil, for topping

For the Gravy

4 tbsp unsalted butter
3 tbsp finely diced onions
1/4 cup all-purpose flour
3 1/2 cups vegetable stock
3 tbsp soy sauce
1/3 cup heavy cream
Salt and fresh cracked black pepper to taste
1 tsp finely chopped fresh thyme and/or fresh sage
1 cup sautéed mushrooms

To make the meatballs, in the bowl of a food processor fitted with a blade attachment, add lentils and mushrooms. Blend and pulse until relatively smooth, about 2 minutes. Mixture will be slightly dry and still a bit chunky. Transfer to a large bowl. To the pureed lentil mixture add onion, garlic, fresh herbs, spices, salt, pepper and breadcrumbs. In a medium bowl whisk eggs until well combined. Whisk in the ricotta cheese, Worcestershire sauce, and mustard. Add the wet ingredients to the lentil mixture and use a wooden spoon to combine all the ingredients. Stir until all the ingredients are evenly combined. Place racks in the center and upper third of the oven and preheat oven to 350 degrees F. Line two rimmed baking sheets with parchment paper. Use a large tablespoon scoop to meatballs onto the prepared baking sheet, leaving 1-inch between each meatball. Drizzle liberally with olive oil and bake for 20 to 22 minutes until cooked through and lightly golden on the bottom. Remove from the oven and allow to rest while the rest of the ingredients come together.

To make the gravy, in a large skillet melt butter over medium heat. Add onions and sauté until softened, about 3 to 5 minutes. Add the flour and whisk immediately, allowing the butter to absorb the flour and whisking constantly for 1 minute. Slowly stream in the vegetable broth, whisking constantly. The mixture will thicken and then appear thin again once all of the vegetable stock is added. Add the soy sauce. Reduce to medium-low heat and simmer until thickened, about 5 minutes. Whisk in the cream, salt, pepper, thyme, and mushrooms. Simmer until thickened again, about 4 minutes more. Keep the gravy warm over very low heat.

Just before serving, toss lentil balls in warm gravy. Enjoy warm.

TRADITIONAL FRIED CHICKEN

4 cups all-purpose flour, divided
2 tbsp garlic salt
1 tbsp paprika
3 tsp pepper, divided
2-1/2 tsp poultry seasoning
2 large eggs
1-1/2 cups water
1 tsp salt
2 broiler/fryer chickens (3-1/2 to 4 pounds each), cut up
Oil for deep-fat frying

In a large resealable plastic bag, combine 2-2/3 cups flour, garlic salt, paprika, 2-1/2 teaspoons pepper and poultry seasoning. In a shallow bowl, beat eggs and water; add salt and the remaining flour and pepper. Dip chicken in egg mixture, then place in the bag, a few pieces at a time. Seal bag and shake to coat. In a deep-fat fryer, heat oil to 375°. Fry chicken, several pieces at a time, for 5-6 minutes on each side or until golden brown and juices run clear. Drain on paper towels.

Hershey Inspired Chocolate Cake

2 cups granulated sugar
1 3/4 cups all-purpose flour
3/4 cup unsweetened cocoa powder
1 1/2 teaspoons baking powder
1 1/2 teaspoons baking soda
1 tsp salt
2 large eggs
1 cup buttermilk
1/2 cup oil (vegetable or canola oil)
2 tsp vanilla extract
1 cup boiling water

For the Frosting

1/2 cup butter
2/3 cup unsweetened cocoa powder
3 cups powdered sugar
1/3 cup milk
1 tsp vanilla extract

Heat oven to 350°F. Grease and flour two 9-inch round baking pans. Stir together sugar, flour, cocoa, baking powder, baking soda and salt in large bowl. Add eggs, milk, oil and vanilla; beat on medium speed of mixer 2 minutes. Stir in boiling water (batter will be thin). Pour batter into prepared pans. Bake 30 to 35 minutes. Cool completely. Frost.

For the Chocolate Frosting:

Combine butter and cocoa powder. Add powdered sugar, milk, and vanilla extract.

Open your heart and kitchen this Valentine's Day

"…You shouldn't face Valentine's Day with a pit in your stomach – instead – fill your stomach… Warm your heart by warming up your belly"

Valentine's Day – it's not just for lovers anymore.

Valentine's Day should be a day to open your heart to all things and all people you hold dear.

So many people get bogged down and feel pressure to do something special or make some sort of extra effort on February 14. And the truth is, you should be showing love and respect and admiration for the person or people you love all year long. If the only day of the year that you give or get love is on Valentine's Day, then you have bigger problems than what to fix for dinner, my friend.

So, let's end the madness and take away the stress for Valentine's Day. If you have someone you hold dear, then great and yes, by all means celebrate the day with all the paper hearts and chocolate candy you want to. But not glitter. Knock it off with the Valentine's Day glitter bomb cards. They just aren't funny. Glitter never goes away.

But if you don't – or if you feel crazed by this "Hallmark Holiday" that requires you to buy 36 roses – stop. If you want to buy flowers or spend time with a loved one, why do you have to wait until Valentine's Day to do it?

And we all know – love comes in many forms, shapes, sizes, and color. Valentine's Day should be a day to open your heart, not drain your wallet.

Make this Valentine's Day a chance to show your heart to people you love – and maybe even to people you don't.

Don't get me wrong. I am a romantic and I like romance and I think expressing love for the people you have in your heart is a beautiful thing. I do it through cooking. But you shouldn't face Valentine's Day with a pit in your stomach – instead – fill your stomach.

Instead of the usual candy and flowers, try some of these recipes. Warm your heart by warming up your belly. If you are spoken for, dinner is ready. If you are single, invite a friend or "friend" over and spend time in the kitchen.

And go into Valentine's Day with an open heart for everyone. Love is the best gift we can give each other, after all. I think food is in the top five but love is definitely at the top of that list. So use the day to make it even more special – for everyone you love. Happy Valentine's Day!

GROWN UP MAC AND CHEESE

4 ounces thick-sliced bacon
Vegetable oil
Salt
2 cups elbow macaroni
1 1/2 cups milk
2 tbsp unsalted butter
2 tbsp all-purpose flour
4 ounces Gruyere cheese, grated
3 ounces extra-sharp Cheddar, grated
2 ounces blue cheese, such as Roquefort, crumbled
1/4 tsp freshly ground black pepper
Nutmeg
Breadcrumbs
2 tbsp freshly chopped basil leaves

Preheat the oven to 400 degrees. Place a baking rack on a sheet pan and arrange the bacon in 1 layer on the baking rack. Bake for 15 to 20 minutes, until the bacon is crisp. Remove the pan carefully from the oven. Transfer the bacon to a plate lined with paper towels and crumble when it is cool enough to handle. Drizzle oil into a large pot of boiling salted water. Add the macaroni and cook according to the directions on the package, 6 to 8 minutes. Drain well.

Meanwhile, heat the milk in a small saucepan, but don't boil it. Melt the butter in a medium pot and add the flour. Cook over low heat for 2 minutes, stirring with a whisk. While whisking, add the hot milk and cook for a minute or 2 more, until thickened and smooth. Off the heat, add the Gruyere, Cheddar, blue cheese, 1 teaspoon salt, pepper, and nutmeg. Add the cooked macaroni and crumbled bacon and stir well. Place the breadcrumbs in a plastic bag, seal and pound with a tenderizer until the crumbs are pulverized. Sprinkle the bread crumb mixture and basil leaves over the top of the pasta. Bake for 35 to 40 minutes or until the top is browned.

PASTA WITH PECORINO AND PEPPER

1 tablespoon whole black peppercorns
salt
1/2 pound dried Italian egg pasta.
1 cup freshly grated aged Pecorino cheese, plus extra for serving
2 tbsp heavy cream
1 tbsp unsalted butter
2 tbsp minced fresh parsley leaves

Crush the peppercorns until you have a mixture of coarse and fine bits. You can also grind them. Set aside. Fill a large, heavy-bottomed pot with water and bring to a boil over high heat. Add 1 tablespoon salt and the pasta and cook according to the directions on the package until al dente. Ladle 1 cup of the pasta cooking water into a glass measuring cup and reserve it. Drain the pasta quickly in a colander and return the pasta to the pot with a lot of the pasta water still dripping. Working quickly, with the heat on very low, toss the pasta with 1/2 cup of the grated Pecorino, the crushed peppercorns, cream, butter, parsley, and 1 teaspoon salt, tossing constantly. If the pasta seems dry, add some of the reserved cooking water. Off the heat, toss in the remaining 1/2 cup Pecorino. Serve immediately with a big bowl of extra grated Pecorino for sprinkling.

CHAMPAGNE RISOTTO

4 thin slices prosciutto
3 cups reduced-sodium chicken broth
12 asparagus spears, cut diagonally into 1-inch pieces
2 tbsp butter, divided
1 shallot, finely chopped
3/4 cup medium-grain white rice
3/4 cup Champagne
1/4 cup freshly grated Parmesan
1/4 tsp salt
1/2 tsp freshly ground black pepper

Preheat the oven to 450 degrees. Place the slices of prosciutto on a lightly greased baking sheet. Bake until the prosciutto slices are almost completely crisp, about 6 to 8 minutes. The slices will crisp up even more as they cool. Reserve for garnish. In a medium saucepan, bring the chicken stock to a boil. Reduce heat to a simmer. Blanch the asparagus in the chicken stock for 2 minutes. Remove the asparagus with a slotted spoon. Set the asparagus aside and keep the chicken stock at a low simmer. In another medium saucepan, melt 1 tablespoon of the butter. Add the shallot and cook until tender, about 3 minutes. Add the Arborio rice and stir to coat in the butter. Continue toasting the rice, stirring constantly, for about 3 minutes more. Add the Champagne and simmer until the liquid has almost evaporated, about 3 minutes. Add 1/2 cup of the simmering broth and stir until almost completely absorbed, about 2 minutes. Continue cooking the rice, adding the broth 1/2 cup at a time, stirring constantly and allowing each addition of broth to absorb before adding the next, until the rice is tender but still firm to the bite and the mixture is creamy, about 20 minutes total. Remove from the heat. Gently stir in the asparagus, remaining butter, Parmesan, salt, and pepper. Spoon the risotto into serving dishes and garnish by breaking the crisp prosciutto into smaller pieces over the top of the risotto. Serve immediately.

STRAWBERRY TRIFLE

Marinated Strawberries:

1 quart fresh strawberries, halved
1/3 cup aged balsamic vinegar
Whipped Cream:
3 cups heavy cream
2 tsp vanilla extract
1/4 cup confectioners' sugar

Trifle:

One 1-pound fresh pound cake
1/3 cup amaretto liqueur

2 amaretto cookies, for garnish
Demerara sugar, for garnish

For the marinated strawberries: In a small, shallow casserole dish, toss the strawberries with the vinegar and let stand at room temperature for 15 to 20 minutes. After the strawberries have marinated, check for sweetness, adding sugar if desired.

For the whipped cream: In a large bowl, using an electric mixer, whisk the cream to soft peaks. Add the vanilla and confectioners' sugar. Whip to stiff peaks. Set aside.

For the trifle: Using a serrated knife, slice the pound cake lengthwise into 1/2-inch-thick slices. You will only need four slices. Using a 2-inch cookie cutter, cut out circles from each cake slice. Line up two highball glasses and place one cake circle in the bottom of each. Brush the cakes with amaretto liqueur. Add 2 tablespoons of marinated strawberries and spread evenly. Using a different tablespoon, add a large dollop of whipped cream and spread evenly. Add a second layer of cake, pressing down lightly. Brush with amaretto liqueur. Add 2 tablespoons of marinated strawberries and spread evenly. Top with a large dollop of whipped cream, spreading evenly. Use the remaining cake, cream and strawberries to create a more humble trifle dish.

Cover the trifles with plastic wrap and refrigerate until ready to serve

Chocolate Fondue for Two

3/4 cup heavy cream
1 pound milk or dark chocolate, broken into pieces
1 pint fresh strawberries
1 store-bought angel food cake, cut into 1-inch pieces
8 ounces dried fruit, such as pineapple slices and figs

In a small saucepan, over low heat, warm the cream and chocolate. Stir until the chocolate melts. Transfer the fondue to a serving bowl. Serve immediately with forks and foods for dipping strawberries, angel food cake, and dried fruit

And now something for the guys

Exploring the tasty pros and cons of having a groom's cake

Most people outside of the South had probably never heard of a groom's cake until it showed up in that memorable scene from the movie *Steel Magnolias* – in all its armadillo glory. Since that movie's debut more than 30 years ago, the groom's cake has moved more north to become a featured staple at weddings now. Where – face it – most of the wedding is usually all about "the bride," the groom's cake is a fun dessert that is all about the guy and usually served at the rehearsal dinner. And if the bridal party has no groom or has two grooms, it's still a way to have some fun and lighten up the bridal party a bit.

Like most wedding customs, the idea of serving a nontraditional groom's cake does have special meaning. It may have become popular over the years in the states that have also brought us country music, honey coated accents, and creole, but it actually started in Jolly Ol' England in the late 19th century. The traditional wedding cake – with its white icing, rosettes, lace fondant and vanilla crème was deemed too "feminine" for the groom and it was thought the groom should have a cake of his own. Enter the liquor-infused fruit cake, which served as the first groom's cake. Yes, the first groom's cake was nothing but an obnoxious drunken fruitcake. But then again, there is usually one of them at every wedding anyway.

In later years, the groom's cake flavors began to include chocolate, orange, raspberry and red velvet.

By the way, custom dictates that if a single lady takes a slice of groom's cake home with her and sleeps with it under her pillow (hopefully wrapped), she will dream of her future husband.

A groom's cake still remains an option – usually served at the rehearsal dinner. Traditionally, it is a gift from the bride and her family to the groom. Since custom says the groom's family pays for the rehearsal dinner, it's just a nice gesture for his future in-laws to pick up the dessert. And the bride is usually in on the design process of the cake. A groom's cake is also a great way to end an argument – if the bride wants a lemon curd wedding cake and the groom would like a simple marble, a groom's cake is a great compromise.

The groom's cake today is simply a cake entirely influenced by the groom, representing his tastes, favorite flavors, and hobbies. The cake can range from a chocolate replica of his car, to an ambitious rendering of his favorite or least favorite animal, it could be an homage to a sports team, an edible tribute to *Star Wars*, or any style that brings a smile and usually a laugh to those who cut into it. It is intended to be over the top, gawdy and even silly. It is supposed to be the antithesis of the elegance presented by the wedding cake. I have seen groom's cake that looked like record players, motorcycles, Buzz Lightyear, circus animals, golf balls, and yes, I have seen one or two gray armadillos – just don't ask me to make one for you – I don't have the counter space.

German Chocolate Blackberry Grooms Cake

2 1/2 recipes for Chocolate Cake
2 recipes for Chocolate Ganache Frosting
Pecan Filling
4 wooden skewers
1 dozen Chocolate-Covered Twigs
3 dozen fresh blackberry
4 dozen fresh blackberries

Prepare the 2 1/2 recipes for cake and ganache frosting according to their own methods. Make one recipe at a time and bake layers. Wrap each layer in plastic wrap; freeze at least for two hours. Then cut domed top off each layer using a serrated knife. Cut 1 (13- x 9-inch) and 1 (9- x 5-inch) rectangle from sturdy cardboard; cover with aluminum foil. Spread a small amount of Chocolate Ganache Frosting on 1 side of 13- x 9-inch cardboard rectangle; place 1 (13- x 9-inch) cake layer on top. Spread 2 1/2 cups Pecan Filling over cake layer, leaving a 1-inch border. Top cake with the remaining 13- x 9-inch layer. Cut 4 wooden skewers to height of 13- x 9-inch tier; insert skewers vertically into cake tier, evenly spaced and level with top of tier, about 3 inches from sides. Assemble 2 (9- x 5-inch) layers on cardboard as directed above, using remaining 1/2 cup Pecan Filling and omitting wooden skewers. Spread top and sides of both tiers with frosting, smoothing with a wet metal spatula. Position 9- x 5-inch tier in the center of 13- x 9-inch tier; place cake on stand. Insert a coupler into a decorating bag. Fit coupler with metal tip #32; fill with frosting. Pipe a shell border on top and bottom edges of each tier. Pipe vines onto tiers using metal tip # Pipe leaves onto vines using metal tip. Attach Chocolate-Covered Twigs to cake with a small amount of frosting. Arrange leaves and blackberries on tops and sides of tiers.

Decadent Dirt Cake: Signature Groom's Cake

1 cup (2 sticks) butter
2 cups granulated sugar
1 1/3 cups good quality dark chocolate
2 tbsp extremely strong coffee

1 1/2 cups self-rising flour
1 cup all-purpose flour
1/4 cup cocoa
2 cups very hot water
3 large eggs, beaten
1 1/2 tsp vanilla
1/4 cup coffee-flavored liqueur

Grease and lightly flour a large Bundt pan or alternatively use a vegetable release spray. Place the rack at the center of the oven and preheat to 300 degrees F. Melt, do not boil, butter, sugar, chocolate, and coffee in a medium-sized saucepan with the hot water, until the sugar is dissolved. Cool completely and pour into a large mixing bowl. Set the mixer on slow to medium speed. Sift together the combined flours and cocoa. In a separate bowl, combine the beaten eggs, vanilla, and coffee-flavored liqueur. Add the flour mixture alternately with egg mixture to the basic chocolate mixture. This is a thin mixture do not over beat. Pour the mixture into the prepared pan and place into the preset oven. Bake for 1 1/4 to 1 1/2 hours at 300 degrees F. Check with a skewer to be sure the cake is cooked through. Cool the cake for 20 minutes before removing it from the pan. Top with whipped cream if desired.

PRINCE WILLIAM'S CHOCOLATE BISCUIT CAKE

½ tsp. softened butter for greasing pan
8 oz. rich tea biscuits, broken into pieces
½ stick unsalted butter, softened
½ cup extra fine granulated sugar
½ cup chopped chocolate or chocolate chips
1 egg, beaten
8 oz. chocolate for icing
Cinnamon for dusting

Lightly grease a 6" spring form pan. Set aside. Cream the butter and sugar in a bowl until mixture has lightened in color. Melt 4 oz. chocolate in a double boiler. Add butter and sugar mixture to the chocolate stirring constantly. Add the egg and continue to stir. Fold in biscuit pieces until they are all coated with the chocolate mixture. Spoon the chocolate coated biscuits into the cake pan. Press firm with the back of a spoon to fill in any gaps - the bottom of the cake will be the top when turned out. Chill the cake in the refrigerator for 3 hours. Remove cake and unmold on a wire rack. Melt the 8 oz of chocolate and pour over the cake. Spread smooth with an off-set spatula. Allow chocolate coated cake to sit at room temperature until chocolate is set. Transfer to a serving platter, slice and serve.

TRADITIONAL CHOCOLATE AND CANDIED GROOM'S CAKE

1 cup (2 sticks) butter
1 cup water
1/4 cup cocoa powder
1/2 cup golden raisins
1/2 cup dried cranberries
2 cups plus 1 tsp all-purpose flour
2 cups granulated sugar
2 eggs
1/2 cup sour cream
1 tsp baking soda
1/2 tsp salt

Preheat oven to 350 degrees F. Coat 2 (9-inch) baking pans with cooking spray and dust with flour. In a small saucepan, melt butter over medium heat; stir in water and cocoa powder. Remove from heat and pour into a large bowl; allow to cool. In a medium bowl, combine raisins, dried cranberries, and 1 teaspoon flour; toss until evenly coated then set aside. Beat remaining cake ingredients, including 2 cups flour, into chocolate mixture. Gently fold in dried fruit then pour into baking pans. Bake 30 to 35 minutes, or until toothpick inserted in center comes out clean. Allow to cool 10 minutes then remove from pans to wire rack to cool completely. For an extra fancy touch, garnish this with shaved chocolate.

Eating Right doesn't mean being boring... or skipping anything

The first step to healthy living isn't at the gym – it's at the refrigerator.

I know what I'm about to say might seem like a Weight Watchers or Nutra-System infomercial but it's a true statement. I'm skinnier than I was when you first met me. My weight has bounced up and down my entire life. Yes, it happens to guys too. At times I thought – who trusts a skinny chef? A heavy chef is a happy chef, right?

But a couple of health scares, hospital visits, surgeries and lectures from doctors about diet and exercise and I realized if I wanted to be the best me for as long as I could be for my family, my friends and the readers I write for (is that "for whom I write?") I needed to start making better choices. And that started with food.

But how do you tell someone who loves to eat and loves to cook to slow down? To not taste what I am preparing? To not constantly sample? Well... for starters, you don't.

What I learned in my own weight loss and routine was that I don't have to give anything up. I can still eat Gibbles potato chips (just not a whole bag) and I can still have Twizzlers, and bread, and ice cream, and bacon – but not all in one sitting. I also got a dog in 2011 and her need for nightly neighborhood walks got me off the couch. And got me walking my neighborhood – a neighborhood I had lived in for six years and had never really explored. Now that I have, I have to say, it's pretty nice. It has sidewalks and everything.

In the last ten to 15 years, my weight has been up and down – all you have to do is look back at old pictures of me and watch my weight change (not to mention my hair color – seriously – white blonde? The Fu-Manchu mustache? What was I thinking?)

Today, I'm at the lightest I have been since my early 30s. I have lost and kept off more than 50 pounds. And I feel healthier. I'm less moody and more awake.

And I think I have learned a few secrets. So I thought I would share those with you. That said, these are the tricks (involving food) that helped me. They might not help you. Talk to your doctor first. You wouldn't trust your doctor to tell you how to cook a soufflé so don't trust medical advice from a chef. This is just from me – personally – to you. But maybe it can help a bit.

Don't give it up

Dieting doesn't mean starving. Or saying goodbye to favorite foods. You can still eat the foods you enjoy but the key is to do it in smaller portions. Trust me. After awhile, you will be taking doggie bags home from restaurants and noticing you are full a lot sooner. The worst thing you can do is deprive yourself because then once you get a bite of the forbidden foods, you won't be able to help yourself.

Have a Plan

I know it's easy to grab burgers and pizza on the way home because you're already tired from a long day of work. But think ahead. If you know you're going out to dinner, think about what you will order. Make sure you fit in the good stuff like whole grains, fruits, vegetables and nuts.

Stop calorie counting

Trust me. You don't need to. If you are making it a habit to eat healthy foods and you are eating them until you are satisfied – not stuffed – you won't need to keep track of calories. Your body will tell you when it's had enough.

Don't Eat Boring

Nutritionists are always saying to eat more vegetables, and that's true so cook them in a way that isn't boring. Add exotic spices. Switch to Virgin Olive Oil instead of frying in butter. Look for recipes in which fruits are used in various and colorful ways. Every food on your dinner plate does not have to be beige.

Taste the Rainbow.

That said….look for color. Eat foods rich in color. Greens, oranges, reds, purples, yellows. "Eating the rainbow" supplies your body with a range of disease-fighting vitamins and antioxidants. You can also blend the rainbow with some sherbet or yogurt and make some killer smoothies.

Prep and store ahead

Want to save money and your health? Pack. Even more important than shopping for healthy food is actually eating them. Put foods in portion controlled containers and take them to work. Have them handy in the car on a trip and around the house when you feel a twinge of hunger. It's all about convenience—if food is in front of you, you're going to eat it. So keep a healthy container of nuts and fruits handy.

It's okay to snack

People think when they are trying to lose weight they can't snack. This isn't true. Snacking actually can control your appetite. Just snack on healthy foods – fruits, vegetables and nuts. Even popcorn is a good option. When you have the urge to snack, just make sure you have healthy choices available like dried fruit or yogurt.

Stop Feeling Guilty

You're human. You're going to have cravings. You're going to want cake. Have it. Just don't eat it every day. Feeling guilty about your food choices can actually undermine a weight loss goal. Guilt makes you give up. Don't throw in the towel...until you have abs you can show.

Lunch is the Most Important Meal of the Day

Everyone says breakfast is the most important meal of the day but that may not be true. In fact, your biggest and most important meal of the day is lunch – when your digestion is at its peak and you can feed your body when it actually needs fuel – to get you through the day. And a nice lunch means you won't gorge at dinner.

Follow the 80/20 rule.

There are two ways you can think about 80/20 eating. One: eat healthy 80% of the time and save 20% for splurges. This allows you to attend that birthday party, have a hot dog at the ball game, eat the holiday cookies and candy. And you won't stress out over it. Another version of this rule suggests stopping eating when you're 80% full. You're more full than you think. And being in tune with your body will prevent overeating.

Am I personally where I want to be? No. Have these tips worked for me? They sure have. It just took me a lot of trial and error to figure it out. I eat when I'm hungry and I stop when I'm full. That seems like a no-brainer, doesn't it? And I reward myself from time to time with a sugary treat. Like you, I'm a work in progress too. And yes, I have been known from time to time to still overindulge – and my body lets me know later with frequent trips to the restroom and restless nights.

Once you start eating better, you will feel better and your body won't want the "junk" anymore. Trust me. It won't.

Getting in control of your diet is getting ahold of your health. The first step to healthy living isn't at the gym – it's at the refrigerator. Here is what I tell myself: "I didn't gain all the weight overnight…I'm not going to lose it overnight." Be patient. Be forgiving. But don't starve yourself.

And talk to your health care provider. Every body (two words intentionally) is different.

MARCH

March-ing into Spring

With pecans, popcorn, and something on a stick

March is a strange month.

It's the month that is supposed to show winter the door and bring us the first flirtations of spring. It's the month of Ides and of St. Patrick. It's the month of quite a few birthdays in my family. I tend to keep the local economy in business in March with the purchase of gift cards.

It's also the month of a lot of strange observations. Consider these "other" holidays that fall into the third page of the calendar. March 2 is Old Stuff Day (does this refer to people or "spring cleaning?" Or both?) "If Pets Had Thumbs Day" is March 3…which is the day I suppose you're thinking the cat or dog isn't cleaning up its own stuff.

March 5 is Multiple Personality Day – finally, a day all of me can celebrate! No, we can't! Oh yes, we can!

March 11 is "Worship Your Tools Day" (really?) National Pi Day (not pie) is March 14. Why March 14? Because 3.14 is the value of Pi. Don't believe me? That's okay. March 15 is "Everything You Think is Wrong Day." Goddess of Fertility Day is March 18 – the day after St. Patrick's Day (wonder if there is a connection?) but March 18 is also ironically National Plant a Seed Day and National Sacrifice Day. What are we sacrificing exactly?

If you don't like any of these so far, maybe the aliens will have better ideas when they take you into space on March 20 for Extraterrestrial Abductions Day. But if you're still here on March 29, go shopping because it's "National

Mom and Pop Business Owners Day" followed by a day that is truly laughable – "I am in Control Day" on March 30.

As far as food, oh yes, March has its official days for culinary delights as well. Here are a few observations with some recipes to help mark the occasions.

March 1

National Peanut Butter Lovers' Day
Peanut Butter and Sweet Potato Stew

Yup, that's right...a stew.... A stew! Gesundheit!

6 small sweet potatoes, peeled, cut crosswise into 3/4-inch slices
3 red onions, thinly sliced
1 14.5-oz. can diced tomatoes
5 sprigs plus 1/2 cup chopped fresh flat-leaf parsley
1 1/2 tsp ground cumin
1/2 tsp ground allspice
Salt and pepper to taste
1/2 cup creamy or crunchy peanut butter

Stir together potatoes, onions, tomatoes, parsley sprigs, cumin, allspice, salt, pepper and two cups water in a slow cooker until thoroughly combined. Cover and cook for 4 to 5 hours on high. Discard parsley sprigs. Just before serving stew, stir in chopped parsley and peanut butter. Serve hot.

March 7

National Crown Roast of Pork Day
Crown Roast of Pork

1/2 bunch thyme, leaves only
1/2 bunch fresh sage, leaves only
2 cloves garlic, gently smashed and paper removed
Salt and freshly ground black pepper
Extra-virgin olive oil
10 pounds pork rib roast
Stuffing (use a favorite recipe)
Gravy (use a favorite recipe)

Preheat oven to 375 degrees. Set rack on the bottom third of the oven so the roast will fit completely inside. In a small mixing bowl, combine thyme, sage, garlic, and salt and pepper, to taste, and mash to break up herbs and garlic. Add oil, about 1 cup, and combine with mixture. Take crown roast of pork and make a small cut into the meat in between each rib so you can wrap it into a circle easily; save the scraps. Rub the pork all over with the herb mixture. With the ribs on the outside, wrap the rack around onto itself so the ends meet and secure with kitchen twine so it holds its crown shape. Place in a roasting pan. Add the scraps into the bottom of the pan alongside the roast. This will help add flavor to your sauce. Set aside to bring the pork to room temperature prior to cooking. Fill the cavity with Stuffing. Cover with foil and then place the whole roast in the oven and bake for 2 hours and 20 minutes. About 30 to 45 minutes prior to being finished, remove the foil to brown the stuffing and create a crust. Remove from the oven, loosely cover with foil and allow to rest for 30 minutes before cutting. Serve with your own gravy on the side.

MARCH 10

Popcorn Lovers' Day
Browned Butter and Parmesan Popcorn

1 package of popped popcorn. Standard sized bag
5 tbsp spoons unsalted butter
3 tbsp grated Parmesan cheese
Popcorn or kosher salt, to taste

Pop the popcorn according to the package directions. Brown the butter: Melt the butter in a skillet or small saucepan over medium heat. Swirl or stir the butter with a wooden spoon as it starts to foam and sputter. Remove the butter from the heat as soon as it begins to turn golden brown and smells nutty. Drizzle the browned butter over the popcorn, sprinkle with Parmesan and salt. Toss well before serving.

March 14

National Potato Chip Day
Home Made Potato Chips

Make 'em at home...ask the kids to help.

1 large potato, sliced very thin
1 tbsp vegetable oil
Salt, or other spices, to taste

Pour the vegetable oil into a plastic bag. Put the potato slices in the bag and shake the bag until all the slices are coated with oil. Coat a large dinner plate lightly with oil or cooking spray. Arrange potato slices in a single layer on the dish. Cook in the microwave for 3 to 5 minutes, or until lightly browned. Remove chips from plate, and toss with salt –or other seasonings. Be sure to let cool completely. Repeat process with the remaining potato slices.

March 25

Waffle Day
Best Belgian Waffle Mix

2 cups flour
4 tsp baking powder
1/2 tsp salt
1/4 cup sugar
2 eggs, separated
1/2 cup oil
2 cups milk

Preheat the Waffle Iron. Sift the dry ingredients together in a large bowl. Separate the eggs. In small bowl, beat egg whites until stiff. Mix together the egg yolks, milk and oil and stir slightly. Add to dry ingredients and mix well. Fold in beaten egg whites. Pour batter into heated waffle iron and bake until desired finish.

MARCH 28

Something on a Stick Day

What's the most traditional "stick food" that comes to mind...that's right!

The All American Corn Dog

Ingredients:
1 package hot dogs
1/2 cup yellow cornmeal
1/2 cup all-purpose flour
2 tbsp sugar
2 tsp baking powder
1/8 tsp salt
1 large egg
1/2 cup whole milk
Vegetable oil, for frying

What else you will need: lollipop sticks or wooden skewers, deep-fry thermometer

Cut each hot dog in half then insert the stick into the cutoff end of each hot dog. Thoroughly dry off the hot dogs with paper towels. In a large bowl, whisk together the cornmeal, flour, sugar, baking powder and salt. In a liquid measuring cup, whisk together the egg and milk. Pour the wet ingredients into the dry ingredients and stir until combined using a spoon or spatula. Add 4 inches of oil to a large, heavy-bottomed stock pot. Attach the deep-fry thermometer then heat the oil over medium-high heat until the thermometer reaches 360ºF. Line a plate with paper towels. Dip each hot dog in the batter until completely coated, lightly shake off the excess then then lower it into the hot oil. Fry the corn dog until golden and crispy, about 3 minutes, then transfer it to the paper towel-lined plate. Repeat the breading and frying process with the remaining hot dogs. Serve immediately.

March 31

National Clam on the Half Shell Day
Baked Clams on the Half

Ingredients:
12 clams
1 cup plain dried bread crumbs
1/4 cup chopped fresh parsley leaves
1 tbsp finely chopped garlic
1/2 cup olive oil

Scrub the clams under cold running water. Pry them open and rinse out any sand or grit. Gently separate the top and bottom shells, loosening and allowing the clam to divide, with some remaining on the top shell and some remaining on the bottom shell. Use a knife to loosen the clam in the shell, removing any sand or grit that may have been under the clam. In a small bowl, toss together the bread crumbs, parsley, and garlic. Use a fork to stir the olive oil into this mixture. It should be moist but not oily. Fill each clam with a portion of the topping mixture, spreading it evenly over the clam to the edge of the shell. Bake until the topping begins to brown slightly, about 5 minutes. Remove from the oven and adjust oven to broil. Place the clams under the broiler and cook until golden brown, about 2 minutes. Serve immediately.

The perfect time to hit the sauce

Yes, March is "sauce appreciation month" (yes, really)

It's March.

And after making it through a long hard winter (well, almost but close enough) March is a good time to hit the sauce. No no no…not *that* sauce. I am talking about actual sauces – that kind you eat not drink. Yes, believe it or not, the month of March is National Sauce Appreciation Month!

And no matter what it's called, we are hooked on sauces.

Foodies everywhere love a good sauce – on pastas, salads, steaks, potatoes, greens….and yes, even ice cream (What? You've never heard of caramel sauce?)

Gravies, salad dressings, mayonnaise, mustards, relish, ketchup, salsa and chutneys are all in the sauce "family." They may all be cousins and called different names but they are all sauces.

Sauces are mainly used to enhance flavors or textures – what would a peanut butter sandwich be without a "sauce" of jelly? But did you know sauces were originally used to disguise the taste of either poorly preserved food or food that was about to go bad? It's true. Those potatoes smell a little old? Put some gravy and butter on it and no one will notice. That is where it originated.

How many parents out there have covered broccoli in melted cheese to get your kids to eat their vegetables? To this day, seeing someone poor A1 over a steak without first tasting it sends shivers down the spine of a good chef.

To me, a great sauce can highlight a dish. Pouring a Hollandaise over asparagus – or a flavorful gravy over stuffing – or a robust tomato sauce over a delicate pasta. The phenomenon of puree-ing something into a liquid and pouring it onto another food (which is the basis for any sauce) is even in pop culture if you think about it. People riding the "Gravy Train" are said to have it made. How many times have you been "in a jam" when someone didn't "cut the mustard?" Calling someone "saucy" means that person has an extra something in his or her personality – usually a kick or a bite to it. And I bet you can't hear the phrase "Pork chops and applesauce" without smiling. See, you're doing it now. (Thanks, Peter Brady!)

I bet you use sauces more than you know. Chili sauce, mustard, ketchup, jelly, jams, gravy, marshmallow crème, salsa, melted peanut butter, chocolate syrup – you go it – if you can pour it over something else to enhance (or hide) another food…guess what? It's a sauce!

Basic Pizza Sauce

1 (15 ounce) can tomato sauce
1 (6 ounce) can tomato paste
1 tbsp ground oregano
1 1/2 tsp dried minced garlic
1 tsp ground paprika

In a medium bowl, Mix together tomato sauce and tomato paste until smooth. Stir in oregano, garlic and paprika.

Tzatziki Sauce with Dill

1 cheesecloth
1 (16 ounce) container plain yogurt
1 cucumber - peeled, seeded, and grated
1 clove garlic, minced
1 tbsp fresh lemon juice
1 tbsp chopped fresh parsley
1 tbsp chopped fresh dill
Salt and ground black pepper to taste

Line a colander with two layers of cheesecloth and place over a bowl. Scoop yogurt onto the cheesecloth and cover the colander with plastic wrap. Put in refrigerator to drain, eight hours or even overnight. Place grated cucumber in a fine mesh strainer over a bowl; drain until most of the water is released, allow for one to two hours. Stir the drained yogurt, drained cucumber, garlic, lemon juice, parsley, and dill together in a bowl; season with salt and pepper. Cover bowl with plastic wrap and refrigerate at least two hours before serving.

Southern BBQ Sauce

1 gallon white vinegar
1 1/3 cups cayenne pepper
1 1/8 cups ground black pepper
3/4 cup mustard powder
1/2 cup salt
3 lemons
2 (10 fluid ounce) bottles Worcestershire sauce

Combine the vinegar, cayenne pepper, black pepper, mustard powder, and salt, lemons, and Worcestershire sauce in a large pot; bring to a simmer. Bring to a boil, then turn heat to low and simmer for at least 30 minutes.

Hollandaise with Hazelnut Butter

1/2 cup hazelnuts
2 tbsp butter, softened
1 cup butter
3 egg yolks
1 pinch salt
1 pinch white pepper
1 tbsp fresh lemon juice

Preheat the oven to 400 degrees. Place the hazelnuts on a baking sheet and toast in the oven for about 8 minutes, or until fragrant. Remove from the oven and cool. When cool enough to handle, place the nuts on a kitchen towel, fold the towel over to cover them and rub to remove the skins. Place the cooled hazelnuts into a food processor or blender and grind to a fine powder. Add 2 tablespoons of butter to the nuts and blend thoroughly. Set the hazelnut butter aside. Melt 1 cup of butter in a small saucepan, and keep hot. In the container of a blender, combine the egg yolks, salt, pepper and lemon juice. Cover, leaving the hole in the lid open, and blend for about 5 seconds. Continue to blend at high speed while pouring butter in through the lid in a thin stream. Stir in the hazelnut butter while still warm. Keep warm until serving or serve immediately.

Authentic Mole Sauce

2 cups chicken broth
2 dried guajillo chiles, stemmed and seeded
2 dried ancho chiles, stemmed and seeded
3 dried chipotle chiles, stemmed and seeded
1 dinner roll, torn into pieces
2 corn tortillas, cut into 1-inch strips
2 tomatoes, cut in half crosswise
5 tomatillos, cut in half crosswise
1 tbsp lard
1 onion, halved and thinly sliced
1/2 head garlic, peeled and sliced
1/3 cup chopped peanuts
1/4 cup raisins
2 tbsp cumin seeds
1 tbsp dried thyme
3 cinnamon sticks
5 whole cloves
6 whole allspice berries
5 ounces dark chocolate, coarsely chopped
1 additional cup chicken broth
3 tbsp white sugar
1 tsp salt

Roast chiles in a dry pan over medium heat, stirring constantly, until warm and aromatic, about 3 minutes. Transfer to the blender with chicken broth. Heat 2 cups chicken broth in a saucepan until it begins to simmer, about 5 minutes. Pour broth into a blender. Toast dinner roll pieces and tortilla strips in a dry pan over medium heat, stirring constantly, until lightly browned, about 3 minutes. Transfer to the blender with chicken broth and chiles. Allow the chiles and toasted bread and tortillas to soak, fully submerged, in the chicken broth until softened, about 10 minutes. Blend the mixture until smooth. Cook tomatoes and tomatillos in a dry skillet on medium-high heat until soft and blackened, 3 to 4 minutes per side. Place tomatoes in the blender with the chile puree. Melt lard in a large skillet over medium heat. Stir in onion, garlic, peanuts, raisins, cumin seeds, thyme, cinnamon sticks, cloves, and allspice berries; cook and stir until onions are soft and golden, 5 to 8 minutes. Remove the cinnamon sticks and other whole spices; add onion mixture to the blender with the chile-tomato mixture and blend until smooth.

Pour chile puree into a large saucepan over medium heat. Stir in chocolate, one cup of chicken broth, sugar, and salt. Bring mixture to a simmer; stir until chocolate is melted and sauce is thickened and slightly reduced, 10 to 15 minutes.

Easy Alfredo Sauce

1/4 cup butter
1 cup heavy cream
1 clove garlic, crushed
1 1/2 cups freshly grated Parmesan cheese
1/4 cup chopped fresh parsley

Melt butter in a medium saucepan over medium low heat. Add cream and simmer for 5 minutes, then add garlic and cheese and whisk quickly, heating through. Stir in parsley and serve.

Super Simple Cocktail Sauce

2 tbsp finely grated raw horseradish
1 tsp dark brown sugar
1/8 tsp fresh lemon juice
Lemons
6 tbsp ketchup

In a small bowl combine horseradish, brown sugar, lemon juice and ketchup. Mix well. Chill in refrigerator.

Easy Pesto

1/4 cup almonds
3 cloves garlic
1 1/2 cups fresh basil leaves
1/2 cup olive oil
1 pinch ground nutmeg
Salt and pepper to taste

Preheat oven to 450 degrees. Place almonds on a cookie sheet, and bake for 10 minutes, or until lightly toasted. In a food processor, combine toasted almonds, garlic, basil, olive oil, nutmeg, salt and pepper. Process until a coarse paste is formed.

New Orleans Remoulade Sauce

1 cup mayonnaise
1/4 cup chili sauce
2 tbsp Creole mustard
2 tbsp extra-virgin olive oil
1 tbsp hot sauce
2 tbsp fresh lemon juice
1 tsp Worcestershire sauce
4 medium scallions, chopped
2 tbsp chopped fresh parsley
2 tbsp chopped green olives
2 tbsp minced celery
1 clove garlic, minced
1/2 tsp chili powder
1 tsp salt, or to taste
1/2 tsp ground black pepper
1 tsp capers, chopped

Mix together mayonnaise, chili sauce, mustard, olive oil, hot sauce, lemon juice, and Worcestershire sauce. Stir in scallions, parsley, olives, celery, capers, and garlic. Season with chili powder, and salt and pepper. Cover, and refrigerate

Attention "Basketball Widows"

Riding the Ides: How to Survive March Madness

So you thought the Super Bowl party was the last big sporting event you would have to have at your house? Oh but no. You think your husband asked for that big screen TV for one single event? Well, he might have but chances are, he's about to park himself in front of the television every night for nearly a month as men's college basketball season begins to come to a close with what is now known as March Madness.

This yearly round-the-clock sporting event makes "basketball" widows out of the best of marital partners who would rather watch anything than anything else with a ball in it. Over the first two full days of the tournament, the field of 64 teams is pared to 32. In the next two days, the field is trimmed to 16 – the Sweet 16, as it is often called. During the second week of the tournament, the field is trimmed from 16 to four. These teams comprise the tournament's Final Four. And then the final four determines a national college championship team. Yes, I know…catch your breath. And it has not even started yet.

But there are two options for surviving the month and coming out on the other side and riding the "tides of Ides" – one is to plan something on your own – stay busy. Read. Go to the movies or even entire vacations with friends. Trust me. He won't know you're missing until the game is over.

The other option is to "join him." Pull up a seat, learn the stats and cheer along. And a great way to disturb the sanctity of the man cave during March Madness is with food – you'll be a hit even when his favorite team misses.

And let's face it – with all that money he has riding on the bracket, you might have to get used to not eating in restaurants for a while.

"Restaurant" Buffalo Chicken Wings

1/2 cup all-purpose flour
1/4 tsp paprika
1/4 tsp cayenne pepper
1/4 tsp salt
10 chicken wings
Enough oil for deep frying
1/4 cup butter
1/4 cup hot sauce
Dash ground black pepper
Dash garlic powder

In a small bowl mix together the flour, paprika, cayenne pepper and salt. Place chicken wings in a large nonporous glass dish or bowl and sprinkle flour mixture over them until they are evenly coated. Cover dish or bowl and refrigerate for 60 to 90 minutes.

Heat oil in a deep fryer to 375 degrees. The oil should be just enough to cover wings entirely, an inch or so deep. Combine the butter, hot sauce, pepper and garlic powder in a small saucepan over low heat. Stir together and heat until butter is melted and mixture is well blended. Remove from heat and reserve for serving. Fry coated wings in hot oil for 10 to 15 minutes, or until parts of wings begin to turn brown. Remove from heat, place wings in serving bowl, add hot sauce mixture and stir together. Serve.

Cheesy Hash Brown Casserole

1 (32 ounce) package frozen hash brown potatoes
8 ounces cooked, diced ham
2 small cans condensed cream of potato soup
16 ounces sour cream
2 cups shredded sharp Cheddar cheese
1 1/2 cups grated Parmesan cheese

Preheat oven to 375 degrees. Lightly grease a 9x13 inch baking dish. In a large bowl, mix hash browns, ham, cream of potato soup, sour cream, and

Cheddar cheese. Spread evenly into prepared dish. Sprinkle with Parmesan cheese. Bake 1 hour in the preheated oven, or until bubbly and lightly brown. Serve immediately.

Totchos Libre

32 ounces package frozen Tator Tots
1 pound lean ground beef
3/4 cup water
1 ounce packet taco seasoning mix
1 cup shredded Mexican cheese blend
1 cup shredded pepper jack cheese
1/2 cup sour cream
1/2 lime, juiced
1 tomato, chopped
1/2 cup chopped black olives
1/2 cup fresh jalapeno pepper slices
1 avocado - peeled, pitted, and cut into chunks
1/4 cup chopped scallions
1/4 cup chopped cilantro

Preheat oven to 400 degrees. Spread potatoes onto a baking sheet. Bake in the preheated oven until nuggets are golden brown and crisp, 22 to 24 minutes. Heat a large skillet over medium-high heat. Cook and stir beef in the hot skillet until browned and crumbly, 5 to 7 minutes. Add water and taco seasoning to beef; bring to a boil, reduce heat to low, and simmer until liquid reduces, about 5 minutes. Set oven rack about 6 inches from the heat source and preheat the oven's broiler. Arrange potatoes on an oven-proof platter and cover evenly with ground beef; spread Mexican cheese and pepper jack cheese over the top. Cook potatoes under the broiler until cheese melts, 1 to 3 minutes. Whisk sour cream and lime juice together in a bowl. Top potato nuggets with tomatoes, black olives, jalapenos, avocado, sour cream mixture, scallions, and cilantro, respectively.

TAILGATE CHILI

2 pounds ground beef
1 pound bulk Italian sausage
3 medium cans chili beans, drained
1 can chili beans in spicy sauce
2 cans diced tomatoes with juice
1 can tomato paste
1 large yellow onion, chopped
3 stalks celery, chopped
1 green bell pepper, seeded and chopped
1 red bell pepper, seeded and chopped
2 green chile peppers, seeded and chopped
1 tbsp bacon bits or real crumbled bacon
4 cubes beef bouillon
1/4 cup chili powder
1 tbsp Worcestershire sauce
1 tbsp minced garlic
1 tbsp dried oregano
2 tsp ground cumin
2 tsp Tabasco sauce
1 tsp dried basil
1 tsp salt
1 tsp ground black pepper
1 tsp cayenne pepper
1 tsp paprika
1 tsp sugar

Heat a large stock pot over medium-high heat. Crumble the ground chuck and sausage into the hot pan, and cook until evenly browned. Drain off excess grease. Pour in the chili beans, spicy chili beans, diced tomatoes and tomato paste. Add the onion, celery, green and red bell peppers, chile peppers, bacon bits, bouillon, and beer. Season with chili powder, Worcestershire sauce, garlic, oregano, cumin, hot pepper sauce, basil, salt, pepper, cayenne, paprika, and sugar. Stir to blend, then cover and simmer over low heat for at least 2 hours, stirring occasionally. After 2 hours, taste, and adjust salt, pepper, and chili powder if necessary. The longer the chili simmers, the better it will taste. Remove from heat and serve, or refrigerate, and serve the next day.

Brown Sugar Smokies

1 pound bacon
16 ounces "Little Smokie" sausages
1 cup brown sugar

Preheat oven to 350 degrees. Cut bacon into thirds and wrap each strip around a little sausage. Place the wrapped sausages on wooden skewers, several to a skewer. Arrange the skewers on a baking sheet and sprinkle them liberally with brown sugar. Bake until bacon is crisp and the brown sugar melted.

Beer Margaritas

12 ounce can frozen limeade concentrate
12 ounces tequila
12 ounces water
12 ounces beer
1 lime, cut into wedges

Pour limeade, tequila, water, and beer into a large pitcher. Stir until well-blended, and limeade has melted. Add plenty of ice, and garnish with lime wedges. Adjust with additional water, if needed.

If you're lucky enough to be Irish…you're lucky enough.

*For the rest of you, Ireland offers a bounty of
earthy and hearty culinary offerings*

Did you hear the story about the Irishman who sent away for his DNA results? An envelope came back a month later in the mail that confirmed not only did his family tree start in Dublin but his blood alcohol content was near the legal limit. Only a person with an Irish background can get away with telling that joke. And that's why I told it.

In investigating my family history, I learned that my surname "Hand" in Gaelic – loosely translated – means "prince or ruler," that my family's roots can be traced to Mayo and Roscommon Counties in the province of Connacht in central Ireland. And that my ancestors had their own tartan colors, coat of arms and everything.

I learned that the Hands have been coming to America for quite some time. The first record of Irish settlers in my family tree shows up in 1621 when Thomas Hand arrived in what is now Virginia. And a John Hand – who settled in Lynn Massachusetts in 1635 – was one of the eight men to buy Montauk Point Long Island and established the town of Easthampton. I come from a long line of Irish Hands – many of whom worked with their hands – as laborers, craftsmen, service personnel, and yes, even cooks.

My father's name was even Patrick – that's just how Irish I am. And so, for this St. Patrick's Day, I would like to offer a taste of the country from where my name originates. Some of these are traditional and some of these dishes have a twist.

I think this time of year, everyone claims to be a wee bit Irish. But I really am. My father's family was made in Ireland and my surname has roots there. Apparently, it was O'Hand years ago and someone along the way – perhaps at Ellis Island – got confused, wrote the name down wrong, dropped the O, and forever more, my last name is associated with that limb on your body that has five digits. But I suppose it could be worse.

And so, as a result, I have a special fondness for Ireland and for all things Irish. James Joyce and George Bernard Shaw were Irish. Galway crystal, Riverdance, Pierce Brosnan, U2, shorthand and the Titanic. All made in Ireland. And yes, Ireland is known for corned beef and potatoes but it's also known for fresh ingredients. Think of the sweetest smelling basil and thyme, aromatic sprigs of mint, the smell of yeast and salt from a bakery. Soda bread, potato bread, black pudding, skirts and kidneys, shepherd's pie, oatmeal, whiskey, Guinness, Irish cream, and Maureen O'Hara are all delicious Irish imports.

Legend has it that it's good luck to kiss an Irishman on St. Patrick's Day. So yes, I suppose then you could kiss me for luck. I am Irish after all. On my Dad's side. That makes me half Irish. So I guess it's up to you which half you think will bring you the luck.

Did I also mention the Irish are also notorious flirts?

And so I offer this Irish blessing:

May you always walk in sunshine.
May you never want for more.
May Irish angels rest their wings
Right beside your door.

Corned beef and Cabbage

4 1/2 pounds corned beef brisket
5 black peppercorns
1/2 teaspoon garlic powder
1 onion, peeled and left whole
2 bay leaves
1 pinch salt
1 small head cabbage, cored and cut into wedges
6 large potatoes, quartered
4 large carrots, peeled and sliced
1/4 cup chopped fresh parsley
2 tbsp butter

In a 6 quart Dutch oven, Place the beef brisket, peppercorns, garlic powder, onion, bay leaves and salt. Fill pan with water to cover everything plus one inch. Bring to a boil and cook for 20 minutes. Skim off any residue that floats to the top. Reduce heat to a simmer and cook for 2 to 3 hours, until meat can be pulled apart with a fork. Once the meat is done, add the cabbage, potatoes and carrots, pressing them down into the liquid. Simmer for an additional 15 minutes or until the potatoes are tender. Skim off any oil that comes to the surface. Stir in the butter and parsley. Remove the pot from the heat. Remove meat from the pot and place onto a serving dish and let rest for 15 minutes. Also remove vegetables to a bowl and keep warm. Slice meat on the diagonal against the grain. Serve meat on a platter and spoon juices over meat and vegetables.

Traditional Fish and Chips

4 large potatoes, peeled and cut into strips
1 cup all-purpose flour
1 tsp baking powder
1 tsp salt
1 tsp ground black pepper
1 cup milk
1 egg

1 quart vegetable oil for frying
1 1/2 pounds cod fillets

Place potatoes in a medium-size bowl of cold water. In a separate medium-size mixing bowl, mix together flour, baking powder, salt, and pepper. Stir in the milk and egg; stir until the mixture is smooth. Let mixture stand for 20 minutes. Preheat the oil in a large pot or electric skillet to 350 degrees F. Fry the potatoes in the hot oil until they are tender. Drain them on paper towels. Dredge the fish in the batter, one piece at a time, and place them in the hot oil. Fry until the fish is golden brown. If necessary, increase the heat to maintain the 350 degrees F. Drain well on paper towels. Fry the potatoes again for 1 to 2 minutes for added crispness.

IRISH STEW

3 tbsp canola oil, divided
1-1/2 pounds boneless beef chuck steak, cut into 1-inch pieces
2 medium onions, chopped
2 garlic cloves, minced
2 cans beef broth
1/3 cup dry red wine
1 tbsp thyme
1 tbsp Worcestershire sauce
1 tsp salt
3/4 tsp pepper
3 tbsp cornstarch
3 tbsp cold water
1-1/4 pounds sweet potatoes, cut into 1-inch cubes
1 pound baby portobello mushrooms, halved
4 medium carrots, cut into 1/2-inch slices
2 medium parsnips, cut into 1/2-inch slices
1 medium turnip, cut into 3/4-inch cubes

Preheat oven to 325. In an ovenproof Dutch oven, heat 2 tablespoons oil over medium-high heat. Brown beef in batches. Remove with a slotted spoon. Add remaining oil to pan. Add onions; cook and stir 2-3 minutes or until tender. Add garlic; cook 1 minute longer. Add broth and wine, stirring to remove browned bits from pan. Stir in thyme, Worcestershire sauce, salt and pepper. Return beef to pan; bring to a boil. Bake, covered, 1-1/4 hours. In a small bowl, mix cornstarch and cold water until smooth; gradually stir into stew. Add sweet potatoes, mushrooms, carrots, parsnips and turnip to pan. Bake, covered, 45-60 minutes longer or until beef and vegetables are tender. If desired, strain cooking juices; skim fat. Return cooking juices to Dutch oven.

"Heart of Ireland" Rutabaga Pie

3 cups diced peeled rutabagas
2 cups diced peeled potatoes
1 pound ground beef
1/2 cup chopped onion
1/2 cup sliced celery
1/4 cup steak sauce
1 tsp salt
1/4 tsp pepper
Pastry for double-crust pie

In a large saucepan, cook rutabagas and potatoes in boiling salted water just until tender; drain and set aside. In a skillet over medium heat, cook beef, onion and celery until meat is browned and vegetables are tender; drain. Add rutabagas, potatoes, steak sauce, salt and pepper. Line a 9-in. pie pan with bottom pastry. Fill with rutabaga mixture. Top with remaining pastry; flute edges and cut slits in top. Bake at 425° for 10 minutes. Reduce heat to 350°; bake 35-40 minutes longer or until crust is golden.

Irish Flag Salad

6 ounces fresh baby spinach
2 medium pears, thinly sliced
2 medium oranges, peeled and sectioned
2 tbsp crumbled feta cheese
2 tbsp chopped pistachios

For the dressing:
3 tbsp canola oil
2 tbsp orange juice
1 tbsp lemon juice
1 tsp honey
1/2 tsp grated orange zest
1/4 tsp salt

Divide spinach among four plates; top with pears, oranges, cheese and pistachios. Whisk the dressing ingredients; drizzle over salads. Serve immediately.

TRADITIONAL IRISH SODA BREAD

3 cups all-purpose flour
2/3 cup sugar
3 tsp baking powder
1 tsp salt
1 tsp baking soda
1 cup raisins
2 large eggs, beaten
1-1/2 cups buttermilk
1 tbsp canola oil

Preheat oven to 350°. In a large bowl, combine first five ingredients. Stir in raisins. Set aside 1 tablespoon beaten egg. In a bowl, combine buttermilk, oil and remaining eggs; stir into flour mixture just until moistened (dough will be sticky). Transfer to a greased 9-in. round baking pan; brush top with reserved egg. Bake 45-50 minutes or until a toothpick inserted in the center comes out clean. Cool 10 minutes before removing from pan to a wire rack to cool. Cut into wedges.

Chocolate Beer Cupcakes

1 cup Irish stout beer (such as Guinness)
1 cup butter
3/4 cup unsweetened cocoa powder
2 cups all-purpose flour
2 cups white sugar
1 1/2 tsp baking soda
3/4 tsp salt
2 large eggs
2/3 cup sour cream
2/3 cup heavy whipping cream
8 ounces bittersweet chocolate, chopped
2 tbsp butter
1 tsp whiskey
1/2 cup butter, softened
3 cups confectioners' sugar
3 tbsp Irish cream liqueur

Preheat oven to 350 degrees F. Line 24 muffin cups with paper liners. Bring beer and 1 cup butter to a boil in a saucepan and set aside until butter has melted, stirring occasionally. Mix in cocoa powder until smooth. Whisk together flour, sugar, baking soda, and salt in a bowl until thoroughly combined. Beat eggs with sour cream in a large bowl with an electric mixer on low until well combined. Slowly beat in the beer mixture, then the flour mixture; beat until the batter is smooth. Divide batter between the prepared cupcake cups, filling each cup about 2/3 full. Bake in the preheated oven until a toothpick inserted into the center of a cupcake comes out clean, about 17 minutes. Cool the cupcakes completely. Cut cores out of the center of each cupcake with a sharp paring knife. Discard cores. Bring cream to a simmer in a saucepan over low heat; stir in bittersweet chocolate until melted. Mix in 2 tablespoons butter and whiskey until butter is melted; let mixture cool to room temperature. Filling will thicken as it cools. Spoon the filling into the cored cupcakes. For frosting, whip 1/2 cup butter in a bowl with an electric mixer until fluffy, 2 to 3 minutes. Set mixer to low speed and slowly beat in confectioners' sugar, 1 cup at a time, until frosting is smooth and spreadable. Beat in the Irish cream liqueur;

adjust thickness of frosting with more confectioners' sugar if needed. Spread frosting on filled cupcakes.

ICED GUINNESS CAKE

1 can Guinness beer
1/2 cup butter, cubed
2 cups sugar
3/4 cup baking cocoa
2 large eggs, beaten
2/3 cup sour cream
3 tsp vanilla extract
2 cups all-purpose flour
1-1/2 tsp baking soda
For the Icing:
8 ounces cream cheese, softened
1-1/2 cups confectioners' sugar
1/2 cup heavy whipping cream

Grease a 9-in. springform pan and line the bottom with parchment paper; set aside. In a small saucepan, heat beer and butter until butter is melted. Remove from the heat; whisk in sugar and cocoa until blended. Combine the eggs, sour cream and vanilla; whisk into beer mixture. Combine flour and baking soda; whisk into beer mixture until smooth. Pour batter into prepared pan. Bake at 350° for 45-50 minutes or until a toothpick inserted in the center comes out clean. Cool completely in pan on a wire rack. Remove sides of pan. In a large bowl, beat cream cheese until fluffy. Add confectioners' sugar and cream; beat until smooth (do not over-beat). Remove cake from the pan and place on a platter or cake stand. Ice top of cake so that it resembles a frothy pint of beer.

REAL IRISH COFFEE

To make a proper Irish coffee, start by warming up a stemmed glass with a swirl of hot water. Dump out the water and pour in a shot of Irish whiskey. Fill the glass 3/4 full with strong coffee and stir in a tablespoon of brown sugar. Next, whip some fresh cream just a little bit so that it's fluffy but still pourable. Slowly pour the whipped cream over the back of a spoon into the coffee, so that the cream remains floating on top. Don't stir! Serve the drink immediately so that everyone can enjoy the sensation of sipping the hot, sweet bite of the spiked coffee through the layer of cool, fluffy cream

THE IRISH COCKTAIL

Mix 2 ½- 3 ounces whiskey with 2 dashes of Pernod Absinthe, 2 dashes of curacao, 1 dash of Maraschino liqueur and 1 dash of Angostura Bitters. Stir mixture over ice. Strain into a chilled sherry glass. Flame a piece of orange peel and squeeze the zest over the cocktail. Garnish with an olive

IRELAND AND THE SIMPLE POTATO

When you put sour cream and chives on your potato the next time, remember this story.

The potato was introduced to Ireland as a garden crop of the gentry. By the late 17th century, it had become widespread as a supplementary rather than a principal food because the main diet still revolved around butter, milk, and grain products. In the first two decades of the 18th century, however, it became a base food of the poor, especially in winter.

Between 1845 and 1852, the Great Famine (in Ireland, known as the Gorta Mór) impacted the island because about two-fifths of the population was solely reliant on this cheap crop for a number of historical reasons. During the famine (in which the potato crop was virtually annihilated due to disease) approximately one million people died and a million more left Ireland, causing the population to fall by between 20% and 25%.

The Potato Famine was a watershed in the history of Ireland and its impact permanently changed Ireland's demographic, political and cultural landscape.

A column twenty years in the making

Hey good lookin'…what you got gluten-free?

Gluten is a protein found in most grains. The gluten found in wheat, barley, and rye are known to cause serious health problems (like Celiac disease) to annoying digestion problems in others. Because removing gluten from your diet can also change your overall intake of fiber, vitamins and other nutrients, it's important to know how to choose your foods in order to meet your overall nutritional needs. A doctor or a dietitian can help you make appropriate dietary choices to maintain a well-balanced diet.

Folks with a gluten sensitivity issue usually need to avoid anything with the following ingredients: Wheat, barley (including beer), rye, triticale, and in some cases oats (because they could have been manufactured in facilities where wheat and barley are also handled.)

In general, eating habits of those who need to avoid gluten can be challenging because it means in most cases, these folks can't or won't digest most common breads, cakes, pies, candies, cereal, cookies, French fries, gravy, lunchmeats, salad dressings, soy sauce, and some meats and seafoods, and even some prescription medications.

Dining out presents its own challenges. Thankfully, many restaurants now carry gluten free options on their menus in response to customer demand.

For those with a gluten sensitivity, it's not all bad news. Some early clinical studies have looked at the benefits of eliminating or just limiting gluten from the diet and they have included weight loss, improved gastrointestinal health, and even improved athletic performance.

Believe it or not, after 20 years of writing a food column for newspapers and magazines, I have never shared my recipes for gluten free desserts. Never. Not in two decades. Friends and family who are gluten intolerant or have an allergy have asked me privately for my gluten-free recipes and I have happily offered up some of my favorites but I have never included them in a cooking column. Until now.

Basic Gluten-Free Flour Mix

4 cups superfine brown-rice flour
2/3 cup tapioca flour or starch
1 1/3 cups potato starch

To measure brown-rice flour and tapioca flour, use a large spoon to scoop flour into a measuring cup, then level it off with the back of a knife. Do not use the measuring cup itself to scoop your flour when measuring; it will compact the flour and you will have too much for the recipe. Add both flours to a large resealable plastic bag, along with potato starch and tapioca flour; reseal and shake until well combined. Keep refrigerated until ready to use, up to 6 months.

Chocolate Layer Cake

For the cake:

Vegetable oil cooking spray
11/2 cups sugar
3/4 cup brown-rice flour
1/2 cup almond flour
3/4 cup unsweetened Dutch-process cocoa powder
1/4 cup quinoa flour
2 tsp baking soda
1 tsp baking powder
3/4 tsp coarse salt
2 large eggs
3/4 cup warm water
3/4 cup low-fat (1 percent) buttermilk
1 ounce (2 tablespoons) unsalted butter
1 tsp pure vanilla extract

For the Frosting:

1 1/4 cups sugar
1/4 cup water

1 tbsp plus 1 tsp corn syrup
5 large egg whites
3/4 tsp pure vanilla extract
Pinch of salt

Preheat oven to 350 degrees. Lightly coat two 8-inch cake pans with cooking spray. Line bottoms with parchment; spray parchment. Whisk together dry ingredients in a large bowl. Add remaining ingredients, and mix until smooth, about 3 minutes. Divide batter between pans. Bake cakes until they pull away from sides of pans, about 1 hour. Let cool in pans on wire racks. Cakes will keep, covered, for up to one day.

Make the frosting: Place sugar, water, corn syrup, and whites in a heatproof mixer bowl over a pot of simmering water. Cook, whisking occasionally, until sugar dissolves and mixture registers 160 degrees on a candy thermometer. Attach bowl to mixer. Whisk hot sugar mixture on high speed until stiff, glossy peaks form, about seven minutes. Whisk in vanilla and salt.

Assemble the cake: Place a cake layer on a plate. Spread 2 cups frosting on top. Place remaining cake layer on top of frosting. Frost top and sides with remaining frosting. Cake is best eaten within 1 hour of frosting.

HAZELNUT-VANILLA SHORTBREAD

3 ounces (6 tablespoons) unsalted butter, softened
1/2 vanilla bean, split and scraped, pod reserved for another use
1/2 cup sugar
1 cup brown-rice flour
3 ounces blanched hazelnuts, finely ground (1 cup)
1/2 tsp coarse salt

Preheat oven to 350 degrees. Line an 8-inch square baking pan with parchment, leaving a 2-inch overhang on 2 sides. Cream butter, vanilla seeds, and sugar with a mixer until fluffy. Reduce speed to low; add flour, hazelnuts, and salt. Press into pan; freeze until firm, about 30 minutes. Score shortbread into 18 pieces; bake until gold, 55 to 60 minutes. Let cool for 15 minutes; unmold using overhang. Let cool on a wire rack. Cut into pieces. Shortbread will keep, covered, for up to 3 days.

Polenta "French Toast"

For the Polenta:

6 1/2 cups water
1/2 tsp coarse salt
2 cups cornmeal (not quick-cooking)
1/2 cup pure maple syrup
1 cup raisins
2 tsp ground cinnamon
Finely grated zest of 1 orange
1/8 tsp freshly grated nutmeg
1 cup low-fat (2 percent) milk

For the French Toast:

Vegetable oil cooking spray
1/4 cup corn flour
1/2 cup pure maple syrup
1/2 cup raspberries

For the polenta: Bring water and salt to a boil in a 2-quart pot. Add cornmeal in a slow, steady stream, stirring constantly. Cook, stirring often, until mixture begins to thicken, about 4 minutes. Reduce heat to medium-low, and cook, stirring often, for 1 hour. Stir in syrup, raisins, cinnamon, zest, nutmeg, and milk. Cook for 30 minutes. Spread polenta onto a parchment-lined rimmed baking sheet, and let cool. Cover, and refrigerate overnight.

Make the "French toast": Cut cold polenta into 4-inch squares; cut each square into 2 triangles. Heat a large nonstick pan over medium heat. Coat pan with cooking spray. Toss polenta triangles with corn flour, dusting off excess. Add to pan; cook until golden brown, about 2 minutes per side. Serve with maple syrup and raspberries.

Banana Walnut Muffins

1 1/4 cups brown-rice
1/2 cup toasted walnuts, finely ground
1/2 cup potato starch
1/4 cup tapioca flour
1 1/2 tsp baking powder
1 tsp xanthan gum
1/2 tsp salt
2 large eggs, separated
1/2 cup safflower oil
1/2 cup packed light-brown sugar
1 1/2 cups mashed overripe bananas (3 to 4)
2 tsp pure vanilla extract

Preheat oven to 350 degrees. Line a 12-cup muffin tin with baking cups. Whisk together brown-rice flour, ground walnuts, potato starch, tapioca flour, baking powder, xanthan gum, and salt. Whisk together yolks, oil, sugar, bananas, and vanilla. Fold flour mixture into banana mixture. Whisk whites until stiff peaks form. Working in 3 batches, fold whites into batter. Fill each baking cup with batter. Bake until light golden brown and a toothpick inserted into the centers comes out clean, 22 to 24 minutes. Let cool slightly. Turn out muffins onto a wire rack, and let cool completely.

Almond Torte with Pears and Whipped Cream

For the Cake:

1 1/4 cups whole natural almonds (about 6 ounces), toasted
1 tsp cornstarch
4 large eggs, separated
3/4 cup sugar
2 tsp finely grated lemon zest (from 1 lemon)
1/2 tsp pure vanilla extract
1/2 tsp coarse salt

For the poached pears and topping:
3/4 cup plus 2 tablespoons sugar
1 cinnamon stick
5 wide strips lemon zest (from 1 lemon)
4 firm, ripe Anjou or Bartlett pears, peeled, cored, and quartered
1 cup heavy cream
1/4 cup sour cream

Make cake: Preheat oven to 350 degrees. In a food processor, blend almonds and cornstarch until finely ground, about 15 seconds. In a large bowl, using an electric mixer, beat egg yolks, sugar, lemon zest, vanilla, and salt until light and fluffy, 4 to 5 minutes. Gently fold in almond mixture. In another large bowl, whisk egg whites until stiff peaks form. Fold one-third the whites into almond mixture; fold almond mixture into remaining whites just until combined. Pour batter into a 9-inch springform pan. Bake until a toothpick inserted in center of cake comes out clean, 25 to 30 minutes. Let cool in pan.

Make pears and topping: In a large saucepan, bring 4 cups water, 3/4 cup sugar, cinnamon, and lemon zest to a boil. Reduce to a simmer, add pears, and cover pan with a piece of parchment to keep pears submerged. Cook until pears are tender when pierced with a paring knife, about 15 minutes. With a slotted spoon, transfer to a plate. Bring liquid to a boil and reduce until thick and syrupy, 15 to 20 minutes. Let cool to room temperature.

In a large bowl, whisk heavy cream until soft peaks form. Whisk in sour cream and 2 tablespoons sugar; continue to whisk until soft peaks return. Serve cake with pears, syrup, and whipped cream

Banana, Coconut, and Cashew-Cream Tart

Tart Shell:

1 1/2 cups whole pecans
Pinch of coarse salt
1 1/2 cups pitted dates
2 tsp pure maple syrup

For filling:

1 cup raw cashews, soaked overnight and thoroughly drained
1/2 cup water
2 tbsp plus 2 tsp pure maple syrup, and more to taste
1 vanilla bean, split and scraped
3/4 cup desiccated coconut
3 or 4 ripe but firm bananas

Coarsely chop pecans and salt in a food processor. Add dates; pulse until thoroughly combined, 15 to 20 seconds. Add syrup; pulse just until combined and mixture sticks together. Press nut mixture firmly and evenly into a 9-inch pie plate, wetting your fingers as needed. Set tart shell aside.

Make filling: Grind nuts to a coarse paste in a blender. Add water, syrup, and vanilla scrapings; blend until smooth, about 5 minutes, scraping sides as needed. Mixture should be the consistency of thick pancake batter. Set aside 2 tablespoons coconut; add remainder to blender, and process to combine. Pour into prepared shell, spreading evenly.

Thinly slice bananas on the bias; arrange in slightly overlapping rows, beginning at edge of tart. Sprinkle with reserved coconut; serve immediately.

APRIL

Call it a hunch, but I'm ready for brunch

That "popular" meal between Breakfast and Lunch...

Brunch. I've always thought it was a strange concept and a strange meal. I don't know who came up with the idea but I am convinced it was a restauranteur who didn't like opening his business at 7 a.m. but still liked scrambled eggs and pancakes.

When I lived outside Canton, Ohio I worked at a restaurant called the 356th Fighter Group. I don't mind giving them a free plug in this story because a bad flood a couple of years ago sadly put this landmark place out of business. I was a chef there and I can honestly tell you that in all of my years of culinary experience, no one did brunch like this place. On Sundays, the 356th would be converted and nothing but brunch was on the menu – all freaking day.

And people would wait sometimes up to two hours in the lobby to get in for brunch. I know this because my only job was to work the omelet station and it was not unusual to make 500 omelets on any given Sunday. I had never experienced anything like it before or since. Until working every Sunday for a man named Bob Scofield (he didn't like getting up at 7 a.m. either), I was never a big fan of the theory of "brunch." It never made sense to me – this combination of breakfast and lunch. I never understood why anyone would want to get pancakes and then wait 20 minutes and dig into lasagna. Until I spent time talking to people in line at my omelet station and I realized brunch is not just a meal – it's a complete social event that totally revolves around food.

Brunch is not hurried. It usually involves a group of friends who want to enjoy a longer and lazier get together. At brunch, you get to visit and laugh and partake in good food – and for some it's a reason to drink alcohol before noon. Being invited for brunch is still a special invitation and the food served at brunch is still on a menu all its own.

SAUSAGE HASH BROWN CASSEROLE

1 pound hot pork sausage
15 ounces of frozen hash brown potatoes, thawed
1 cup shredded Cheddar cheese
1 1/2 tsp salt, divided
1/2 tsp ground black pepper
1 cup milk
3 large eggs, beaten

Preheat oven to 350 degrees. Grease a half-casserole baking dish or deep-dish pie plate. Heat a large skillet over medium-high heat. Cook and stir sausage in the hot skillet until browned and crumbly, 5 to 7 minutes; drain and discard grease. Stir hash browns, cooked sausage, Cheddar cheese, 1/2 teaspoon salt, and black pepper together in a large bowl. Whisk milk, eggs, and remaining salt together in another bowl. Pour hash brown mixture into prepared baking dish; pour egg mixture evenly over hash brown mixture. Bake in the preheated oven until bubbling and golden, about 45 minutes.

ORANGE PECAN FRENCH TOAST

1 cup packed brown sugar
1/3 cup butter, melted
2 tbsp corn syrup
1/3 cup chopped pecans
12 slices of thickly cut bread
1 tsp grated orange zest
1 cup orange juice
1/2 cup milk
3 tbsp white sugar

1 tsp ground cinnamon
1 tsp vanilla extract
5 eggs
Confectioners' sugar for dusting

In a small bowl, stir together the brown sugar, melted butter, and corn syrup. Pour into a greased 9x13 inch baking dish, and spread evenly. Sprinkle pecans over the sugar mixture. Arrange the bread slices in the bottom of the dish so they are in a snug single layer. In a medium bowl, whisk together the orange zest, orange juice, milk, sugar, cinnamon, vanilla, and eggs. Pour this mixture over the bread, pressing on the bread slices to help absorb the liquid. Cover and refrigerate for at least one hour, or overnight. Preheat the oven to 350 degrees. Remove the cover from the baking dish, and let stand for 20 minutes at room temperature. Bake for 35 minutes in the preheated oven, until golden brown. Dust with confectioners' sugar before serving.

AMISH CASSEROLE

1 pound sliced bacon, diced
1 sweet onion, chopped
4 cups frozen shredded hash brown potatoes, thawed
9 eggs, lightly beaten
2 cups shredded Cheddar cheese
1½ cups small curd cottage cheese
1¼ cups shredded Swiss cheese

Preheat oven to 350 degrees F. Grease a 9x13-inch baking dish. Heat a large skillet over medium-high heat; cook and stir bacon and onion until bacon is evenly browned, about 10 minutes. Drain. Transfer bacon and onion to a large bowl. Stir in potatoes, eggs, Cheddar cheese, cottage cheese, and Swiss cheese. Pour mixture into prepared baking dish. Bake in preheated oven until eggs are set and cheese is melted, 45 to 50 minutes. Let stand 10 minutes before cutting and serving.

BRUNCH CUPS

Cooking spray
18 refrigerated biscuits (unbaked)
8 ounces breakfast sausage
7 large eggs
1/2 cup milk
Salt and ground black pepper to taste
1 cup mild shredded Cheddar cheese Directions

Preheat oven to 400 degrees F. Grease 18 muffin cups with cooking spray. Roll out biscuit dough on a lightly floured surface to form 5-inch rounds. Place each round in the prepared muffin cups, pressing into the base and sides to form a dough cup. Cook and stir sausage in a skillet over medium-high heat until browned and cooked through, 5 to 10 minutes; drain fat. Spoon sausage into dough cups. Whisk eggs, milk, salt, and pepper together in a bowl until well-beaten. Pour egg mixture into each dough cup, filling each just below the top of the biscuit dough. Sprinkle Cheddar cheese on top of egg mixture. Bake in the preheated oven until eggs are set and biscuit dough is golden, 15 to 18 minutes.

EASY WAFFLES

2 cups all-purpose flour
4 tsp baking powder
1/4 tsp salt
1 1/2 cups milk
6 tbsp vegetable oil
2 eggs, separated

Preheat waffle iron. In a large mixing bowl, sift together flour, baking powder and salt. Stir in milk, oil and egg yolks until mixture is smooth. In a separate bowl, beat egg whites until soft peaks form. Gently fold egg whites into batter. Spray preheated waffle iron with non-stick cooking spray. Pour mix onto hot waffle iron. Cook until golden; serve hot.

PICKLED BLOODY MARY

3 cups bottled Bloody Mary mix
1 tbsp prepared horseradish
1 tsp chopped fresh dill
1 tsp hot pepper sauce
2 tbsp dill pickle juice
1/2 cup kosher salt
1 tsp ground black pepper
1 tsp celery seed 1 lime, juiced
1.5 ounces vodka
6 dill pickle spears
1 fresh lime, cut into wedges

In a large pitcher, stir together the Bloody Mary mix, horseradish, dill, hot pepper sauce, and dill pickle juice. Taste and adjust seasoning if desired. In a shallow dish, stir together the kosher salt, pepper and celery seed. Pour the lime juice onto a saucer. Dip each glass into the lime juice to coat the rim, then into the spice mixture. Fill each glass with ice. Pour one shot of vodka into each glass if using. Fill with the Bloody Mary mixture. Garnish each glass with a wedge of lime and a dill pickle spear.

MANGO MIMOSAS

12 ounce can apricot-mango nectar
12 ounce can pineapple juice
3/4 cup cold water
6 ounce can frozen orange juice concentrate, thawed and undiluted
Bottle of cold champagne

Stir together apricot nectar, pineapple juice, water, and orange juice concentrate in a large pitcher until combined. Pour in bottle of sparkling wine just before serving.

Picture it! Sicily...2021!

A Taste of Sicily
Taking a bite out of the 'Italian Boot'

Ah, Sophia.

If it wasn't for that 4 -foot 5-inch character from our favorite 1980s television comedy, face it, many of us may have never heard of the country of Sicily. The Golden Girl brought this region located near the tip of Italy's boot to the forefront of mainstream attention. Ask anyone from that region and there is a big difference between being Italian and being Sicilian. Those culinary differences arguably have to do with taste – seasonings, ingredients, and even just a small variation in recipes used from one culture to the other. What foods came first, Italian or Sicilian is like asking the age-old "chicken and egg" question. Both are so closely related that it is sometimes hard to tell them apart – unless you have a sophisticated Mediterranean trained palette.

One of my most favorite and most requested adult cooking classes I have taught is "Taste of Sicily." I get more requests to teach and reteach and reteach this cooking class than any other I teach throughout the year. And my "continuing education" students always want recipes to take home. It could be the herbs used, it could be the ingredients, it could be even be the warm and fuzzy memories we have of that character with the grey curls and the pearl handled purse.

ITALIAN LEMONADE

2 cups lemon juice, about 12 to 15 lemons
2 cups Basil Simple Syrup, recipe follows
2 cups cold or sparkling water
Ice
Lemon twists, for garnish
Basil Simple Syrup:
1 bunch fresh basil, washed and stemmed
2 cups sugar
1 cup water

Mix lemon juice, Basil Simple Syrup, and water together in a pitcher. Store in the refrigerator until ready to serve. Pour over ice filled glasses and garnish with a lemon twist.

Basil Simple Syrup:

In a saucepan combine basil, sugar, and water and simmer until the sugar is dissolved, 5 minutes. Cool, strain the simple syrup, and store in the refrigerator.

MEDITERRANEAN SALAD

3 tbsp extra-virgin olive oil, plus 1/4 cup
2 cloves garlic, minced
1 (1-pound) box couscous (or any small pasta)
3 cups chicken stock
2 lemons, juiced
1 lemon, zested
1/2 tsp salt
1/2 tsp freshly ground black pepper
1 cup chopped fresh basil leaves
1/2 cup chopped fresh mint leaves
1/4 cup dried cranberries
1/4 cup slivered almonds, toasted

In a medium saucepan, warm 3 tablespoons of the olive oil over medium heat. Add the garlic and cook for 1 minute. Add the couscous and cook until toasted and lightly browned, stirring often, about 5 minutes. Carefully add the stock, and the juice of 1 lemon, and bring to a boil. Reduce the heat and simmer, covered, until the couscous is tender, but still firm to the bite, stirring occasionally, about 8 to 10 minutes. Drain the couscous. In a large bowl, toss the cooked couscous with the remaining olive oil, remaining lemon juice, zest, salt, and pepper and let cool. Once the couscous is room temperature, add the fresh herbs, dried cranberries, and almonds. Toss to combine and serve.

INSALATA PANTESCA

4 ounces fingerling potatoes
1 small red onion, peeled and thinly sliced
4 medium red heirloom tomatoes, cored and cut into 1-inch cubes
2 medium green heirloom tomatoes, cored and cut into 1-inch cubes
2 medium yellow heirloom tomatoes, cored and cut into 2-inch cubes
1/4 cup green (preferably Picholine) olives, pitted
1 tbsp capers
1 tbsp Champagne wine vinegar
1/4 tsp salt
1/2 tsp freshly ground black pepper
1 tbsp minced oregano leaves
1/4 cup extra-virgin olive oi
Lemon juice, to taste
1/2 cup caperberries

In salted boiling water, cook the potatoes until tender. Drain and allow to cool to room temperature. Peel and cut into 4 to 6 pieces. Transfer to a medium bowl. Add the red onions, tomatoes, olives and capers. In another bowl, combine the vinegar, salt, pepper and oregano. Slowly whisk in the olive oil. Pour over salad mix. Taste and season with lemon juice. Divide salad into 2 and mound onto salad plates. Surround with caper berries.

Involtini di Maialle

1 pork tenderloin cut into scaloppini (about 12 slices 1/2- inch thick)
12 fresh sage leaves
6 slices Parma prosciutto
6 pieces of fontina Cheese 1/4 by 3/4 by 2
1 cup flour for dredging
3 tbsp olive oil
2 tbsp chopped shallots
2 cups shiitake mushrooms sliced
1/2 cup sherry wine
1/2 cup veal stock
1 pound spinach Sautéed with garlic and oil

Pound the scaloppini between 2 pieces of plastic wrap to about 1/4 inch, top each piece with a sage leaf broken into pieces, 1/2 a slice of prosciutto and pound again to press together, add a piece of cheese. And roll into a cigar shape. Dredge in flour, and sear quickly in olive oil in a large sauté pan, remove and set aside. Add shallots, and mushrooms to the pan and cook for 2 minutes, deglaze the pan with sherry wine, add stock and pork, and cook for 2 minutes until sauce is reduced. Serve the rolls of pork, with mushroom sauce and Sautéed spinach.

Pasta con Sarde a Mare

1/4 cup olive oil
1 cup sliced onions
8 anchovy fillets
1 fennel bulb cooked al dente, julienned
1 cup basic tomato sauce
1/4 cup pine nuts
1/4 cup dried currants
1/2 cup fresh dill
8 saffron threads
1 pound percatelli pasta
Toasted bread crumbs

Sauté the onions for 5 minutes until soft, add anchovies and cook until dissolved, add fennel, tomato, pine nuts, currants, salt and pepper to taste. Bring to boil, and reduce to simmer. Cook for 15 to 20 minutes, add fresh dill. Meanwhile, cook the pasta al dente, drain and add saffron dissolved in 3 tablespoons of water, let stand for 2 minutes to color the pasta, top with sauce and serve with toasted bread crumbs on top.

Spring is in the air — and in your supermarket.

April Flowers bring May appetites…

Yes…. April. The first full month of spring. The birds are chirping. The flowers are blooming. The snow shovels are put away and the lawnmowers are out. The weather is hopefully going to be a little warmer – and I am optimistic for a less wet season than last year this time. And best of all – for chefs and foodies everywhere - it's the season the farmers' markets start opening up outside again. And that means more produce, from artichokes to watercress, is in season, and it's time to start cooking up a green storm. It's April — the month of spring produce. Put away the comfort foods, lose that little bit of winter bulk, and enjoy a variety of fresh fruits and greens making their way into our markets and onto your table. Here are some recipes I personally cannot wait to get back to this month:

SHEET PAN ORANGE CHILI SALMON

1 to 1.25 pounds skin-on salmon fillet
1 orange, sliced into thin rounds
1/2 cup unsalted butter, melted
3 to 4 tbsp honey
3 to 4 tbsp orange juice
2 tsp Chili Seasoning Mix
1/2 tsp salt
1/2 tsp freshly ground black pepper
1 tbsp finely chopped fresh parsley

Preheat oven to 375F and place a piece of foil on the baking sheet to cover it completely. Place salmon on the foil (with the longer side parallel with the longer side of the sheet pan) with the skin-side down. Raise the edges of the foil up about 2 inches (or enough so that when you pour the buttery mixture over the top it will be contained in the foil). Nestle orange slices underneath the salmon, spaced evenly around the fillet; set aside. In a microwavable bowl, add the butter and heat on high power to melt, about 1 minute. Stir in the honey and orange juice. Pour or spoon about two-thirds of the mixture over the salmon; reserve remainder. Evenly season with Chili Seasoning, salt, and pepper. Seal up the foil. Likely you will need to add another sheet of foil on top in order to seal it. Crimp or pinch the top and bottom pieces of foil together; get it as air-tight as possible. Bake for about 15 minutes. Remove salmon from the oven and remove the top piece of foil or open up the packet so salmon is exposed but keep the edges raised to contain the buttery mixture. Set your oven to its highest broil setting. Spoon the reserved buttery mixture over the salmon. Broil salmon for about 5 to 10 minutes, or until as golden as desired. Keep a close eye on it because all broilers are different. Garnish with parsley and serve.

CAJUN SHRIMP KALE CAESAR SALAD

1 pound medium shrimp, peeled and deveined
2 tbsp olive oil
2 cloves garlic, minced
2 tsp Cajun seasoning
Salt and freshly ground black pepper, to taste
1 bunch of kale, tough stems removed, cut into ribbons
1/2 cup freshly grated Parmesan
2 cups croutons.

For the Dressing

1/2 cup mayonnaise
1/3 cup freshly grated Parmesan
1/4 cup freshly squeezed lemon juice
2 tbsp olive oil
1 tsp Worcestershire sauce

1 anchovy fillet, rinsed, dried and chopped, optional
2 cloves garlic, minced
Salt and freshly ground black pepper, to taste

To make the dressing, whisk together mayonnaise, Parmesan, lemon juice, olive oil, Worcestershire, anchovy, garlic, salt and pepper, to taste; set aside. Preheat oven to 400 degrees F. Lightly oil a baking sheet or coat with nonstick spray. Place shrimp in a single layer onto the prepared baking sheet. Add olive oil, garlic and Cajun seasoning; season with salt and pepper, to taste. Gently toss to combine. Place into oven and roast just until pink, firm and cooked through, about 6-8 minutes; set aside. To assemble the salad, place kale in a large bowl; top with shrimp, Parmesan, salt and pepper, to taste. Pour the dressing on top of the salad and gently toss to combine. Serve immediately, garnished with croutons.

BERRY WITH ARUGULA AND PROSCIUTTO PIZZA

Store-bought or homemade pizza dough
Extra virgin olive oil
1/2 cup fresh ricotta cheese
8 ounces fresh mozzarella cheese sliced
About 12 strawberries sliced
1/2 cup raspberries
1 sprig fresh rosemary
2 cups arugula leaves
4 slices prosciutto
Parmesan cheese ribbons
2 sprigs fresh mint leaves
Sea salt
Red pepper flakes
Cornmeal

Preheat oven and pizza stone or baking sheet to 475 degrees. Divide pizza dough ball into 6 sections. Stretch dough to form a rough circle or oblong shape and place on a pizza paddle or piece of parchment paper sprinkled with cornmeal. Brush the dough with a little olive oil and some sea salt flakes. Spread 2 tablespoons or so of the ricotta cheese on the crust then layer with half of the mozzarella cheese. Top with half of the strawberries and half of the raspberries and sprinkle with fresh rosemary leaves. Cook for 10-15 minutes or until cheese is melted and crust is golden. Top with arugula leaves then tear the prosciutto into strips and add to the arugula with the Parmesan cheese ribbons. Sprinkle with more fresh rosemary leaves, fresh mint and drizzle of olive oil. Season with flaked sea salt and red pepper flakes if desired. Serve immediately.

BROCCOLI CHEESE TORTELLINI WITH FRIED LEMON

8 ounces cheese tortellini
2 heads broccoli, florets roughly chopped
2 lemons, thinly sliced
2 tbsp olive oil
2 large handfuls baby spinach
1 tbsp chopped fresh chives
4 tbsp butter
1 cup grated manchego cheese
1 cup grated parmesan cheese
1 pinch of crushed red pepper flakes
Salt and pepper

Bring a large pot of salted water to a boil. Add the tortellini and broccoli and cook according to package directions until the tortellini is al dente, about 4-6 minutes. During the last minute of cooking, add the lemon slices. Just before draining, remove 1 cup of the pasta cooking water. Drain. Pick out the lemon slices. Return the pot to the stove and set over medium heat. Add the olive oil and lemon slices. Fry until lightly golden on each side, about 30 seconds to 1 minute. Remove the pot from the heat. Add the tortellini, broccoli, spinach, chives, butter, cheese and a splash of the pasta cooking water. Toss until the cheese has melted, adding more water, little by little to create a loose sauce. Season with crushed red pepper, salt and pepper.

Asparagus Tart with Balsamic Reduction

1 sheet frozen puff pastry, thawed, cut into 4 squares
12-ounces asparagus spears, trimmed, cut into thirds
1 cup shredded Gruyere cheese
2 tbsp grated Parmesan
1 tbsp olive oil
Salt and freshly ground black pepper, to taste
1/4 cup balsamic vinegar

Preheat oven to 400 degrees F. Line a baking sheet with parchment paper or a silicone baking mat; set aside. Place puff pastry squares onto prepared baking sheet. Using a fork, pierce each square to create a 1/2-inch border. Sprinkle Gruyere and Parmesan evenly over the top. Arrange asparagus spears in a single layer over the cheese, alternating ends and tips. Drizzle with olive oil; season with salt and pepper, to taste. Place into oven and bake until golden brown, about 15-20 minutes. Meanwhile, to make the balsamic reduction, add balsamic vinegar to a small saucepan over medium heat. Bring to a boil until thick and reduced, about 4-5 minutes. Serve asparagus tart squares immediately, drizzled with balsamic reduction.

Polenta Stacks with Eggplant, Tomato and Mozzarella

Polenta
1/2 tsp salt
2 cups water
1/2 cup yellow cornmeal
1/4 cup freshly grated Romano cheese
1 tbsp butter
1/4 cup chopped fresh basil
Stacks
2 large Japanese eggplants, each cut into six 1/2-inch-thick rounds
Olive oil
4 large plum tomatoes, each cut into 1/2-inch-thick rounds
Balsamic vinegar
Dried oregano

1 7 3/4-ounce package small fresh mozzarella balls in water, drained
12 fresh basil leaves

For polenta: Bring 2 cups water and salt to boil in heavy small saucepan. Gradually whisk in cornmeal. Reduce heat to medium-low; simmer until polenta is very thick, whisking constantly, about 6 minutes. Remove from heat. Add cheese and butter; whisk until melted. Mix in basil. Season generously with pepper. Spread in 9x9x2-inch metal baking pan. Chill until cold, about 1 hour.(Can be made 1 day ahead. Cover, keep chilled.)

For Stacks: Preheat broiler. Place eggplant on baking sheet. Brush with oil on both sides; sprinkle with salt and pepper. Broil until brown, about 4 minutes per side. Arrange 12 tomato slices on large plate (discard end slices). Drizzle each slice with a few drops of vinegar. Sprinkle eggplant and tomatoes with oregano.

Preheat oven to 375°F. Oil baking sheet. Cut polenta into 25 squares. Place 12 squares on sheet. Top each with eggplant round. Cut cheese into 1/3-inch thick slices; place atop squares. Top each with tomato slice (save remaining polenta and cheese for another use). Bake polenta stacks until heated through and cheese melts, about 15 minutes. Top each stack with 1 basil leaf.

SHRIMP WITH ORANGE BUTTER AND FENNEL AND ORANGE SALAD

2 oranges
1 large bulb fennel, thinly sliced (about 2 cups)
4 tsp plus 1 tbsp extra-virgin olive oil
2 tsp white wine vinegar
salt
12 large shrimp, peeled and deveined
2 tbsp butter

Zest and juice 1 orange; reserve. Cut the peel and white pith from the remaining orange. Slice the orange into half-moons and put into a bowl. Add the fennel, 4 teaspoons olive oil, vinegar, and 1 teaspoon salt; toss to coat and set aside. Toss the shrimp with the remaining 1 tablespoon olive oil; sprinkle with salt. Sear the shrimp in a hot skillet for 45 seconds, then flip. Add 2 tablespoons orange juice, 1 teaspoon orange zest, and butter; cook until the shrimp is opaque in the center, 1 to 2 minutes. Serve the fennel salad with the shrimp.

FRESAS AL VINO

3 tbsp sugar
4 packets Splenda
1/4 tsp cinnamon
1 cup red wine
2 tsp lime juice
1 lb. ripe strawberries, hulled and sliced lengthwise
1 cup mango sorbet
4 mint sprigs

Stir sugar, Splenda, cinnamon and a pinch of salt into wine until completely dissolved. Add lime juice. Pour over strawberries in a bowl and marinate, covered, in the refrigerator at least 1 hour. Serve in teacups or chilled wine glasses over 1/4 cup sorbet or frozen yogurt. Garnish with a sprig of mint

You really are what you eat

Celebrating 35 Super Healthy Foods

Getting enough nutrients, vitamins, minerals, and antioxidants are an essential part of maintaining a healthy lifestyle. If you eat greasy chips all day, yeah, you're going to see a result on your body and in your health – not to mention your spouse and doctor will be nagging at you nonstop. Trust me, I love pork rinds and corn chips as much as the next guy and no one is telling you that you can't have those things – but everything in moderation right? Slow your roll and introduce some healthy foods into your diet. Books upon books written by people much more experienced than I am can tell you which is which and why fresh and health is better, and so my humble offering here is for 35 "super foods."

Eating deliberately and eating well helps us feel better, look better and age well – and while we all can't be forever 35, these 35 super foods just might help slow down the clock a bit.

1. Almonds

Contrary to popular belief, almonds are not nuts. They are actually "drupes," a type of seed. Whether eaten raw or toasted, almonds are a delicious source of protein. Just one handful will give you a fourth of your recommended daily protein needs. Vitamin E found in almonds works to lower cholesterol levels as well as the risk of developing breast cancer. Studies have also shown that almonds can help prevent or delay Alzheimer's.

2. Apples

You know the old saying about an apple a day? It could be true. Antioxidants found in this fruit have been linked to improving brain health and preventing dementia. Apples can also lower bad cholesterol levels, reduce the risk of stroke and prevent diabetes. Apples and apple skins contain lots of vitamin C, fiber, calcium, and potassium.

3. Avocado

Avocados are low in sugar, unlike most fruits. Half an avocado holds nearly 5 grams of fiber, which is a lot. Avocado is reported to help protect the body against cancer, heart disease, and diabetes. You'll find folate, potassium, copper and vitamins E, K1, C, and B6 in avocados.

4. Barley

Barley was one of the first-ever cultivated grains. Barley is great for maintaining low blood pressure. Magnesium, calcium, and potassium found in barley naturally decrease blood pressure levels. Fiber, folate, vitamin B6 and other minerals work to strengthen your heart and bones.

5. Bell Peppers

One red bell pepper can provide 169 percent of the recommended daily intake for vitamin C. These peppers also include vitamin B6, which is great for red blood cell formation and vitamin K1, which is essential for blood clotting and bone health.

6. Black Beans

Black beans are rich in fiber and protein. These legumes are related to peas, peanuts, and lentils. Vitamins and other nutrients found in black beans are great for your health. One of the main benefits of consuming black beans is strengthening your bones. Black beans contain calcium, copper, zinc, manganese, and magnesium. All of these vitamins help to build and maintain bone strength and structure.

7. Blueberries

Just one cup of blueberries provides 24 percent of your daily vitamin C requirements. Blueberries contain a powerful antioxidant, iron, calcium, magnesium, and vitamin K. Eating foods high in calcium, magnesium, and potassium like blueberries helps to lower blood pressure and manage type 1 and type 2 diabetes.

8. Broccoli

Part of the cruciferous vegetable family, broccoli is known as one of the healthiest vegetables. Studies have shown that eating broccoli can help fight cancer. One cup of broccoli contains more than 100 percent of your daily needs of vitamin K. Broccoli also contains a lot of vitamin C which can improve your skin and make you look younger.

9. Buckwheat

Buckwheat contains no gluten, so it's ideal for those with a gluten intolerance. One cup of cooked buckwheat contains nearly six grams of protein and five grams of fiber. It's rich in vitamins K and B-6, niacin, folate, and riboflavin. The fiber found in buckwheat contributes to lower cholesterol levels as well as reduced risk of diabetes, heart disease, obesity, and stroke. Buckwheat can also help regulate your digestive system.

10. Bulgur Wheat

This whole grain is rich in iron, manganese, and magnesium and lower in calories than other whole grains like brown rice and quinoa. The fiber in bulgur wheat can help keep your heart healthy and regulate blood sugar. These whole grains also work to help grow good bacteria in your gut.

11. Cabbage.

It is believed that eating cabbage can help protect healthy tissue during cancer treatment. Sulforaphane found in cabbage can help lower your risk of developing cancer. Other antioxidants in cabbage work to reduce heart inflammation. When fermented, like kimchi or sauerkraut, cabbage becomes packed with probiotics which are great for your immune system.

12. Chia Seeds

Loaded with antioxidants, chia seeds provide a wealth of health benefits. Chia seeds benefit your health without raising blood sugar levels. The fiber content also makes you feel fuller longer. These seeds are ideal for vegetarians and vegans because of their high protein content.

13. Chicken

Chicken helps control the body's homocysteine amino acid levels which can lead to heart disease if they get too high. It also contains vitamins and minerals that promote healthy bones, boost metabolism and keep your blood vessels healthy.

14. Edamame

Edamame provides all of the essential amino acids the body needs to get from protein, so it's an excellent plant-based protein source. You can also get vital omega-3 fatty acids and other healthy fats from these beans. Edamame help with the prevention of age-related mental disorders, breast and prostate cancer, depression and heart disease.

15. Eggs

One of the best ways to get choline into your system is by eating eggs. Eggs also contain vital antioxidants that promote good eye health. For those avoiding meat, eggs are a wonderful source of protein.

16. Greek Yogurt

In Greek yogurt, the whey is removed via straining. Getting rid of the whey removes lactose, leading to a thicker, less sweet creamy yogurt. Greek yogurt contains many vital nutrients including protein, calcium, probiotics, iodine and vitamin B-12. Protein and calcium in the yogurt promote good bone health and can reduce the risk of developing osteoporosis.

17. Kale

Kale provides a wealth of nutrients including calcium, fiber, antioxidants, and other vitamins. Kale's high fiber content is effective at lowering blood sugar levels and preventing diabetes. This vegetable contains vitamin B6, potassium, fiber and vitamin C. The high water and fiber content promotes a healthy digestive system and the beta-carotene makes skin and hair healthy.

18. Kidney Beans

Kidney beans are a fantastic source of carbohydrates, fiber, and protein. One serving of kidney beans contains 127 calories, 8.7 grams of protein, and 22.8 grams of carbs. Kidney beans are a great source of vital nutrients like iron, folate, copper, potassium and vitamin K1.

19. Kiwi

Originally called the Chinese Gooseberry, Kiwi is technically a berry. They have a high vitamin C content, making them great for your skin and collagen production. Studies have shown that kiwis can help improve your sleep quality. Kiwis have a lot of fiber and potassium which is essential for a healthy heart.

20. Mushrooms

Mushrooms are technically vegetables because they belong to the fungi family. And mushrooms can prevent inflammation and along with vitamin D, slow the growth of cancer cells. The high fiber content of mushrooms can improve blood sugar levels and help those with diabetes become healthier.

21. Nut Butters

Peanut butter is just one of them. But you can get a nut butter packed with protein and fiber by eating butters made from almonds, cashews, sunflower and macadamia nut. Nut butters are also known for helping improve cholesterol levels. But if you have a nut allergy, steer clear.

22. Oats

One of the most popular health foods out there today is oats. Oats can be found in oatmeal, baked goods, and cereal. Eating oats can lead to a healthier heart and improve blood pressure and of course, cooked oats are known to soothe irritated skin when applied topically.

23. Olive Oil

Consuming olive oil can reduce your risk of inflammation, thrombosis and cardiovascular issues. It can also prevent stroke and possibly reduce your risk of developing breast cancer. Olive oil has also been proven to help maintain healthy cholesterol levels. It's not only consumed, but olive oil has also been used in soaps, medicine, and cosmetics.

24. Onions

"Organosulfur compounds" found in onions are beneficial for reducing the risk of cancer, especially colorectal and stomach kinds. The high levels of vitamin C found in alliums build collagen which is necessary for improving skin and hair. Eating onions is also said to help reduce depression and insomnia.

25. Oranges

Just one orange can provide you with 130 percent of your daily vitamin C needs. Eating citrus fruits can help lower your risk of stroke. The potassium in oranges works to lower blood pressure and make your heart healthier.

26. Pumpkin

Pumpkin is loaded with vitamins and minerals but low in calories. In addition to its "meat," nutrients can be found in the pumpkin's leaves, seeds, and juice. This fruit contains beta-carotene, a powerful antioxidant. That's how it gets its vibrant orange color.

27. Quinoa

Pronounced keen-wah, this grain is naturally free of gluten. One cup of this whole grain is 222 calories and contains over 8 grams of protein, 5.2 grams of fiber and a ton of nutrients. The vitamins and minerals you can get from quinoa include iron, manganese, B-2, and lysine.

28. Salmon

Salmon's omega-3 fatty acids can help reduce heart rates and heart failure. Selenium found in salmon is said to help support a thyroid health. Omega-3 fatty acids also decrease depression, aggression, and impulsivity.

29. Sardines

Because sardines only eat plankton, they don't have high levels of mercury like most fish. The fish are loaded with vital omega-3 fatty acids that help with heart disease prevention. You can get a lot of vitamin B-12 from sardines which helps boost your energy and keeps your cardiovascular system working smoothly.

30. Spinach

Spinach has been known to reduce blood sugar levels as well as instances of neuropathy in diabetics. Chlorophyll found in leafy greens like spinach has been shown to block carcinogenic effects in the body, preventing cancer growth in the body.

31. Sweet Potatoes

One medium-sized potato provides more than 400 percent of the daily vitamin A requirement. These potatoes are known as complex carbohydrates making them better for you than regular potatoes. Sweet potatoes won't raise blood sugar levels like starchier foods. Potassium found in sweet potatoes can also help maintain healthy blood pressure levels. And their fiber content promotes healthy digestion and regularity.

32. Tomatoes

Despite botanically being a fruit, tomatoes are generally eaten and prepared like a vegetable. Tomatoes are one of the best sources of the antioxidant lycopene, which has been linked to many health benefits, including reduced risk of heart disease and cancer.

33. Walnuts

Walnuts are high in omega-3 fatty acids, monounsaturated and polyunsaturated fatty acids, making them great for your heart. These fats can lower bad cholesterol as well as reduce the risk of stroke, heart attack, and cardiovascular disease.

34. Watercress

It is reported that Hippocrates prescribed watercress to his patients. Watercress sandwiches (sandwiches wrapped in watercress instead of a bun) were common until the 19th Century Just one cup of watercress contains 100 percent of the daily recommended amount of vitamin K. Magnesium, potassium and calcium found in this leafy green can help reduce blood pressure levels.

35. Whole Grain Pasta

Whole grain kinds of pasta can lower your risk of diabetes, obesity, stroke and heart disease. Another benefit is that the way whole grain pasta is processed leads to a higher level of micronutrients.

Are you getting fresh with me?

How you can recreate the "farm to table"
experience in your own kitchen

Think back, if you can, to the homemade food that came from your grandmother's kitchen. There was a time when "farm to table" wasn't a novelty but the norm.

The idea of frozen and canned fruits and vegetables is relatively new to the culinary world. Pre packaged and processed foods only came around during World War II, when the government needed new ways to get supplies to soldiers. After the war, the "convenience" of canned or frozen foods found its way off the battlefield and into the average home.

Lately, we have heard the phrase "Farm to Table" tossed around as a new idea but it means nothing more than using the freshest ingredients from your local farmers and food vendors. It also means growing your own fruits and vegetables and using them in your every day life. Before we had super markets and mega stores, this is always how it was done.

For a chef who loves to cook with fresh ingredients, this movement is a long time coming. As someone who has made his living working in various restaurants, I can tell when I am actually dining out if the food is processed or fresh. For the record, I shouldn't have to tell you, fresh is always best.

From meats to greens to fruits and even flowers, we are about to enter a season where "farm to table" is something everyone can do. Try it, you'll like it.

Where to Start? Buy Local!

Farmer's Markets – and every single community big and small has them – are great places to find the freshest sweet corn, the reddest, ripest tomatoes and the most fragrant, flavorful strawberries. Taste heirloom vegetables and fruits and sample hard-to-find foods like ramps, morel mushrooms, cardoons, and quince. In late April, these outdoor markets open up in large cities and small towns – and all of these foods should be available and plentiful. At many farmer's markets, the vendors also often will offer recipes and cooking tips if you spend some time and talk to them. And some will have their own prepared and organic offerings like house-made jams and hearth-baked breads, free-range chickens and fresh eggs. Good cooking – at home or in any restaurant – starts with good ingredients. A great meal is only as good as its worst ingredient. When you use the freshest materials you can find and work them into your recipes, you honestly can't go wrong.

Asparagus

Try using fresh asparagus of all colors–green, purple, or white. It really is a true gift of spring time. Grill it or roast it. Include it in a quiche or frittata. Put it on a homemade vegetarian pizza.

Basil

Basil is a wonderful and fragrant summer delight that can highlight any meal. Serve it fresh in a pesto, on fettucine, in a roui, or blend it into a cream sauce for chicken or fish.

Beans and Peas

Green beans, string beans, English peas, and sugar snap peas. Go get them. So fresh this time of year that they should snap. Serve up peas with mint, stir fry beans with shrimp or chicken.

Beets

Did you know that both the green tops and the roots are edible? This time of year, a hearty beet salad is delicious. You can also soak them in vinegar, Sautee them with greens and bake them.

Cherries, Raspberries, and Strawberries

The fresh fruits of summer, this is the season that is begging for berries. Try adding them to iced tea and to your salads. And of course, serve them on their own with cream or frozen yogurt.

Corn

Knee high by the Fourth of July? Remember that adage. One of my favorite recipes is simply to wrap it in foil and throw it into a dying bonfire…wait awhile and fish them out of the ashes. Peel back the foil and the husk and taste summer.

Cucumbers

Crisp, refreshing cucumbers are just reminders of warmer weather ahead. Try a cool cucumber soup, salad or salsa. Or you can simply slice them up and place them in ice water for a refreshing beverage that might surprise you.

Eggplant

The eggplant is that great purple "fruit" that is both versatile and remarkable for recipes. Serve it up in a summer ratatouille, bread it and bake it with fresh mozzarella, or slice it up with some fresh basil.

Grapes, Plums, and Blackberries

It may be a couple more months – usually late summer – before this trio is in season but nothing says warm weather than these beautiful offerings perfect in jams, syrups, and pies.

Leafy Greens

Dark leafy greens are high in fiber, vitamins, and minerals. Recipes include dandelion salad (yes, you read that right), escarole and beans, collard greens and the every popular kale.

Tomatoes

Tomatoes are often the stars of the Farmer's Market season. And for good reason. There is nothing more flavorful than a ripe homegrown or farmed grown tomato. And there are so many varieties of them – from beefsteak to cherry. Try a fresh tomato salad, or craft a Caprese with fresh mozzarella cheese, create a bruschetta, or a chutney. Grab some green ones and fry them up.

Zucchini

If your neighbor wants to give you some zucchini, take if. Create a recipe from it and invite the neighbor back over for a taste. Try lemon zucchini bread, calabacitas, zucchini with eggs, or sauté the zucchini the same way you would a summer squash.

Variety is the "Spice" of Life

Here are the 40 Spices Everyone Should Have in the Kitchen!

They life begins at 40, right? Whoever said that deserves to be drawn and quartered and covered in Tabasco. But I digress. Life actually begins whenever you say it begins. If you are "finding yourself" at 30 or 40 or looking for a second act at 60, life has no "starting gate." You get there when you get there. However, that said, 40 is a nice round number for the spices everyone should have in the pantry. And don't worry if the only spices you know are Ginger Spice, Scary Spice or Old Spice, it's okay. I'm not only going to tell you what you want…what you really really want… I am going to tell you what these spices are and exactly how best to use them. After all, variety is the "spice" of life. Put down that salt and pepper shaker…quit dousing your steaks with ketchup. I'm about to give you some tips on how to put some spice back in your life – at least in the kitchen. The other rooms of the house are entirely up to you.

Allspice

Allspice is a key ingredient in "jerk" seasoning but you can also use it in pickling too. It's good cooked with pot roast, stews, sausages, ham, and fish. And it tastes great on root vegetables. And because of its sweet flavor, you can find it sprinkled on puddings, cakes, and pies.

Basil

Mediterranean and Italian cuisine influenced, use basil with pesto; tomato and minestrone soups; blend it with meatballs, chicken, and lamb; potato salad; and zucchini. Throw some Basil on the coals of your grill after your meal is cooked and the mosquitoes will stay away while you feast!

Bay Leaves

Bay leaves are wonderful in hearty soups, stews, pot roast, marinades for chicken, and spaghetti sauce. The leaves release their oils over a long time. But you should always remove them from your dishes just before your serve them. Keeping a bay leaf in your flour container will also keep bugs out.

Caraway seeds

With a tangy flavor and similar to dill, caraway seeds are edible in whole but you usually find them ground up.

Cardamom

Sprinkle in over pork, cabbage, carrots, a citrus salad…or even put it in your coffee.

Note: keep it in a dark place. Cardamom loses flavor when exposed to air.

Cayenne

Some like it hot! To cool your mouth after being exposed to cayenne, drink milk, eat yogurt, or a banana. Water doesn't help because the hot part of the chili is an oil, which the water can't dissolve and will usually spread. To use, add just a dash to curries, hamburgers, casseroles, and even dips. Use sparingly.

Celery Seed

There are three types – white, green, and turnip rooted, and they are all slightly bitter. Use to flavor fish, winter salads, egg dishes, and even sprinkle some in tomato juice or Bloody Marys.

Chili Powder

Not just for chili – but essential when making chili, of course. Use for beef dishes, marinades, sprinkle over grilled corn and rice.

Chives

It's a cousin to the onion, believe it or not. Use it to add some flavor to chicken, potatoes, cream soups, eggs, carrots, and cauliflower. Sprinkle it in sour cream and you have an easy chip dip.

Cilantro

Some people don't like cilantro – can't stand the taste or the smell. It has a spicy and peppery taste. It is used mostly in Mexican and Asian dishes like salsas, stews, soups, sauces, dips, curries, and vegetables.

Cinnamon

One of my favorites. Use in pies, cakes, sweet rolls, fruit, and hot drinks. Put a cinnamon stick in your coffee or hot cocoa. And do you know sprinkling some cinnamon on your window sills will keep pests away?

Coriander

Both sweet and tart, coriander adds rich flavor to meat loaf, spicy meat mixtures, sausage, stews, ham or pork roast, poultry stuffing, and cooked beets. It's also an ingredient in gingerbread, sweets and breads, baked apples, and fruit salad.

Cumin

A strongly flavored spice, add it to beef, roast pork, chicken marinades, vegetable salads, cabbage dishes and sauerkraut, black beans, and even sugar cookies. Flavor doesn't blend well with other flavors; use sparingly.

Dill

For more than just pickles, use it with chicken, lamb chops, and with shellfish. Try it sprinkled over cucumbers, squash, cauliflower, potato salad, coleslaw, cottage cheese, and even hot buttered popcorn.

Fennel

It can taste a bit like licorice and it's great for fish; in fact, it's called the "fish herb." If you have a whole plant, throw the long stalks on the charcoal when grilling fish.

Five Spice Powder

Different brands vary, but this blend includes a combination of five of the following spices: Star Anise, Fagara (Szechuan Pepper), cassia or Cinnamon, Fennel, Clove, Ginger, and licorice root.

Garlic

It is so good for you it's ridiculous. While it may not smell great and it keeps vampires away, garlic is amazing for your blood and digestive system. It is widely used in Italian, Mediterranean, and Mexican cuisine. Garlic powder accents beef, pork, lamb, and game. Of course, garlic bread is a dinnertime staple.

Ginger

Use fresh, powdered, or pickled form with steak, meatloaf, chicken, and fish and seafood. Boil some and use it in teas to help with a sore throat. Use powdered form in cakes, cookies, puddings, and sweet breads. A key ingredient in many Oriental cuisines.

Herbs De Provence

It's basically a blend of Oregano, Savory, Rosemary, Thyme, and Marjoram. May also contain lavender, Basil, or Fennel seeds. Use it to season kabobs, chicken, pork, stews, tomato dishes, and pizza.

Italian Seasonings

A blend of Marjoram, Basil, Oregano, Thyme, and Rosemary. May also contain Savory or Sage.

It's great with dips, herb breads, and tomato dishes. Mix with olive oil to create a quick and easy rub for chicken. Crumble over pizza sauce before layering on the toppings.

Marjoram

It is similar to Oregano but milder and can be used on hamburgers, meat loaf, stews, chicken pot pie, fish dishes and sauces, and poultry stuffing. Try it with cabbage, carrots, peas, beans, and summer squash.

Mint

The most popular are peppermint and spearmint. You can use mint on everything from roast lamb to fruit salad. You can garnish a summer time drink with it. And did you know allowing the steam from boiled peppermint to permeate your house not only smells good, it's a natural insect and critter repellant.

Mustard

Use ground Mustard seeds on ham, pork, in barbecue and cocktail sauces, salad dressings, chowders, baked beans, cabbage, and squash. And have faith, will you?

Nutmeg

I was once called this a nickname in my early professional years. Use nutmeg with chicken, lamb, and vegetable stew. You can also add it to desserts, sauces, milk- or cream-based custards, white sauces, and eggnog. Also good for candied yams; green, leafy vegetables such as spinach; tomatoes; green beans; corn; eggplant; onions; and mashed potatoes.

Oregano

Its most common uses are in pizzas and spaghetti sauces but try some oregano in chili, hamburgers, meat loaf, lentil soup, stuffings, and on top of eggplant dishes.

Paprika

It's a dried and powdered fruit of a red sweet pepper. Use as flavoring or as a garnish. Try it over poultry, stews, vegetables, deviled eggs. Paprika loses its flavor quickly though so be sure to store it away from heat and direct light.

Parsley

Available fresh or dried, parsley is great with soups, stews, sauces; herb butter for bread, fish, and poultry; salads, potatoes, and omelets. Parsley brings out the flavor of other herbs. And do you know where there is a custom of leaving a sprig of fresh parsley on your plate? You are supposed to eat it after your meal as a natural breath neutralizer.

Peppercorns

I love fresh peppercorns. It has a strong flavor and aroma, and is one of the world's oldest known spices. Available in white, black, green and even pink, each one has its own different flavor. Peppercorns are available whole and ground and you can use them on just about anything – but I would recommend you invest in a pepper mill or grinder so your pepper is always ground fresh right when you need it.

Poppy Seeds

Crunchy, slightly sweet seeds from the same plant that produces opium, but don't worry the narcotic alkaloids are removed during processing. I promise that episode of Seinfeld is slightly exaggerated. Try them on buttered noodles; mashed potatoes; and steamed vegetables such as cabbage, spinach, carrots, onions, and zucchini.

Rosemary

Robustly flavored spice with needle-like leaves and a taste reminiscent of pine trees, its uses include roasts, carrots, winter squash, cauliflower, beans, and potatoes. Often used with pasta dishes as a spice and garnish. Not a dessert spice, but goes with breads and yogurt dips.

Saffron

Difficult to grow and harvest, saffron is a yellow spice that comes whole or powdered. It is also actually one of the most expensive spice in the world (an ounce can cost $150). Fortunately, one or two threads is enough to flavor most dishes. If you have saffron in your spice cabinet, you have arrived.

Sage

Sage is in the "mint" family and has a sweet, earthy, herbal taste and smell. It comes whole, rubbed (crushed), or ground. You can use it in veal, beef stew, hamburgers, turkey and chicken, pork, stuffing, fish chowder, cornbread, stewed tomatoes, cheese spreads, vegetables, and breads. Burning whole stalks of sage is said to sanitize and purify the air and is a common practice when homes are being "blessed."

Salt

Yes. Good ol' salt. The most popular and yet sometimes overlooked spice. Use a pinch of it to bring water to a boil faster and to bring out flavors of foods. Use sparingly. Salt is one of those spices in which each person's tolerance varies.

Savory Spice

In summer and winter varieties, savory spice is best used with sausage, chicken, lamb, and vegetable soup. The most popular herb for beans, but also use with Brussels sprouts, turnips, cabbage, green beans, peas, potatoes, and tomatoes. And you can rub savory spice leaves on bee stings to instantly relieve the pain!

Sesame

The oil from the seeds, used to make sesame oil, is high in vitamin E, cholesterol-free, and high in polyunsaturates. Sesame is wonderful in breads and rolls or mixed into cakes and cookies. Used to make a "Sesame butter" called tahini, a paste made from ground-up seeds. Lightly toast Sesame seeds in a dry skillet before use to release their nutty flavor.

Seven Spice

A Mediterranean spice with origins in the Middle East, you can usually find this spice in specialty stories and markets. It is amazing with fish, stews, on vegetables, rice, and even mixed with fresh greens and salads.

Tarragon

A rich, sweet herb with a slight licorice taste, it is most often used in French cuisine. It's strong, so use near the end of cooking.

Thyme

Use in meatloaf, pot roast, hamburgers, lamb, game, fish dishes, clam chowder, hearty soups and stews, poultry and stuffing, and most vegetables. Make Thyme for good cooking!

Turmeric

Available powdered and, occasionally-especially in stores that sell Asian foods-you may find whole, dried pieces of the root. Best in curried lamb, chutney, legumes, and zucchini. Can use as a substitute for Saffron, but expect the taste to differ.

Vanilla

Available as whole beans or an extract. Choose beans that look moist and are flexible, not stiff, and keep both beans and extract away from heat or light. Use it in drinks, sweet dishes, baked goods. And here's a storage tip – keep your whole beans with sugar in a sugar container. The sugar will take on the Vanilla flavor, making it great for baking use, and the beans will last for years

MAY

Honor Thy Mother...

The gift of cooking is a gift of love

My Mom passed away in June, 2013 and I still miss being able to cook for her. I cook like she does – by taste – and I have also been accused of organizing my kitchen at home a bit like she used to. Which means none at all sometimes. The rolling pins will be mixed in with the spices. The aluminum foil can be found with trash bags. I used to think my Mom did this so no one else would be tempted to use her kitchen – for lack of finding anything. And I probably do that for the same reason. When it came to the kitchen, my Mom could be a bit territorial.

Evidence of my Mom's love for cooking became obvious to my two brothers and sister and me when we were in her house after her death. In boxing up items that each child wanted to keep, we found just as many cookbooks as family photo albums. For every loose photo we found in a box, we found a recipe card. In her last years, my mother kept up subscriptions to three magazines – the one that publishes my monthly column (Allegany Magazine), Cooking Illustrated and Gourmet.

My Mom – Virginia Lou Hand – loved the very idea of cooking – of the notion of translating your thoughts and love for someone into food. If she liked you, she cooked for you.

I get that expression from her.

I was actually born in mid May and so for "Ginny Lou," I was a belated Mother's Day present. And so, for my mother and me, Mother's Day always held special significance. We each got presents that month. From each other.

Even in the year she died, I called a florist and sent her flowers for Mother's Day and the very next week, she sent me flowers right back. There were years we would laugh because the arrangements would look exactly the same. Sometimes it became a contest. My Mom and I thought a lot alike. She was even a teacher too.

There are times now – even going on eight years since her passing – when I discover a new technique or a new recipe and I want to call her up and tell her how I made it.

Anytime I was having a bad day, our "go-to" dessert was ice cream. My Mom and I had ice cream to soothe each other's mental battle wounds of the day. It was our thing. My brothers and sister had their own favorites but for my Mom and me – it was ice cream. Actually, it was all desserts. The sweeter the better. But ice cream was at the top of that list. Ice cream always made us smile.

So I thought to celebrate all mothers I'd suggest a few desserts – all with Mom in mind – and all of them go great with a side of ice cream.

MOTHER'S DAY PIE

1 cup white sugar
2 tbsp all-purpose flour
1/4 tsp salt
6 tbsp butter
1 tsp vanilla extract
3 eggs
1 (12 fluid ounce) can evaporated milk
1 cup shredded coconut

Preheat oven to 325 degrees F (165 degrees C). Generously grease and flour a 9 inch pie plate. In a medium bowl, mix together sugar, flour, and salt. Stir in melted butter or margarine and vanilla extract. Add eggs one at a time, mixing well after each addition. Mix in evaporated milk followed by coconut. Pour mixture into pie plate. Bake in preheated oven for 35 to 40 minutes. Chill before serving.

MOTHERS DAY POUND CAKE

1 tsp butter
1 cup butter
1 1/3 cups white sugar
2 tsp vanilla extract
4 eggs
1/4 tsp salt
1 lemon
4 2/3 cups sifted all purpose flour
2 tsp baking powder
1/2 cup milk

Preheat oven to 350 degrees F (175 degrees C). Grease a 9 1/2-inch square baking pan with 1 teaspoon butter and set aside. Melt 1 cup butter in a saucepan over low heat; stir in the sugar until thoroughly combined. Stir in the vanilla. Whisk in the eggs, one by one, whisking well between each egg. Stir in the salt and lemon zest. Transfer to a large mixing bowl In a separate bowl, sift the flour and baking powder together. Gently stir the flour mixture into the egg mixture. Stir in the milk, folding the batter lightly with a spatula until thoroughly combined. Pour the batter into the prepared baking pan. Bake in the preheated oven until a toothpick inserted near the center of the cake comes out clean, 50 to 60 minutes. Let cool in pan on a wire rack for 10 minutes; invert the cake onto a second wire rack and let cool completely.

MOM'S APPLESAUCE CAKE

3 1/2 cups all-purpose flour
1/2 tsp salt
2 tsp ground cinnamon
1 tsp ground cloves
3 tsp baking soda
1/2 cup butter
2 cups packed brown sugar
2 eggs, beaten
3 cups unsweetened applesauce

1/2 cup raisins
1/2 cup dates, pitted and chopped
1 cup chopped walnuts
1/2 cup butter
1 cup packed brown sugar
1/4 cup milk
1 tsp vanilla extract
2 cups sifted confectioners' sugar

Preheat oven to 300 F. Grease and flour a tube pan. Whisk together flour, salt, cinnamon, cloves, and soda. Set aside. Cream together 1/2 cup butter and 2 cups brown sugar, beating until light and fluffy. Mix in eggs. Add flour mixture into creamed mixture alternately with applesauce, beginning and ending with flour mixture. Stir in the raisins, dates, and walnuts. Pour batter into prepared pan. Bake in preheated oven until a tester inserted in the center of the cake comes out clean, about 1 1/2 hours. Cool on wire rack. To make icing, melt 1/2 cup butter or margarine in a small saucepan over low heat; stir in 1 cup brown sugar. Boil for 2 minutes. Stir in milk, and continue to stir until the mixture returns to a boil. Remove from heat, and cool for 5 minutes. Beat in vanilla and confectioners' sugar. Frost cooled cake.

MOTHER'S TURTLE PIE

1 (9 inch) baked pie shell
12 individually wrapped caramels, unwrapped
1 (14 ounce) can sweetened condensed milk, divided
1/4 cup margarine
2 (1 ounce) squares unsweetened baking chocolate
2 eggs
2 tbsp water
1 tsp vanilla extract
1 pinch salt
1/2 cup chopped pecans

Preheat oven to 325. Place pie shell in a 9-inch pie dish. Heat caramels and 1/3 cup sweetened condensed milk together in a saucepan over low heat until caramels are melted, 3 to 5 minutes. Spread caramel mixture into the bottom of pie shell. Heat margarine and chocolate together in a saucepan over low heat until melted and smooth, 3 to 5 minutes. Remove from heat. Beat eggs, remaining sweetened condensed milk, water, vanilla extract, and salt together in a large bowl until smooth. Stir chocolate mixture into egg mixture; pour over caramel mixture. Top pie with pecans. Bake in the preheated oven until center of pie is set, about 35 minutes. Cool pie for 1 hour at room temperature. Chill in refrigerator.

GRANDMA'S LEMON PUDDING CAKE

1 tbsp unsalted butter
2/3 cup superfine sugar, plus more for dusting
2 eggs, separated
2/3 cup reduced fat buttermilk
2 tbsp lemon juice
1 tbsp lemon zest
1/4 cup all-purpose flour
1/4 tsp salt
Garnish:
3 cups fresh berries (raspberries, strawberries, blueberries, blackberries)
2 tbsp confectioners' sugar

Preheat oven to 325 degrees F. Butter and lightly sugar 4 ramekins (about 1-cup size). In a mixer, add egg yolks, buttermilk, lemon juice and lemon zest and beat until well combined. Reduce the speed to low and sift in flour, sugar and salt. Continue to mix until combined. Beat egg whites until you get stiff peaks then combine the 2 mixtures by gently folding them together, a little at a time. Divide evenly amongst ramekins then bake in a water bath - set ramekins in a roasting tray and fill with water halfway up the sides of the ramekins. Bake for 45 minutes until the top springs back when gently pressed and the cakes have a nice golden brown color. Allow to cool slightly, then carefully invert onto a plate. Serve with fresh berries and dust with powdered sugar.

One of the best days of the year to take Mom to brunch – or better yet, to attempt to make it yourself – is this month, the very merry month of May.

And trust me, these recipes are not hard to make and Mom will appreciate the extra effort. Mother's Day Brunch is nice way to make our Moms feel important and loved by doing something that is just for her. Feel free to serve any or all of these with a single rose placed in a keepsake vase – on a tray or at the table as a whole family – I bet your mom doesn't care how well it turns out. I bet more than your food, she wants your company.

Chicken Sausage Patties

1 tbsp butter
1 green apple, finely chopped
1 small onion, finely chopped
Salt and pepper
1 tsp fennel seed
1 1/2 pounds ground chicken breast
1 1/2 tsp poultry seasoning, half a palm full
1 tsp allspice, 1/3 palm full
1 tsp sweet paprika, 1/3 palm full
Extra-virgin olive oil, for drizzling

Heat a small nonstick skillet over medium heat. Add butter and melt. Add apples and onions and season with a little salt, pepper and fennel seeds. Gently sauté the mixture 5 minutes to soften and remove from heat to cool. Heat a griddle pan or large nonstick skillet over medium-high heat. Place chicken in a bowl and season with salt and pepper, poultry seasoning, allspice, paprika and a healthy drizzle of extra-virgin olive oil. Add in the apples, onions and fennel and mix the sausage. Score meat into 4 sections and form 3 small, thin patties from each section, 2 1/2 inches across, 12 small patties total. Cook patties 3 to 4 minutes on each side and serve warm.

Herb-Roasted Potatoes

2 pounds red new potatoes, quartered
1/4 cup extra-virgin olive oil

Leaves from 1/4 bunch fresh thyme
Salt

Preheat the oven to 375 degrees F. Toss together the potatoes, oil, and thyme, and sprinkle with salt. Dump the potatoes out on a baking sheet and roast until tender and crisp on the edges, 30 to 40 minutes.

Herbed-Baked Eggs

1/4 tsp minced fresh garlic
1/4 tsp minced fresh thyme leaves
1/4 tsp minced fresh rosemary leaves
1 tbsp minced fresh parsley
1 tbsp freshly grated Parmesan
6 extra-large eggs
2 tbsp heavy cream
1 tbsp unsalted butter
Salt
Freshly ground black pepper
Toasted French bread or brioche, for serving

Preheat the broiler for 5 minutes and place the oven rack 6 inches below the heat. Combine the garlic, thyme, rosemary, parsley, and Parmesan and set aside. Carefully crack 3 eggs into each of 2 small bowls or teacups (you won't be baking them in these) without breaking the yolks. (It's very important to have all the eggs ready to go before you start cooking.) Place 2 individual gratin dishes on a baking sheet. Place 1 tablespoon of cream and 1/2 tablespoon of butter in each dish and place under the broiler for about 3 minutes, until hot and bubbly. Quickly, but carefully, pour 3 eggs into each gratin dish and sprinkle evenly with the herb mixture, then sprinkle liberally with salt and pepper. Place back under the broiler for 5 to 6 minutes, until the whites of the eggs are almost cooked. (Rotate the baking sheet once if they aren't cooking evenly.) The eggs will continue to cook after you take them out of the oven. Allow to set for 60 seconds and serve hot with toasted bread.

Mascarpone and Marmalade Stuffed French Toast

6 eggs
1/2 cup heavy cream
1/2 orange, juiced
1 1/2 tsp orange zest
1/2 tsp ground cinnamon
1/4 tsp freshly grated nutmeg
1/2 tsp vanilla extract
3 tbsp sugar
1/4 tsp salt
8 slices (3/4-inch) day-old brioche
16 tsp mascarpone
8 tsp orange marmalade
2 tbsp butter
Confectioners' sugar, for dusting
Maple syrup, for serving

In a mixing bowl whisk together the eggs, cream, orange juice, zest, cinnamon, nutmeg, vanilla, sugar, and salt. Lay the brioche slices flat on a clean work surface. Spread 1 side of each slice with 2 teaspoons of the mascarpone. Spread 2 teaspoons of the marmalade over the mascarpone on half of the slices. Place the slices together to form 4 sandwiches. Working 1 at a time, dip the sandwich in the egg mixture, letting it sit about 1 1/2 minutes per side. Transfer to a plate and repeat with the remaining sandwiches. Preheat a large nonstick skillet over low heat. Add 1 tablespoon of the butter. When the butter has melted, add 2 of the sandwiches and cook until golden brown on both sides, about 5 minutes per side. Repeat with the remaining butter and sandwiches. Cut the French toast "sandwiches" in half and serve hot, dusted with powdered sugar and drizzled with maple syrup, as desired.

Orange Glazed Blueberry Scones

2 cups unbleached flour, plus more for rolling berries
1 tbsp baking powder

1 tsp salt
1/3 cup sugar
1/4 cup unsalted butter, chilled and cut in chunks
3/4 cup buttermilk or cream
1 egg
1 pint fresh blueberries

Preheat oven to 400 degrees. In a large bowl, sift together flour, baking powder, salt and sugar; mix thoroughly. Cut in butter using 2 forks or a pastry blender. The butter pieces should be coated with flour and resemble crumbs. In another bowl, mix buttermilk and egg together, and then add to the flour mixture. Mix just to incorporate, do no overwork the dough. Roll blueberries in flour to coat, this will help prevent the fruit from sinking to the bottom of the scone when baked. Fold the blueberries into batter, being careful not to bruise. Drop large tablespoons of batter on an ungreased cookie sheet. Bake for 15 to 20 minutes until brown. Cool before applying orange glaze.

Orange Glaze:

2 tbsp unsalted butter
2 cups powdered sugar, sifted
2 oranges, juiced and zested

To prepare Orange Glaze: combine butter, sugar, orange zest, and juice over a double boiler. Cook until butter and sugar are melted and mixture has thickened. Remove from heat and beat until smooth and slightly cool. Drizzle or brush on top of scones and let glaze get hazy and hardened.

TRADITIONAL EGGS BENEDICT

1 tsp vinegar
4 eggs
4 thin slices Canadian bacon
2 English muffins

Hollandaise sauce:

3 egg yolks
1 tbsp hot water
1 tbsp lemon juice
1 stick unsalted butter, melted and hot
Salt and pepper
Paprika
Chopped parsley

In a large skillet, bring 2 inches of water and the vinegar to a boil. Crack one egg into a glass. Reduce water to a simmer and pour egg into water in one quick motion. Quickly add remaining eggs. Let eggs cook for 4-5 minutes. The white should be firm but the yellow should be runny. Remove eggs with a slotted spoon and drain on a paper towel. In a non-stick skillet heat the bacon until warm. Toast the English muffins until golden.

For the sauce: Place yolks, water and lemon juice into blender. Blend for 1 minute. With blender running, pour butter through open hole of blender lid. Season with salt and pepper and keep warm.

To assemble eggs benedict: Top each muffin with bacon and a poached egg. Pour warm sauce over everything. Serve immediately.

MOTHER'S DAY FRENCH TOAST

Fruit Filling

1 cup sliced fruit or small berries
1/2 tsp lemon juice
1/2 tsp lemon zest
2 tbsp sugar

French Toast

4 thick slices of bread
1 cup milk

2 tsp vanilla extract
4 egg whites
2 eggs
4 tsp butter
2 tbsp sugar

Garnish

1/2 Cup Fresh fruit
1/4 Cup Fruit syrup

Fruit Filling: Mix together the cup of sliced fruit or small berries, the lemon juice and zest and 2 tablespoons of the sugar. Set aside to soak and sweeten the fruit.

French Toast: Pre-heat oven to 400°F. Combine milk, sugar, vanilla and eggs in a mixing bowl. Beat until frothy foam can be seen. Put it in the refrigerator for a few minutes until you have the bread ready. Cut the thick bread slices into two thick halves. Just as if you were cutting a sandwich in half. Cut a slit in each of the bread pieces to form a hole for the fruit filling. Put about 1 tablespoon of the fruit filling in each piece of bread and secure the slit with toothpicks to keep the fruit inside. Don't fill them so full that the fruit spills out. Place the filled bread slices in a 13" X 9" baking dish.

Beat the egg mixture a second time to make sure it's really well mixed and pour half of the egg mixture over the fruit stuffed bread. Flip the bread over and pour the rest of the mixture onto the bread. Make sure that all of the bread is coated. Chill for 30 minutes flipping the bread pieces about 3 or 4 times while they are chilling. Grease another 13" X 9" inch baking pan and put the fruit filled bread pieces in this pan. Bake for 3 - 5 minutes or until the top is golden brown then flip them and bake for another 3 - 5 minutes until the top is golden brown. Serve with warm fruit syrup and the rest of the fruits and berries.

BAKED BLUEBERRY FRENCH TOAST CASSEROLE RECIPE

1 pound loaf rustic bread, cut into 1-inch cubes (about 10 cups of cubes)
1 1/2 cups blueberries
5 large eggs
2 cups milk
1 cup heavy cream
1/2 tsp vanilla extract
8 tbsp sugar, divided
1 tbsp lemon zest
1/8 tsp salt
2 tbsp unsalted butter, diced

Butter a 9x13 baking dish. Spread half of the bread cubes in an even layer in the prepared pan. Top with 2/3 of the blueberries, followed by the remaining bread cubes and blueberries. In a separate bowl, whisk the liquids: Beat the eggs, milk, cream and vanilla. Then add in 6 tablespoons of the sugar, lemon zest, and the salt. Pour the mixture over the bread cubes, pressing down gently – don't burst the whole berries but do make sure the egg mixture is absorbed. Cover dish with plastic and allow the bread to soak in this mixture at least 30 minutes or even overnight in the refrigerator. Preheat the oven to 350°F. Sprinkle the top of the casserole with the remaining sugar and dot with the diced butter. Bake for 45 minutes, until slightly puffed and golden brown. Let cool for about 10 minutes before cutting. Serve with a dusting of powdered sugar over top or a drizzle of maple syrup.

ALMOND FLOUR WAFFLES

1 1/2 cups almond flour or almond meal
1/2 cup tapioca flour
1 tsp baking soda
1 tsp baking powder
Pinch of salt
3 tbsp sugar
3 large eggs
3 tbsp coconut oil, warmed to liquid state

1 cup almond milk, room temperature
1 tsp almond extract
1 tsp vanilla extract

Special equipment:
Waffle maker

Turn on your waffle maker and let it warm until it is hot enough that a drop of water evaporates on contact. Heat the oven to 250°F. Make the waffle batter: Whisk together the dry ingredients in a medium bowl. In a separate bowl, whisk together the wet ingredients. Add the wet ingredients to the dry ingredients and thoroughly whisk together. Allow the mixture to sit for 5 minutes to give the flour time to absorb the liquid. Then grease the waffle maker and make waffles in the waffle iron. If not serving immediately, place waffles in warm oven for five to 10 minutes.

CRANBERRY ORANGE SCONES

1 cup dried cranberries
3 oranges, grated zest
5 cups cake flour
3 tbsp baking powder
1 tsp salt
1/4 cup sugar
6 oz cold diced butter
2 cups cream (approx.)

Preheat oven to 400 degrees. Place flour, baking powder, salt, sugar, butter, orange zest, and cranberries together and mix well. Pour in 2 cups of cream and gently mix, add a little more cream as needed to make nice dough. Shape the dough into 2 circles about 8 inches in diameter. Cut into 8 wedges; bake about 15 to 20 minutes or until lightly browned.

Shakshuka with Swiss Chard Pesto

1 bunch organic swiss chard, stems removed
1 bunch organic cilantro
2 cloves garlic, plus 2 additional cloves (minced)
1 lime, juiced
1/2 cup organic extra-virgin olive oil, plus 2 tablespoons
1 large shallot, diced
1 organic red bell pepper, diced
1 28-ounce can organic crushed tomatoes
1 tsp organic harissa
1 tsp organic ground cumin
1 tsp organic paprika
1 tsp organic ground cinnamon
salt and pepper
8 eggs

In a food processor, combine the swiss chard, cilantro, 2 cloves garlic, lime juice and olive oil. Season with salt and pepper, to taste. Pulse to combine until smooth pesto consistency is reached. Set aside. Meanwhile, in a large cast-iron skillet over medium heat, sauté shallot and bell pepper in olive oil until soft, about 3-5 minutes. Add minced garlic and sauté until aromatic, about 1 minute. Add tomatoes and season with harissa, cumin, paprika and cinnamon; salt and pepper to taste. Reduce heat to medium-low and let simmer for 5 minutes, stirring occasionally. Carefully crack the eggs into the tomato sauce, using a spoon to create a small hole for the egg to fit into. Cover and cook until eggs are just set, about 5 minutes. You can also fry or poach the eggs in a separate pan, if you'd like – but it's a preference. It looks "prettier" but it tastes the same. Remove the cast-iron skillet from the heat and garnish with choice of toppings that could include feta cheese crumbles, 1/4 cup olives or capers. Serve with hard crusted bread or pita.

LEMON POPPYSEED MUFFINS

These are gluten-free and vegan.

1/4 cup vegan butter at room temperature
1 cup coconut or organic cane sugar
1/4 cup vegan yogurt
2 tsp lemon zest
1 tbsp "Egg Replacer" and 2 tbsp water mixed together.
1 tsp vanilla extract
1/2 cup unsweetened almond or coconut milk
2 cups Gluten Free 1-to-1 Baking Flour
2 tsp baking powder
3/4 tsp sea salt
6 tbsp lemon juice
2 tbsp poppy seeds

For the Glaze:

1/2 cup organic powdered sugar
1 1/2 tbsp lemon juice

In a small bowl, mix 1 tablespoon of lemon juice with the almond milk to create a buttermilk. Set aside. Preheat oven to 425 degrees F. Spray a muffin pan with non-stick flour spray or rub with vegan butter and dust with gluten free flour, removing excess.

In a mixer, cream the butter, sugar and vegan yogurt together with the lemon zest for about 3 minutes. While mixing, whisk the Baking Flour, baking powder and sea salt together in another container. Set aside. In the butter sugar mixture, add the Egg Replacer mix and the vanilla to combine for another 30 seconds, scraping down the bowl. Add the rest of the lemon juice and mix to combine for another 30 seconds. The batter will be watery. Add the flour mixture to the bowl, alternating in sets of three with the buttermilk, ending with the flour. Add the poppy seeds and mix one last time to distribute them throughout the batter.

Using a 1/4 cup measuring cup, pour the batter into each of muffin hole; they should be filled about 1/3 high. Bake for 5 minutes, then reduce the temperature to 350 and bake for 18 minutes until a toothpick inserted into a muffin comes out clean. Remove from oven and allow to cool in pan for about 10 minutes.

Make the Glaze: Mix the powdered sugar and lemon juice together. Pour glaze over the cooled muffins - about a teaspoon per cake. Allow to set for about 5 minutes.

Mimosa

Orange Juice
Champagne
Orange slice

Fill champagne flute or glass about 1/4 full with juice. Add champagne to fill the glass. Place orange slice on the rim of the glass for garnish. Serve.

Blissini

1 1/2 cups Prosecco, chilled
1 1/2 cups orange juice, chilled
1 1/2 cups pomegranate juice, chilled
Mint leaves, for garnish

Combine the Prosecco, orange juice, and pomegranate juice and pour into 4 Champagne glasses. Garnish with mint leaves and serve.

Traditional Bloody Mary

1 (46-ounce) can vegetable or tomato juice
1 tsp pepper
1 tsp salt
1 tbsp Worcestershire sauce

1 lemon, juiced
1 cup vodka
1 tbsp celery seed
4 shakes hot sauce
Ice cubes
10 celery sticks, for garnish

Pour the juice into a large pitcher. Add the pepper, salt, Worcestershire sauce, lemon juice, vodka, celery seed, and hot sauce. Stir well. Pour into jars with lids for traveling. Serve over ice with celery sticks as stirrers

The Holiday That Almost Wasn't

Mother's Day was actually first observed in 1908, when a woman from Grafton, West Virginia named Anna Jarvis held a memorial for her mother. Anna's intent was to honor her own mother by continuing work she started and to set aside a day to honor mothers. Her mother had been a peace activist who cared for wounded soldiers on both sides of the Civil War. Anna petitioned Congress that same year to have Mother's Day declared an official holiday. And Congress said no. One congressman even went on record with the reply "where would it end? Next, you'll want a Mother-in-Law's Day." But in 1914, President Woodrow Wilson signed a proclamation making the second Sunday in May an official holiday for mothers.

The quick commercialization of the new holiday, however so angered Anna Jarvis that she returned to Congress and asked them to rescind the holiday. She organized boycotts and threatened lawsuits and even crashed a candy makers' convention in Philadelphia. And in 1925 during a demonstration against the holiday, she was arrested for disturbing the peace. Ironically, she was protesting at a convention of the American War Mothers, an association which was becoming known for Mother's Day flowers as their annual fundraiser

Just in time for Mother's Day…or any day!

Breakfast in Bed? Sure! Why not?
And yes, you can do this!

I actually get asked this question every year in May. Is it actually appropriate to serve your mother or your wife or girlfriend breakfast in bed for Mother's Day? And how hard is it to round up all the kids at seven in the morning and get them excited about cooking on a Sunday?

Well, here's my advice. If the kids can keep a secret and if the mother of your child is not a light sleeper – and chances are if she's a mom she is *not* a light sleeper – breakfast in bed is a perfectly wonderful day to start the day for your Mother. But it *cannot* be your only gift. You can't leave her any dishes or messes in the kitchen to clean up and you have to keep the kids and the dog from jumping into bed with her while she eats.

And remember, presentation is everything so if you're going to make Mom breakfast in bed this year, make sure you also serve her favorite beverage (whether it's black coffee, milk or mimosas or a Bloody Mary – find out and have it on that tray) and also serve a single flower from a whole vase of matching cousins waiting downstairs. And present her with her cards in the morning. Yes, it may seem like you're making a fuss – and you are and you should. This is your Mom we are talking about –she made *you* – the least you can do is make her Nutella pancakes – or any of the other dishes suggested here.

CRESCENT BREAKFAST SQUARES

Cooking spray
2 cans crescent dough
3 tbsp butter, divided
12 large eggs
1/4 cup milk
salt
pepper
1/4 cup finely chopped chives
1/2 pound deli ham
12 slices cheddar
1 tsp minced onion
1 tsp dried garlic
sea salt

Preheat oven to 375° and grease a baking sheet with cooking spray. In a large bowl, whisk together eggs and half-and- half. In a large nonstick pan over medium heat, melt 1 tbsp. butter. When butter is foamy, reduce heat to low and add egg mixture. Cook, stirring often with a spatula, until eggs are just set. Season with salt and pepper and remove from heat.

Unroll one can of crescents onto greased baking sheet and pinch seams together. Add a layer of ham then top with scrambled eggs, chives and cheese. Unroll second crescent dough and place on top of cheese. Pinch together crescent sheets to seal. Melt remaining butter in microwave. Brush melted butter on top then sprinkle with minced onion, dried garlic, and sea salt. Bake until crescent dough is golden and cooked through, about 25 to 30 minutes. Let rolls come down to room temperature before serving.

STRAWBERRY SWEET ROLLS

1 tube crescent rolls
1 cup strawberry preserves
1 cup chopped strawberries
1 tbsp melted butter
sugar

To make the glaze:

4 oz. cream cheese, softened
4 tbsp butter, softened
1 cup powdered sugar
1 tbsp milk
1 tsp pure vanilla extract
1 tsp lemon zest

Preheat oven to 375° and grease an 8"-x-8" baking pan with cooking spray. On a lightly floured surface, unroll dough and separate the sheet into 4 rectangles. Pinch the perforations to seal. Spread strawberry preserves onto each rectangle, then top with chopped strawberries. Starting with one short side, roll up each rectangle and pinch edges to seal. Cut each roll into 4 to 5 slices. Place side by side, cut side up in baking pan. Brush the tops with melted butter and sprinkle with sugar. Bake until golden, about 15 minutes.

Meanwhile, make glaze: In a medium bowl using a hand mixer, beat cream cheese, butter and powdered sugar until well combined. Add milk, vanilla and lemon zest and mix until smooth.

Drizzle baked rolls with cream cheese glaze. Serve warm.

CREME BRULEE FRENCH TOAST

5 eggs
1 cup milk
1/2 cup heavy cream
1 tsp vanilla
1/4 tsp ground nutmeg
1 tsp cinnamon
kosher salt
1 stick melted butter
3/4 cup brown sugar
1/4 cup maple syrup
1 loaf thickly sliced bread

Confectioners' sugar
Syrup (optional)

Preheat oven to 375 degrees. In a small bowl, whisk together melted butter, brown sugar and maple syrup. Pour mixture into a large tall baking dish and spread into an even layer using a spatula. Arrange bread on top in a single layer. In a large bowl, whisk together eggs, milk, cream, vanilla, cinnamon, nutmeg and salt. Pour mixture over bread. If you have time, cover and let soak in refrigerate for at least an hour. Otherwise, bake for about 25 minutes, or until the butter-sugar mixture is bubbling in the bottom of the pan. Serve immediately, sugar side up. Sift powdered sugar on top if desired. Serve with warm syrup.

BACON, EGG, AND CHEESE BREAKFAST BREAD

Cooking spray
6 slices bacon
4 large eggs
1 1/2 cup skim milk
salt
pepper
3 cans refrigerated biscuits
1 1/2 cup shredded Monterey Jack

Preheat oven to 350° and grease a Bundt pan with cooking spray. In a large skillet over medium heat, cook bacon until crisp, 6 minutes. Transfer to a paper towel-lined plate and let drain, then crumble. In a large bowl, whisk together eggs and milk and season with salt and pepper. Quarter biscuits and dip in egg mixture, then add a layer to the prepared Bundt pan. Add a layer of cheese, then bacon, then continue with biscuit pieces until the pan is three-quarters full. Pour remaining egg mixture over top. Bake until egg is cooked through and bread is golden, 35 to 37 minutes. Let cool, then turn out onto a plate and serve.

Nutella Stuffed Pancakes

1 cup Nutella
Pancake batter, prepared according to package instructions
1 cup sliced strawberries, for serving
Maple syrup, for serving

Line a baking sheet with parchment paper. Dollop about 2 tablespoons of Nutella onto the baking sheet and spread into a flat disc, about 2 ½" wide. Repeat with remaining Nutella. Freeze until solid, about 30 minutes to 1 hour. Keep the Nutella discs in the freezer until required. Heat a large nonstick skillet over medium heat. Grease the pan with cooking spray, then spoon a small amount of pancake batter into the pan. Place a Nutella disc in the center of the batter and spoon a bit more batter on top of the Nutella. When little bubbles appear and start to pop (about 2-3 minutes), flip the pancake. Cook until golden on both sides. Repeat with remaining batter. Serve with sliced strawberries and syrup.

Ham and Cheese Breakfast Casserole

10 large eggs
1 1/2 cup milk
2 tsp Dijon mustard
2 tsp fresh thyme leaves, plus more for garnish
1 tsp garlic powder
salt
black pepper
4 cubed French bread "chunks"
1/2 pound ham, chopped
1 1/2 cup shredded Cheddar

Preheat oven to 350. In a large bowl, whisk together eggs, milk, mustard, thyme, and garlic powder and season generously with salt and pepper. Butter a large baking dish. Add bread and top with ham and cheddar. Pour over egg mixture. Bake until eggs are cooked through and ham golden, 45 to 55 minutes. Garnish with more thyme and serve

It's My Party

Blow out my candles and make a wish....

Yes, the month of May contains Mother's Day and yes, it contains Memorial Day and yes, I could have easily offered you recipes and tips for celebrating each. But been there and done that. All you have to do is look at back on the last few chapters of this book and find those recipes. Instead, I thought I would celebrate a little known holiday that happens in the month of May that only a handful of people celebrate. My birthday.

Yes, my birthday is this month, May 17 in fact. That makes me a Taurus and trust me, I live up to the description. So I thought maybe you wouldn't mind indulging me this edition as I suggest a few birthday cake recipes. Any one of these would be great to show up with (May 17) to celebrate my big day. I wouldn't mind a bit…and if you want to make these for someone else's birthday, well, I guess that would be fine too. Did I mention my birthday is May 17?

And if you don't want to make these for my specific holiday, I am pretty sure there is someone in your life celebrating a birthday this year who would appreciate it.

BIRTHDAY PARTY ICE CREAM CAKE

2 1 1/2-quart containers vanilla ice cream
1 9-ounce package chocolate wafers
1 7-to-8-ounce bottle chocolate shell ice cream topping
1 1 1/2-quart container chocolate ice cream
5 cups whipped cream
Rainbow sprinkles, for decorating

Put a 9-inch spring form pan in the freezer for 15 minutes. Meanwhile, let one container vanilla ice cream soften at room temperature. Remove the pan from the freezer. Spread a 1/2-inch-thick layer of softened vanilla ice cream on the bottom and up the sides of the pan. (If the ice cream gets too soft, return to the freezer.) Freeze until firm, about 45 minutes. Pulse the chocolate wafers in a food processor to break into large crumbs. Add the chocolate shell topping and pulse until the crumbs are moist, about 5 pulses; set aside. Let the chocolate ice cream soften at room temperature, about 15 minutes. Spread over the vanilla layer, firmly packing the ice cream into the pan. Spread the chocolate crumb mixture over the chocolate ice cream. Freeze until set, about an hour. Remove the remaining container vanilla ice cream from the freezer 15 minutes before assembling the final layer. Spread the ice cream over the crumb layer, packing it tightly, then smooth the top with an offset spatula. Freeze until firm. To unmold, wipe the outside of the pan with a hot cloth, then run a hot knife around the inside; unlatch and remove the side. If the ice cream cake is too soft, refreeze. Spread 3 cups whipped cream over the top and sides of the cake. Freeze until set. Put the remaining 2 cups whipped cream in a pastry bag fitted with a star tip; pipe along the top and bottom edges of the cake and decorate with sprinkles. Return to the freezer; remove 15 minutes before serving and slice with a hot knife.

CARROT AND PINEAPPLE CAKE

For the cake:

2 cups granulated sugar
1 1/3 cups vegetable oil
3 extra-large eggs, at room temperature
1 tsp pure vanilla extract
2 1/2 cups plus 1 tablespoon all-purpose flour, divided
2 tsp ground cinnamon
2 tsp baking soda
1 1/2 tsp salt
1 cup raisins
1 cup chopped walnuts
1 pound carrots, grated
1/2 cup diced fresh pineapple

For the frosting:

3/4 pound cream cheese, at room temperature
1/2 pound unsalted butter, at room temperature
1 tsp pure vanilla extract
1 pound confectioners' sugar, sifted

For the decoration:

1/2 cup diced fresh pineapple

Preheat the oven to 350 degrees F. Butter 2 (8-inch) round cake pans. Line with parchment paper, then butter and flour the pans. For the cake: Beat the sugar, oil, and eggs together in the bowl of an electric mixer fitted with the paddle attachment until light yellow. Add the vanilla. In another bowl, sift together 2 1/2 cups flour, the cinnamon, baking soda, and salt. Add the dry ingredients to the wet ingredients. Toss the raisins and walnuts with 1 tablespoon flour. Fold in the carrots and pineapple. Add to the batter and mix well. Divide the batter equally between the 2 pans. Bake for 55 to 60 minutes, or until a toothpick comes out clean. Allow the cakes to cool completely in the pans set over a wire rack. For the frosting: Mix the cream cheese, butter and vanilla in the bowl of an electric mixer fitted with the paddle attachment until just combined. Add the sugar and mix until smooth. Place 1 layer, flat-side up, on a flat plate or cake pedestal. With a knife or offset spatula, spread the top with frosting. Place the second layer on top, rounded side up, and spread the frosting evenly on the top and sides of the cake. Decorate with diced pineapple.

Big Sexy Chocolate Birthday Cake

Cake:

4 sticks butter, plus more for greasing
8 heaping tablespoons cocoa, plus more for dusting
4 cups all-purpose flour
4 cups sugar
1/2 tsp salt
2 cups boiling water
1 cup buttermilk
2 tsp baking soda
2 tsp vanilla extract
4 whole eggs, beaten

Frosting:

3 cups heavy cream
24 ounces semisweet chocolate, broken into pieces
2 tsp vanilla extract

For the cake: Preheat the oven to 350 degrees F. Heavily grease and dust with cocoa four 9-inch round cake pans. In a mixing bowl, combine the flour, sugar and salt. In a saucepan, melt the butter. Add the cocoa. Stir together. Add the boiling water, allow the mixture to boil for 30 seconds and then turn off the heat. Pour over the flour mixture and stir lightly to cool. Combine the buttermilk, baking soda, vanilla and beaten eggs. Stir the buttermilk mixture into the butter/chocolate mixture. Divide the batter among the prepared cake pans and bake for 20 minutes. Cool completely before icing. Refrigerate the layers after cooling for best results. For the frosting: Heat the cream until very hot, and then pour over the chocolate pieces. Stir to completely melt, and then pour into the bowl of an electric mixer. Refrigerate to cool. Once completely cooled, add the vanilla and beat with an electric mixer until light and airy. Frost the cake in between each layer, on the top and around the sides.

POPCORN BIRTHDAY CAKE

1 bag microwave popcorn (kettle style)
1/2 stick unsalted butter, plus more for greasing the pan
2 cups marshmallows
3/4 cup candy coated chocolate

Make popcorn according to the instructions on the bag. In a medium saucepan over medium heat, melt the butter. Add the marshmallows stirring with a wooden spoon until melted. Add the popcorn mixing rapidly from bottom to top until well coated. Add the candy coated chocolate, mixing well to distribute evenly. Butter a 9 by 9-inch baking dish with butter and line with plastic wrap. Pour the popcorn mixture into the prepared pan. Press down with the back of spoon and let it cool. Cut in 4 squares and serve

JUNE

It's All About the Burger, Baby

Summertime...and the grillin' is easy

You know the saying– If you can't stand the heat, get out of the kitchen.

In no other time of the year does that advice apply more than right now – in the summer. No one wants to fire up the kitchen stove when it's 90 degrees and still daylight until nine at night. This is grilling season and outdoor dining season. This is that great time of year when your culinary skills are only as good as a full tank of propane under the grill or the charcoal inside of it. This is the season of the year for eating on the patio, the deck, by the pool, on the beach, under an umbrella, on the tailgate of a truck, at a picnic table on the side of the road, and on your back porch. And the formal dining room becomes that place you won't see again until Thanksgiving.

It's the time of year when you sit on the swing, recline in the hammock, or play fetch with the dog while you wait for the grill to heat up.

Some things might change and go in and out of style in the culinary world, but the one thing that has been constant since 1891, when Chef Otto Kuasw in Hamburg, Germany, dreamed it up, is the burger. And when that recipe for ground beef was introduced to the modern American grill, it was a marriage made in heaven and a new summertime tradition was born.

Summer is definitely burger season. So grab your tongs, your spatula, your appetite and your toasted buns and follow me out into the yard.

THE PERFECT GRILLED BURGER

1 pound lean ground beef
1 tbsp Worcestershire sauce
1 tbsp liquid smoke flavoring
1 tsp garlic powder
1 tbsp olive oil
seasoned salt to taste

Preheat a grill for high heat. In a medium bowl, lightly mix together the ground beef, Worcestershire sauce, liquid smoke and garlic powder. Form into 3 patties, handling the meat minimally. Brush both sides of each patty with some oil, and season with seasoned salt. Place the patties on the grill grate, and cook for about 5 minutes per side, until well done.

MILLION DOLLAR RIB EYE BURGER

2 pounds rib-eye steaks
2 tsp sea salt
1/2 tsp black pepper
8-10 slices of Port Salut cheese
8-10 deep fried onion rings
4-5 brioche buns

Filling:

1 1/4 cups dried morel mushrooms
1 shallot, finely chopped
1/3 cup mushroom broth
2 tbsp olive oil
2 tbsp red wine
1/2 tsp Worcestershire sauce
1/4 tsp paprika
1/4 tsp chili powder
salt and pepper

Sauce:

2 tsp chopped shallots
1/3 cup mushroom broth
2 tsp Dijon mustard
1 tsp tomato paste
1 tsp honey
salt and pepper

Place dried morel mushrooms into a medium bowl. Add 2 cups of hot water to bowl and allow mushrooms to steep for 1 1/2 hours. Remove mushrooms from water and place onto cutting board. Using a kitchen strainer, strain liquid mushroom were steeping in, into another bowl to remove impurities. This liquid is your mushroom broth. In a medium skillet heat olive oil, add 1/2 tablespoon diced shallots. Cook for 2 minutes. Cut mushrooms into bite sized pieces and add to skillet. Cook for an additional minute. Add remaining liquid ingredients and seasonings to skillet. Bring to a boil, reduce heat and simmer for 3-5 minutes or until most of the liquid has dissipated. Make sure to stir occasionally. Remove from heat and allow to cool slightly. For sauce, heat oil and add 2 teaspoons diced shallots. Cook for 1-2 minutes, then add remaining ingredients. Bring to a boil, reduce and simmer until sauce has reduced by half. Remove from heat and let cool. The sauce can be made ahead of time. Preheat grill for medium high heat. Cut excess fat off steaks and cut into chunks. Grind meat according to preference. Add salt and black pepper. Form into eight to ten thin patties. Fill up to five of the patties with mushroom filling. Place remaining patties on top and gently, yet firmly seal edges. Make sure not to over fill. Put patties onto grill grate and cook for 5 minutes per side. Move patties to cooler part of grill and cook for an additional 5 minutes or more depending on thickness of patties. Add cheese slices to patties and cook until cheese has melted. Remove from heat, and place onto a baking sheet. Toast buns, cut side down. minutes. Remove from heat. Assemble your burger to your liking, topping the burger with the sauce and the onion rings.

Brat Burger

1 1/2 pounds bratwurst
1 cup sauerkraut
12 pickle slices
4 hamburger buns
Dijon style mustard

Cut casings from bratwursts and combine. Divide into four equal parts and form into patties. Preheat grill. These bratwurst burgers are going to have a higher fat content than regular burgers so grill them at a medium heat and watch for flare-ups. When burgers are cooked through, remove from the grill. Place on bun and top with sauerkraut, pickles and mustard.

Cuban Burger

1 pound ground beef
1/2 pound ground chorizo
2 cloves minced garlic
1/2 tsp black pepper

Preheat your grill for medium heat. Combine meat and spices in a large bowl. Form into 6-8 patties, about 1/2 inch thick. Place on grill and cook 6 minutes per side. Remove from grill and serve on deli rolls with favorite condiments. I'd suggest chili peppers, mustard, fresh tomatoes and thin onion slices.

Stuffed Bacon Cheeseburger

1 1/2 pounds ground beef
1 cup shredded cheddar cheese
1/2 large onion diced
1/4 pound chopped, crisp cooked bacon
1/2 tsp sea salt
2 tbsp beer

In a mixing bowl, combine bacon, onion, cheddar cheese and set aside. Combine beef, salt and beer, mix thoroughly, the shape into 6 thin patties. Put bacon/onion/cheese mixture on three patties. Top with remaining patties and press edges to seal. Grill until well done, about 4 minutes per side.

How would you like that cooked?

Extra rare (or Blue)
Very red and cold

Rare
cold red center; soft

Medium Rare
warm red center; firmer

Medium
pink inside but firm

Medium well
small amount of pink in the center

Well done
gray-brown throughout; no pink at all; firm

Hey, Dad...This One's for You

Recipes and Suggestions That Will
Make Father's Day Delicious

Let's face it. Mother's Day in May gets a lot of attention.

And yes, deservingly so. This book itself spent an awful lot of time on the subject! After all, when is the last time you saw a football player shout out "Hi Dad" after making a touchdown? When is the last time a Marine came home from a Tour of Duty with "Dad" tattooed on his arm?

Often times, our fathers are our first heroes but I wonder if we give them enough credit. My father died in 2006. He had been ill for quite awhile and I happened to be visiting him and my Mom at their house in Florida when he slipped away. My Dad wasn't one for showing public displays of affection. He was one of those fathers who didn't say "I love you" to his kids a lot. We always had to say it first and he would reply back with "love you too." But he did love us – and his four children knew it. He loved us in the way he treated us and the life he provided for all of us. As a kid, we must have moved a half a dozen times and yet everywhere we went my Dad – Patrick – made all of us feel safe.

Our Dads are those guys who give up their time, their money, and their hearts to their children – and how do we show our appreciation? With a tie? Come on...you know your Dad is worth way more than a trip to the local department store.

This year, why not show Dad your appreciation for all he has done and does for you and treat him to something you make by Hand (pun intended) in the kitchen. The way to a man's heart is his stomach, after all – and your Dad is still a man – and probably a hungry one at that.

FATHER'S DAY MANCAKES

8 slices bacon
1/3 cup packed brown sugar
1 tsp vegetable oil, or as needed
1 1/2 cups all-purpose flour
3 tbsp white sugar
1 1/2 tsp baking powder
10 ounces beer
3 tbsp unsalted butter
1/2 tsp salt
1/2 tsp vanilla extract

Preheat oven to 350 degrees. Line a baking sheet with aluminum foil. Place a wire rack on top of baking sheet; place bacon strips on wire rack. Bake in the preheated oven for 10 minutes; remove from oven and sprinkle tops of bacon strips with half the brown sugar. Return to oven and bake 10 more minutes. Remove from oven and flip bacon to other side; sprinkle with remaining brown sugar and bake until bacon is crisp and brown sugar is golden brown, 10 to 15 more minutes. Remove bacon, let cool, and crumble into small pieces. Lightly grease a skillet with vegetable oil and place over medium-high heat. Whisk flour, white sugar, and baking powder in a large bowl; in a separate bowl, whisk beer, melted butter, salt, and vanilla extract. Lightly stir the liquid ingredients into the flour mixture to make a smooth batter. Stir candied bacon pieces into the batter. Pour batter into the hot skillet 1/2 cup at a time and cook until edges are browned, about 2 minutes; flip pancake and cook until golden brown and the center is set, 3 to 5 more minutes.

BACON WRAPPED BURGERS

12 slices uncooked bacon
1/2 cup shredded Cheddar cheese
1 tbsp grated Parmesan cheese
1 small onion chopped
1 egg
1 tbsp ketchup

1 tbsp Worcestershire sauce
1/2 tsp salt
1/8 tsp pepper
1 pound ground beef
6 hamburger buns

Preheat a grill for high heat. In a large bowl, mix together the Cheddar cheese, Parmesan cheese, onion, egg, ketchup, Worcestershire sauce, salt and pepper. Crumble in the ground beef, and mix together by hand. Form into 6 patties, and wrap two slices of uncooked bacon around each one. Secure bacon with toothpicks. Place patties on the grill, and cook for 5 minutes per side, or until well done. Remove toothpicks before serving on hamburger buns.

BEERBECUE BEEF FLANK STEAK

1/2 cup ketchup
1/4 cup molasses
1/3 cup white vinegar
1 tbsp sugar
2 tsp black pepper
1 tsp salt
1/4 tsp cayenne pepper
1/4 tsp cumin
1/4 tsp allspice
1/4 tsp cinnamon
1 cup dark beer
½ pound trimmed beef flank steak
salt and ground black pepper

Pour ketchup, molasses, and white vinegar in a bowl; add white sugar, 2 teaspoons black pepper, 1 teaspoon salt, cayenne pepper, cumin, allspice, and cinnamon. Whisk until sauce is smooth. Pour in beer. Place flank steak into a baking dish, and pour sauce over meat. Poke at least 100 holes per side in the flank steak using 2 forks. Cover container with plastic wrap and marinate beef from 12 hours to overnight. Remove flank steak from marinade and pat the meat dry with paper towels. Pour leftover marinade into a saucepan, place over medium heat, and bring to a boil. Reduce heat to low and simmer for 5 minutes to make a basting sauce. Preheat an outdoor grill for high heat and lightly oil the grate. Season flank steak with salt and black pepper.

Grill flank steak until prepared to desired "done-ness.' Remove from heat and "paint" meat with heated sauce. Place back on the grill just long enough to glaze the sauce.

A Monte Cristo Benedict

2 large eggs
1/4 cup heavy whipping cream
1 tbsp sugar
1 pinch salt
1 pinch cayenne pepper
1/4 tsp cinnamon
1/8 tsp allspice
4 thick slices day-old French bread
1 tbsp butter
8 thin slices cooked ham
4 slices Cheddar cheese
4 slices Havarti cheese
8 poached eggs
2 tsp chopped fresh chives
1 pinch salt
1 pinch cayenne

Preheat oven to 375 degrees. Whisk 2 eggs, cream, white sugar, salt, 1 pinch cayenne pepper, cinnamon, and allspice together in a bowl until batter is thoroughly combined. Lay bread slices into batter, one at a time, and let bread absorb the mixture. Turn bread slices in batter until almost all batter has been absorbed, about 10 minutes. Heat a large skillet over medium heat, and melt butter in the hot skillet. Cook bread slices in the hot butter until browned, 2 to 3 minutes per side. Transfer French toast slices to a baking sheet. Lay ham slices into the hot skillet and cook until meat begins to brown, about 1 minute per side.

To assemble, place a Cheddar cheese slice on a slice of French toast, top with 2 slices of ham, and lay a Havarti cheese slice over ham.

Bake in the preheated oven until French toast pieces are no longer wet, the batter is set, and cheese has melted and begun to brown, about 20 minutes.

Place sandwiches on serving plates and top each with 2 poached eggs. Season with a pinch of salt and the pinch of cayenne pepper.

DAD'S APPLE PIE

1 pastry for a 9 inch double crust pie
1/2 cup unsalted butter
3 tbsp all-purpose flour
1/4 cup water
1/2 cup white sugar
1/2 cup packed brown sugar
8 Granny Smith apples - peeled, cored and sliced

Preheat oven to 425 degrees. Melt the butter in a saucepan. Stir in flour to form a paste. Add water, white sugar and brown sugar, and bring to a boil. Reduce temperature and let simmer.

Place the bottom crust in your pan. Fill with apples, mounded slightly. Cover with a lattice work crust. Gently pour the sugar and butter liquid over the crust. Pour slowly so that it does not run off. Bake 15 minutes in the preheated oven. Reduce the temperature to 350 degrees and continue baking for 35 to 45 minutes, until apples are soft.

The Old Fashioned Old Fashioned

1 1/2 oz Bourbon or Rye whiskey
2 dashes Angostura bitters,
1 Sugar cube
Few dashes plain water

Place sugar cube in old fashioned glass and saturate with bitters, add a dash of plain water. Muddle until dissolved. Fill the glass with ice cubes and add whiskey. Garnish with orange slice, and a cocktail cherry.

Hit Me with Your Best Shot

If whiskey makes you frisky...

...So whiskey it is!

Remember, in those old Westerns (starring everyone from John Wayne to Kevin Costner), the cowboy would saunter up to the bar, dust flying from his hip saw overcoat. He'd take his hat off, damp with sweat and throw it on the bar. Then his eyes squinted and through gritted teeth he would order a shot of whiskey... straight. He'd gulp it quickly, grab his pistol and shoot the bad guy who was trying to launch a sneak attack from an inside balcony.

Whiskey – for better or for worse – was distilled right alongside of American history. Call it whiskey with the E, whisky without the E, Scotch or Bourbon, but this adult libation has been whetting the whistles of cowboys, back rooms at barbershops, with members of the Rat Pack, Don Draper types and "man caves," and "dens" for generations.

But did you know that a splash of this distilled spirit can also be a welcomed addition to chicken and beef? It can put an interesting flavor in brownies and can even be made into a sweet sauce that you can pour over everything from pancakes to ice cream.

As we head into Barbecue Season and Father's Day, why not grab that bottle of Jack and drag it out to the kitchen or the grill? You know where you're hiding that private stash – it's not exactly a secret – behind the Larry McMurtry paperbacks on the living room bookshelf.

WHISKEY GINGER CHICKEN

4 (4-ounce) skinless, boneless chicken breast halves
1/3 cup bourbon
1/3 cup soy sauce
3 tbsp brown sugar
2 tbsp hoisin sauce
1 tsp grated lime rind
2 tbsp fresh lime juice
2 tsp grated peeled fresh ginger
2 tsp dark sesame oil
1/4 tsp crushed red pepper
2 garlic cloves, minced
Cooking spray
1 tbsp water
1/2 tsp cornstarch
1 tsp sesame seeds, toasted

Place each chicken breast half between 2 sheets of heavy-duty plastic wrap; pound to 1/2-inch thickness using a meat mallet or rolling pin.

Combine bourbon and the next nine ingredients. Reserve 1/3 cup marinade. Pour remaining marinade into a zip-top plastic bag; add chicken. Seal and marinate in refrigerator for at least hour, and up to overnight, turning occasionally. Preheat grill to medium-hot using both burners. Turn left burner off but leave the right burner on. Remove chicken from bag; discard marinade. Coat grill rack with cooking spray. Place chicken on grill rack over right burner; grill 2 minutes on each side or until browned. Move chicken to grill rack over left burner. Cover and cook 5 minutes or until done. Slice each breast diagonally into thin strips; place chicken on a platter. Cover loosely with foil.

Combine water and cornstarch, stirring well with a whisk. Place reserved 1/3 cup marinade in a small saucepan; stir in cornstarch mixture. Bring to a boil; cook 15 seconds, stirring constantly. Drizzle sauce over chicken; sprinkle with sesame seeds.

Filet Mignon with Sweet Bourbon Coffee Sauce

1/2 cup water
3 tbsp bourbon
1 1/2 tsp sugar
1/2 tsp beef-flavored bouillon granules
1/2 tsp instant coffee granules
1/2 tsp black pepper
1/4 tsp salt
4 (4-ounce) beef tenderloin steaks, trimmed (about 1 inch thick)
Cooking spray
2 tbsp chopped fresh parsley

Combine first 5 ingredients in a small bowl; set aside. Sprinkle pepper and salt over both sides of steaks. Heat a medium nonstick skillet over medium-high heat. Coat pan with cooking spray. Add steaks; cook 2 minutes on each side. Reduce heat to medium; cook steaks 2 minutes or until desired degree of doneness. Transfer steaks to a platter; cover and keep warm. Add bourbon mixture to pan; cook over medium-high heat until mixture has reduced to 1/4 cup (about 3 minutes). Serve sauce over beef.

Bourbon Brownies

1/4 cup bourbon
1/4 cup semisweet chocolate chips
1 1/2 cups all-purpose flour
1/2 cup unsweetened cocoa
1 tsp baking powder
1/2 tsp salt
1 1/3 cups sugar
6 tbsp butter, softened
1/2 tsp vanilla extract
2 large eggs
Cooking spray

Preheat oven to 350°. Bring bourbon to a boil in a small saucepan; remove from heat. Add chocolate chips, stirring until smooth. Lightly spoon flour into dry measuring cups, and level with a knife. Combine the flour, cocoa, baking powder, and salt, stirring with a whisk. Combine sugar and butter in a large bowl; beat with a mixer at medium speed until well combined. Add vanilla and eggs; beat well. Add flour mixture and bourbon mixture to sugar mixture, beating at low speed just until combined.

Spread batter into a 9-inch square baking pan coated with cooking spray. Bake at 350° for 25 minutes or until a wooden pick inserted in the center comes out clean. Cool in pan on wire rack.

Bourbon Pecan Sauce

1 cup sugar
1/3 cup water
1/3 cup chopped pecans, toasted
2 tbsp fat-free milk
1 1/2 tbsp butter
1 tbsp bourbon
2 tsp vanilla extract

Combine sugar and 1/3 cup water in a small saucepan over medium-high heat. Cook 5 minutes or until sugar dissolves, stirring constantly. Stir in pecans, milk, butter, bourbon, and vanilla extract. Reduce heat, and cook 3 minutes or until mixture is thick and bubbly. Serve over pancakes, waffles or even ice cream.

Orange Whiskey Punch

1⅔ cups Irish whiskey
1⅔ cups strong black tea
½ cup fresh orange juice
½ cup fresh lemon juice
½ cup Oleo-Saccharum
7 dashes Angostura bitters
1½ tsp fresh nutmeg, plus more for garnish

Combine whiskey, tea, juices, Oleo-Saccharum, Angostura bitters, and 1½ tsp. nutmeg in a large bowl or pitcher; cover and chill up to 8 hours. Strain into a punch bowl over ice. Serve punch in cups.

Classic Whiskey Sour

1 1/2 ounces whiskey
4 ounces sour mix
Crushed ice
1 maraschino cherry

Combine whiskey and sour mix in a large old-fashioned glass with ice. Stir, garnish with cherry, and serve

Summer Dishes...

Light, Easy, and Delicious!

Oh...summer.

How I have missed you.

It's finally June and June marks the "official" start of the summer season – at least on the calendar.

I know for some people, summer starts on Memorial Day but according to the 12 months we have observed for more than 2000 years, June is the first month of the warmest season of the year and it brings with it the long days that linger lazily into cool nights. The sun doesn't set until 9 p.m. and white lights that used to be strung only in December get a new life on decks and in trees to illuminate outdoor entertaining.

It's hot outside. So it should not be hot in your kitchen. And just because the days are longer it doesn't mean you should spend longer hours preparing meals – in fact, you should be doing just the opposite. You should be preparing foods that are light and easy to make, easy to transport to pot luck backyard soirees, impressive to guests and most of all, delicious.

Here are some of my "go-to" recipes for light and easy summer cooking.

Dig in!

And don't forget to invite me over...especially if you have a pool.

Barbecue Chicken with Peach and Feta Slaw

5 tbsp olive oil, divided
2 tbsp sherry vinegar
1/2 tsp freshly ground black pepper, divided
3/8 tsp salt, divided
1 1/2 cups sliced fresh peaches
12-oz. package of broccoli slaw
3 skinless, boneless chicken breasts, cut crosswise into one inch strips
1/4 cup barbecue sauce
1 tbsp chopped chives
¼ cup feta cheese, crumbled
1/8 cup bacon slices, cooked and crumbled

Combine 4 tablespoons oil, vinegar, 1/4 teaspoon pepper, and 1/4 teaspoon salt in a large bowl, stirring with a whisk. Add peaches and slaw to vinegar mixture; toss gently to coat. Sprinkle chicken evenly with remaining 1/4 teaspoon pepper and remaining 1/8 teaspoon salt. Heat remaining 1 tablespoon oil in a large nonstick skillet over medium-high heat. Add chicken to pan; cook 6 minutes or until done. Place chicken in a large bowl. Add barbecue sauce to bowl; toss. When serving, sprinkle with chives, feta, and bacon.

Open-Faced Prosciutto and Plum Sandwiches

1/4 cup fig preserves
1 tbsp fresh lemon juice
1/4 tsp grated peeled fresh ginger
3 ounces soft goat cheese
4 slices wheat or whole grain bread, toasted
1 cup loosely packed arugula
2 ripe plums, cut into thin wedges
3 ounces very thin slices prosciutto

Combine first three ingredients, stirring with a whisk; set aside. Spread 3/4 ounce cheese evenly over each bread slice; divide arugula, plum wedges, and prosciutto evenly over sandwiches. Drizzle each sandwich with about 1 tablespoon fig preserves mixture.

Summer Squash Soup with Pasta and Parmesan

6 cups chicken broth
3 cups water
2 1/4 cups uncooked bow tie pasta
2 cups finely chopped yellow squash
2 cups finely chopped zucchini
1 tbsp chopped parsley
1 tbsp chopped basil
1 tbsp lemon juice
1/2 tsp chopped thyme
1/2 tsp chopped oregano
1/2 tsp ground black pepper
2 ounces grated Parmigiano cheese
1/4 cup thinly sliced basil

Bring broth and water to a boil in a Dutch oven. Add pasta, and cook 8 minutes or until almost tender. Add squash and the next 7 ingredients. Reduce heat, and simmer four minutes or until pasta is done and squash is tender. Sprinkle with cheese and basil.

Crab, Corn, and Tomato Salad
with Lemon-Basil Dressing

1 tbsp grated lemon rind
5 tbsp lemon juice, divided
1 tbsp extra virgin olive oil
1 tsp honey
1/2 tsp Dijon mustard
1/4 tsp salt
1/8 tsp ground black pepper
1 cup corn kernels
1/4 cup thinly sliced basil leaves

1/4 cup chopped red bell pepper
2 tbsp finely chopped red onion
1 pound lump crabmeat
8 slices of ripe beefsteak tomatoes
2 cups cherry tomatoes, halved

Combine rind, 3 tablespoons juice, and next 5 ingredients in a large bowl, stirring well with a whisk. Reserve 1 1/2 tablespoons juice mixture. Add remaining 2 tablespoons juice, corn, and next 4 ingredients (through crab) to remaining juice mixture; toss gently to coat. Arrange 2 tomato slices and 1/2 cup cherry tomatoes on each of 4 plates. Drizzle about 1 teaspoon reserved juice mixture over each serving. Top each serving with 1 cup corn and crab mixture.

GRILLED HALIBUT AND FRESH MANGO SALSA

2 cups plum tomatoes, seeded and diced
1 1/2 cups diced peeled ripe mango
1/2 cup diced onion
1/2 cup chopped fresh cilantro
2 tbsp fresh lime juice
1 tbsp cider vinegar
1 tsp sugar
1 tsp salt, divided
1 tsp black pepper, divided
2 cloves garlic, minced
4 halibut fillets
1 tbsp olive oil

Heat and prepare grill. Combine first 7 ingredients. Stir in 1/2 teaspoon salt, 1/2 teaspoon pepper, and garlic. Rub halibut with oil; sprinkle with 1/2 teaspoon salt and 1/2 teaspoon pepper. Place fish on grill rack; grill 3 minutes on each side or until fish flakes easily when tested with a fork. Serve with mango salsa.

Salmon Cake Burgers

1 cup finely chopped red onion
1/4 cup thinly sliced fresh basil
1/4 tsp salt
1/4 tsp freshly ground black pepper
1 pound salmon fillet, skinned and chopped
1 tbsp hot pepper sauce
1 large egg white
Cooking spray
8 slices focaccia, toasted

Combine first five ingredients in a large bowl. Combine hot pepper sauce and egg white in a small bowl; add egg white mixture to salmon mixture, stirring well to combine. Divide the mixture into four equal portions, shaping each into a 1/2-inch-thick patty. Heat a large nonstick skillet over medium-high heat. Coat pan with cooking spray. Add salmon patties, and cook 3 minutes on each side or until desired degree of doneness. Serve patties on toasted focaccia.

Chicago Dogs

8 hot dog buns
2 quarts water
8 beef franks
1 cup finely diced white onion
1 cup diced tomato
1/2 cup sweet pickle relish
1/3 cup prepared mustard
16 sport peppers

Preheat oven to 350°. Wrap buns in foil; bake at 350° for 10 minutes or until thoroughly heated. Remove from oven, and keep warm. Bring 2 quarts water to a simmer in a large saucepan. Add franks; simmer 5 minutes or until thoroughly heated. Drain well. Place 1 frank in each heated bun. Top each frank with equal amounts of onion, tomato, relish, and mustard. Top with peppers

The Power of Five

Easy Summer Recipes with five ingredients or less

I was cleaning up after a banquet at my job one evening when an older gentleman approached me. He recognized me from my magazine column, he said. He told me he had served in the military in California and lived in Anaheim for a time. He had noticed from my bio in Allegany Magazine that I lived in California once too and he asked me if I knew a 'Richard Hand.' I had to say I was sorry, but I don't.

But it got me thinking of all the times people have asked me two things – when they find out my last name is Hand, one, they comment on someone else with my surname that they know and two, they also ask if I can ever include a column that spotlights recipes with five ingredients or less – it must be because a "Hand" has five fingers. And so while I don't know every Hand on the planet, I do have a few favorite recipes that call for five ingredients or less and are perfect for summer. Try them out….and if you know Richard in Anaheim, tell him an old Army buddy is looking for him.

FRESH MOZZARELLA SALAD

4 medium tomatoes or 6 roma tomatoes
4 ounces fresh mozzarella cheese
2 tbsp bottled balsamic vinaigrette salad dressing
¼ cup loosely packed fresh basil leaves, thinly slice
Salt and Pepper

Cut tomatoes into ½-inch slices. Cut mozzarella cheese into ¼-inch slices. Arrange tomato and cheese slices on a serving platter. Drizzle tomato and cheese slices with vinaigrette dressing. Sprinkle with basil, salt, and pepper.

Mushroom Tomato Pesto Pizza

1 12 inch Italian bread shell (such as Boboli brand)
½ c purchased dried tomato pesto
1 cup shredded pizza cheese blend
1 6 oz package refrigerated cooked Italian-style chicken breast strips
1½ c sliced fresh mushrooms

Place bread shell in a 12 inch pizza pan. Spread pesto over bread shell. Sprinkle with half of the cheese. Top with the chicken pieces and mushrooms. Sprinkle with the remaining cheese. Bake, uncovered, in a 400 degree oven for 10 to 15 minutes or until cheese is golden and bubbly.

Cacciatore Style Penne Pasta

1 pound dried penne pasta
8 ounce lean ground beef or bulk Italian sausage
¾ cup chopped green sweet pepper
1 14-ounce jar pasta sauce
1 1/2-ounce can (drained weight) sliced mushrooms, drained

Cook pasta according to package direction; drain. Return to hot pan; cover and keep warm. Meanwhile, in a large skillet cook ground beef and sweet pepper over medium-high heat until meat is brown and pepper is tender. Drain off fat. Stir in pasta sauce and mushrooms; heat through. In a large serving bowl toss meat mixture with hot cooked pasta.

Cheese and Garlic Crescents

1 8-ounce package refrigerator crescent rolls
¼ cup semisoft cheese with garlic and herbs
2 tbsp finely chopped walnuts, toasted

Milk
1 tbsp seasoned fine dry bread crumbs

Unroll crescent rolls; divide into 8 triangles. In a small bowl combine cheese and walnuts. Place a rounded teaspoon of the cheese mixture near the center of wide end of each crescent roll. Starting at the wide end, roll up dough. Place rolls, point sides down, on a greased baking sheet. Brush tops lightly with milk; sprinkle with bread crumbs. Bake, uncovered, in a 375° oven about 11 minutes or until bottoms are browned. Serve warm.

PINEAPPLE FRIES

1 medium fresh pineapple
2 cups frozen raspberries, thawed
1 to 2 tbsp sugar
Nonstick cooking spray
6 giant waffle ice cream cones

Remove crown and cut off top and base of pineapple. Cut off wide strips of peel. Remove eyes by cutting marrow wedge-shape groves diagonally around fruit, following patter of the eyes. Slice pineapple lengthwise into ½-inch slices. Coarsely chop 1/3 cup of the pineapple from an end piece. Set remaining slices aside. For ketchup, in a blender combine raspberries and sugar. Cover and blend until smooth. Press berry mixture through a sieve; discard seeds. Return berry mixture to blender. Add the 1/3 cup chopped pineapple. Cover and blend until smooth. Cover and chill ketchup until ready to serve. Lightly coat pineapple slices with nonstick cooking spray. For a charcoal grill, grill pineapples slices on the rack of an uncovered grill directly over hot coals for 5-7 minutes or until lightly browned, turning once halfway through grilling. (For a gas grill, preheat grill. Place pineapple slices on grill rack over high heat. Cover and grill as above.) Remove pineapple slices from grill; cool slightly. Cut gilled pineapple into about ½-inch strips. Divide pineapple fries among waffle cones; top with some of the raspberry ketchup.

Cotton Candy Cocktail

1 oz amaretto
1 oz limoncello
3 oz pink lemonade
Dash grenadine
Crushed ice, for serving

In a cocktail shaker, add the amaretto, limoncello, lemonade, and grenadine. Shake, and then pour into a rocks glass filled with crushed ice. The look of this is to have it look like a snow cone, with lots of ice sticking out of the glass and pour the drink on top of the ice.

Cilantro Shrimp

1 lb. fresh or frozen jumbo shrimp in shells (20 to 24 shrimp)
2 tbsp snipped fresh cilantro
1 tbsp lemon juice
1 tbsp butter, melted
3 or 4 cloves garlic, minced
1 fresh red Serrano chile pepper, seeded and finely chopped

Thaw shrimp, if frozen. Using a sharp knife, butterfly each shrimp by cutting a deep slit along its back through the shell (do not cut all the way through shrimp), leaving tail intact. Devein shrimp; flatten with your hand. Rinse shrimp; pat dry. In a small bowl combine cilantro, lemon juice, melted butter, garlic, and if desired, Serrano pepper. Brush shrimp with lemon mixture. Place shrimp, split side down, in a lightly greased grill basket. For a charcoal grill, place basket on the rack of an uncovered grill directly over medium coals. Grill for 5 to 8 minutes or until shrimp are opaque, turning basket once halfway through grilling. (For gas grill, preheat grill. Reduce heat to medium. Place shrimp in basket on grill rack over heat. Cover and grill as above.)

OVEN FRIED COCONUT CHICKEN

½ cup flaked coconut
¼ cup seasoned fine dry bread crumbs
2 ½ to 3 pounds meaty chicken pieces
¼ cup butter or margarine, melted

In a shallow bowl stir together coconut and bread crumbs; set aside. Brush chicken pieces with melted butter. Roll chicken pieces in coconut mixture to coat all sides. In a 15x10x1 or a 13x9x2 inch baking pan arrange chicken so pieces don't touch. Drizzle any remaining melted butter over chicken. Bake, uncovered, in a 375° oven for 45-50 minutes or until chicken is tender and no longer pink. Do not turn.

COOKIES-AND-CREAM CUPCAKES

1 package 2-layer-size white cake mix
1 cup coarsely crushed chocolate sandwich cookies with white filling
1 16-ounce can cream white frosting
24 miniature sandwich cookies with white filling

Line twenty-four 2 ½ inch muffin cups with paper bake cups; set aside. Prepare cake mix according to package directions, except fold the crushed cookies into batter. Spoon batter into prepared cups, filling each about half full. Bake, uncovered, in a 350 oven according to package directions. Cool in muffin pans on wire racks for 5 minutes. Remove cupcakes from pans. Cool on wire racks. Pipe or spread frosting onto cupcakes. Top with the miniature cookies.

JULY

Hand Over Your Heart

Tasty Alternatives to Flying the Flag

All summer long, as a veteran of the U.S. Navy I believe in flying the American flag. And I follow the rules about how high it should be on the pole and how to fold it when it comes down and how to dispose of it when the flag needs to be replaced. Hanging in my living room is the flag my Uncle Bill (I was named for him) had on the back of his Swift Boat during the Vietnam War. Its edges are tattered and worn. The flag has seen better and more glorious days but that flag represents not only my service to the country but my uncles and to all service men and women who have given so much to their nation.

Shortly after the devasting tragedies that occurred in New York, Washington and Pennsylvania in September 2001, my father wrote all of his children a letter and placed that letter in the mail. He did not email it, Tweet it, or make it a social media post. He mailed it. His intent behind it was to reassure all four of his adult children that the United States would rise to the occasion and become a stronger country than it was even before 9-11. I thought for this book I would reprint that letter from my dad – along with the recipe that follows (it was a Fourth of July family favorite for us Hands).

Thank you, Dad for reminding us what patriotism, strength and independence is really about. I miss you.

"I can recall December 7, 1941 very well. I was six years old. We returned from mass and went to my Aunt Mary's and Uncle Bru's for breakfast, which was not uncommon. They lived about two blocks from us at that time in Edison Park, Illinois. My uncle Harold was in the Navy, probably stationed at Great Lakes for training. We were listening to the radio. There was no TV then. We heard the

announcement that the Japanese were bombing Pearl Harbor. I was too young to understand the significance, other than the fears among family members that Uncle Harold would be involved. As it turns out, he was assigned later to the European theater.

I can also recall when police action was declared in Korea. I was a lifeguard at Whealen Pool and I was 16 years old. The Selective Service was reactivated and all the lifeguards were concerned about the draft. As it turns out, I was too young for Korea and then too old for Vietnam, although my brother, Bill, served in the Navy on two swift boats in Vietnam rivers and my wife's brother, Marvin, served in the Air Force stationed in Saigon.

I was in in Downtown Chicago when President John F. Kennedy was assassinated. These were all very sad times and I, as well as others, were very depressed.

I was in Louisville, Kentucky on business when Desert Storm started and can recall watching the attack by airplane and missile.

Now in my lifetime I have seen the attacks on soil again – in New York, Washington, and in Shanksville, Pa. This will all have an effect on our lives – as will other events to come in the future that we cannot see coming.

I would urge you to continue to hold your head high, out of reach of these adversities, out of reach of the constant bombardment of bad news. How and how much we are impacted by devasting news – personal and global – is up to us. We determine our own response. We might not be able to control what is happening around us but we can control how much we react.

The United States has weathered other setbacks and will weather this one. The United States rose to greater heights then and it will again. And so will we.

Patrick Hand
1935-2006

RED WHITE AND BLUEBERRY CHEESECAKE

8 sheets Phyllo dough
¼ cup butter, melted
2 (8 ounce) packages cream cheese
½ cup white sugar
1 tsp vanilla
2 eggs
2 cups fresh blueberries
½ cup strawberry jelly

On a flat surface, place one sheet phyllo dough. Brush it with melted butter and cover with another piece of dough. Repeat until all sheets are used. Using kitchen scissors, cut layered dough into a 12 to 13 inch circle. Carefully place circle into a greased 9 inch pie plate. Gently fan edges. Bake at 425 degrees until edges are just golden, 6 to 8 minutes. Allow to cool to room temperature.

In a medium bowl, beat cream cheese, sugar and vanilla with a mixer until light and fluffy. Beat in eggs until well combined. Fold in 1 cup blueberries. Pour filling into prepared crust.

Bake at 350 degrees until set of 40 to 50 minutes. To prevent over browning of crust, gently cover pie with foil for the last 25 minutes of baking. Cool completely.

In a small bowl, beat jelly until smooth. Spread over cheese filling. Arrange 1 cup blueberries on top into a star pattern.

PATRIOTIC POPSICLES

1 ½ cups lightly packed chopped strawberries
3 tbsp sugar
1 cup canned light coconut milk
1 tsp vanilla extract
1½ cups blueberries

Puree the strawberries in a blender or food processor with 1 tablespoon sugar. Pour about 2 tablespoons into each of 9 popsicle molds. Freeze this layer until solid. Mix the coconut milk, another tablespoon of sugar, and vanilla. Pour about 2 tablespoons into the molds. Freeze this layer until slushy – then insert the wooden sticks and freeze until solid. Puree the blueberries in a blender or food processor with the last tablespoon of sugar. Pour about 2 tablespoons into each of the popsicle molds. Make sure not to fill the molds over the "fill" line, since liquid expands as it freezes. Freeze the pops until solid before unmolding. Pop them out and enjoy.

BLUEBERRY SHEET CAKE WITH STRAWBERRY BUTTERCREAM

For the Cake:

2 cups granulated sugar
2 tsp baking powder
1 tsp baking soda
1 tsp table salt
1/4 tsp cardamom
2 1/2 cups all-purpose flour
1 tbsp., divided 1 cup whole buttermilk
1 cup tahini (sesame paste)
3/4 cup water
1/2 cup unsalted butter, melted
2 tsp vanilla extract
2 large eggs
1 1/2 cups fresh blueberries

For the Strawberry Buttercream:

1 cup unsalted butter softened
6 cups powdered sugar
1 tsp vanilla extract
1/4 tsp salt
3 tbsp whole milk, divided
1/3 cup chopped fresh strawberries

Preheat oven to 350°F. Grease and flour a 13- x 9-inch cake pan, and line bottom with parchment paper; lightly grease parchment paper. Whisk together sugar, baking powder, baking soda, salt, cardamom, and 2 1/2 cups of the flour in a large bowl. Whisk together buttermilk, tahini, water, butter, vanilla, and eggs in a medium bowl. Whisk buttermilk mixture into flour mixture until thoroughly combined. Toss blueberries with remaining 1 tablespoon flour; gently fold coated blueberries into batter. Spoon batter into prepared pan. Bake in preheated oven until a wooden pick inserted in center comes out clean, 40 to 45 minutes. Cool in pan on wire rack for 20 minutes. Invert on wire rack and cool completely, about 1 hour.

Prepare the Strawberry Buttercream: Beat butter with a heavy-duty stand mixer on medium speed until creamy. Gradually add powdered sugar, vanilla extract, salt, and 2 tablespoons of the milk, beating until blended. Gently fold in chopped strawberries. Stir in remaining 1 tablespoon milk, 1 teaspoon at a time, until desired consistency is reached. Frost cake with Strawberry Buttercream.

RED WHITE AND BLUE SANGRIA

Red Layer:

2 cups frozen raspberries
3/4 cup white wine
1 tbsp maple syrup

White Layer:

2 1/2 cups ice
1/2 cup white wine

Blue Layer:

3 cups ice
2 ounces vodka
1/4 cup white wine

1 tbsp maple
1 drop blue food coloring

Red Layer: Add ingredients to the blender and blend until smooth. Pour into a large cup or jar and place into the freezer while you create the other layers.

White Layer: Repeat the steps and set aside in the freezer.

Blue Layer: Add everything to the blender and blend until smooth.

Pour the blue layer into glasses, followed by the white layer, and finishing with the red layer.

"Elevated and Celebrated"

A Taste of the Good Ol' American County Fair

Who doesn't love the county fair?

The amusement rides, the animals, the concerts in a great outdoor open setting.

Isn't it amazing to think that in communities and counties all over the United States – from the mountains to the prairies, to the oceans white with foam…. (cue Kate Smith), there is one large sprawling field dedicated to one event that happens one weekend a year? The fairgrounds may be used for many other purposes throughout the year, but for one summer weekend, their original purpose shines under neon and electric lights.

But the one thing that has been tried and true and makes the All-American County Fair such a staple in our culture is the food. There actually is a classification in my business called "fair food." And no, it doesn't mean food that is rated somewhere between poor and good. It means treats that normally you can only enjoy if you get your hand stamped or get a wrist band at the gate and enter the fairgrounds.

It's food that reminds us of summer. Fried, messy, wrapped in foil and carried on paper plates to picnic tables. Yes… it's junk food…. But it's junk food that is somehow elevated and celebrated.

But did you know you could replicate some of these favorite tasty treats in your own kitchen? Try out these recipes and let me know if they taste like your local county fair. If I don't get back to you right away, don't worry – I might be on the Tilt-a-Whirl and will return your message once the ride and my head stop spinning.

Deep Fried Cookie Dough

Premade refrigerated cookie dough
Ready made biscuit dough
oil for frying

Make 1 inch balls with cookie dough and place back in refrigerator until right before frying. Separate each biscuit dough slice into two. Roll out each piece and flatten slightly with rolling pin. Heat oil in pot being used for frying. Wrap dough around cold cookie dough, making sure to seal it properly. Drop into hot oil and fry for a few minutes on each side until golden brown. Repeat with remaining dough. Dust with powdered sugar before serving. You can also add a chocolate drizzle.

Frozen Chocolate Bananas and Bacons

8 ice pop sticks
4 bananas, peeled and halved
3 cups dark chocolate chunks
4 tbsp coconut oil
1 cup chopped peanuts
1 cup crumbled, crisp cooked bacon

Line a sheet pan with parchment paper or foil. Insert the pop sticks as far into the cut ends of the bananas as you can without poking the stick out of the side or other end. Make sure you leave enough room to hold onto. Lay the bananas out on the prepared tray, put in the freezer and freeze for at least 2 hours. Toss together the chopped peanuts and crumbled bacon on a dinner plate. Working quickly, take one frozen banana half at a time, dunk into the chocolate dip and roll around to coat thoroughly, then quickly lift the banana and press into the peanut/bacon mixture. Transfer the coated banana back to the lined pan and repeat until you run out!

To Make the Chocolate Shell Coating: Put the chocolate chunks into a microwave safe container and microwave on high for 1 minute. Remove and stir to check whether the chocolate is melted. If it is not, microwave again in 15 second increments until it is. When chocolate is completely melted, add the coconut oil and stir until smooth.

FUNNEL CAKES MADE EASY

2 eggs
1 cup milk
1 cup water
1/2 tsp vanilla extract
3 cups all-purpose flour
1/4 cup sugar
3 tsp baking powder
1/4 tsp salt
Oil for deep-fat frying
Confectioners' sugar

In a large bowl, beat eggs. Add milk, water and vanilla until well blended. In another bowl, whisk flour, sugar, baking powder and salt; beat into egg mixture until smooth. In an electric skillet or deep-fat fryer, heat oil to 375°. Cover the bottom of a funnel spout with your finger; ladle 1/2 cup batter into the funnel. Holding the funnel several inches above the oil, release your finger and move the funnel in a spiral motion until all the batter is released, scraping with a rubber spatula if needed. Fry 2 minutes on each side or until golden brown. Drain on paper towels. Dust with confectioners' sugar; serve warm.

ITALIAN SAUSAGE SANDWICHES

6 links sweet Italian sausage (Mild Ground)
2 tbsp butter
1 yellow onion, sliced
1/2 red onion, sliced
4 cloves garlic, minced
1 large red bell pepper, sliced
1 green bell pepper, sliced

1 tsp dried basil
1 tsp dried oregano

Place the sausage in a large skillet over medium heat, and brown on all sides. Remove from skillet, and slice. Melt butter in the skillet. Stir in the yellow onion, red onion, and garlic, and cook 2 to 3 minutes. Mix in red bell pepper and green bell pepper. Season with basil, and oregano. Add water if necessary for moisture. Continue to cook and stir until peppers and onions are tender. Return sausage slices to skillet with the vegetables. Reduce heat to low, cover, and simmer 15 minutes, or until sausage is heated through. Serve in a nice thick "Hoagie-style" bun.

SPICY CORN ON THE COB

6 ear corn
¼ cup mayonnaise
2 limes
Ground chipotle
¾ c. grated Manchego cheese

Heat grill to medium. Grill corn, turning occasionally until all sides are charred and kernels are tender, 20 to 25 minutes. Meanwhile, in a small bowl, stir together mayonnaise and juice of half a lime. Remove corn from grill and spread with thin layer of mayonnaise mixture. Sprinkle each cob with a pinch of chipotle and 1/8 cup cheese. Serve immediately.

CARAMEL APPLE PIE

1 refrigerated pre-ready pie crust.
1 cup butterscotch caramel ice cream topping
4 tbsp all-purpose flour
8 cups baking apples, peeled, cored, sliced 1/2 inch
1/2 cup packed brown sugar
1 1/2 tsp cinnamon
1 tsp milk
2 tsp sugar

Preheat oven to 400°F. Place cookie sheet on bottom oven rack. In small bowl, mix 1/2 cup topping and 2 tablespoons flour; spread in bottom pie crust. In large bowl, mix apples, brown sugar, 2 tablespoons flour and the cinnamon. Spoon over caramel. Gently press apples. Cut small shapes from top crust to allow steam to escape. Place crust over apples. Seal edge and flute. Brush crust with milk; sprinkle with sugar. Bake 60 to 70 minutes or until apples are tender and crust is golden brown. In small microwavable bowl, place remaining 1/2 cup topping. Microwave uncovered on High 30 to 45 seconds or until warm. Spoon over each slice of pie after it is cut.

Fresh Foods at our Finger tips

17 Reasons to Love the Month of July
...well, 18 if you count the weather

Welcome to the lazy hazy days of ...well...you get it.

It's July! The month of tank tops, flip-flops, poolside drinks and park picnics. It's the month of Frisbee, volleyball, and croquet playing. It's also one of my favorite months of the year for food – fresh produce in particular. This is the month to take advantage of everything the local Farmer's Markets have to offer. I can't say enough nice things about the jobs our local farmers do and the good they bring to our tables and this time of year, the open markets everywhere give all of us a chance to taste our hometown. Summertime...and the eatin' is easy.

But what's in season? To answer that, simply grab a basket and let's stroll the produce aisle together. You coming?

Avocados

A friend of mine says "I love guacamole. But I can't stand avocado." So let's not tell him! It's our secret. Avocado on toast is one of the simplest dishes you can make. The avocados you'll find in stores are probably from South of the Border, where avocados are in season year-round, but they are at their best when you find them at your local markets right now. Avocado by itself sliced up is a great treat but try making it into a hummus, put it in a grilled cheese sandwich, try it in a breakfast.

Blackberries

They are so great, they leave a mark on your fingers when you pick them. Plump, juicy, sweet blackberries are a snack and dessert alone. But they are also fantastic options for dishes like muffins, jam, pancakes, and cobbler.

Blueberries

While we're on the subject of blackberries, how about their distant cousin – blueberries. Blueberries are not only delicious, they are healthy – nature's own little vitamin pill – loaded with antioxidants. Throw a handful in your ice cream, oatmeal, cereal and even inside a salad.

Cherries

Sweet, red cherries make their best presentation in July. Yes, they can be eaten alone (watch out for the pits), or you can bake them into a pie, add them to cocktails, and mix them into cakes and cookies. Cherries pair nicely with chocolate, for instance.

Corn

When you think summer, don't you think sweet roasted corn on the cob? Try roasting it and carving it off into dishes like salad, breads, and even soups. Corn also freezes nicely off the husk.

Cucumbers

Crisp cucumbers always remind me of summer. And their hydrating qualities make them an excellent juicing ingredient. Cucumber salads are popular this time of year. But I like to simply slice fresh cucumbers and soak the slices with a touch of lemon in a pitcher of water. Cucumber water is one of the most refreshing drinks you will ever taste. Try it. I promise.

Fresh Greens

Who doesn't love a fresh greens salad? Check your local market for arugula, spinach, lettuce, spinach, Swiss chard and watercress this month. And when you make that salad, break the fresh leaves apart. Don't chop them. Just tear, break, and toss with your favorite salad ingredients.

Green Beans

Who doesn't have a great memory of sitting on the back porch as a kid helping Grandma snap fresh green beans? There's a reason this is such a great childhood memory of summer. Maybe that's what's wrong with society today. Not enough back porch bean snapping. Fresh green beans go great with almonds, basil, a little butter and Parmesan.

Kale

Kale is the "it" produce at the moment. Everyone seems to love kale. And for good reason! It's tremendously good for you and totally delicious, given the right preparation. You can chop kale for stir-fries, serve it mixed in with greens, salt and pepper it and roast it, or throw chunks of it in a smoothie and blend it with fruits. It also makes a great dressing and can be blended in with guacamole. Just don't tell my friend the guac has both avocado and kale!

Mango

Remember the Saturday Night Live sketch – "everybody loves Mango." I know I do. I love the rich sweet summer smell of a fresh mango. Some people call mangos tropical peaches. Alone or mixed in with favorite fruits, they can be lovely salads, ice cream toppings, smoothie ingredients, or desserts.

Peaches

Speaking of which….fresh, local peaches epitomize summer. Feel free to eat them, slice them up with ice cream, bake them into a pie, use them in jams, stir them into salsas, and dip them into yogurt

Peppers

Peppers! All kinds of peppers – all in season in July and ready for the pickings. And did you know that green, yellow, orange and red bell peppers are all the same variety of pepper, just picked at different stages? Green peppers are the youngest. The more red the pepper, the more time it had to mature before picking.

Plums

I can't resist a plump, juicy plum, can you? I do like a sweet variety but I know folks who like their plums a little on the tart side. Treat plums as you would their first cousin – the peach. Serve them raw or roasted or baked to bubbly perfection, in salads or desserts.

Radishes

The understated and often ignored radish – the "backstage crew" of the summer basket. But I actually love radishes! Raw, chopped radishes lend a spicy crunch to salads. And nothing beats a great plate of tangy pickled radish

Raspberries

The raspberry season in the summer is brief. And this is it. Raspberries don't "keep" as long as other berries and they are fragile even when plucked from the vine. Ripe raspberries are sweet, tender but not mushy, and pretty much perfect as is. They go great with cream, lemon, vanilla, almonds, honey and other berries.

Strawberries

Strawberries are here! July is the month for them. Succulent, beautiful, tasty, tangy strawberries. Who doesn't think of strawberries when you think of summer? They go great in ice cream, alone with pound cake and whipped cream, in salads – but have you ever tried strawberries on pizza? No? You've been missing out!

Tomatoes

Tomatoes are in full bloom right now. Ripe tomatoes don't need much help when it comes to preparation—a sprinkle of sea salt and a drizzle of olive oil is about all you need. Raw and roasted tomatoes are also amazing with garlic and basil. Just make sure you use them before you lose them.

P.S.: Have you hugged a Chef today? July is National Chef Appreciation Month!

Snap! Crackle! Pop! Wow! Hosting the Summer Blockbuster Block Party

Throwing a Super Party and Being the Hero of your own Backyard

Boom. Pow. Pop. You're invited! To the summer blockbuster of the year... and it's happening in your own backyard. Can't get enough of the superhero summer season? Bring it to your next pool party barbecue or birthday! Superheroes don't have to be just for the kids (*Deadpool*, anyone?) and neither do superhero themed soirees. So, this summer, whether it's by the beach, by the pool, in the yard, or on the porch, you can be a super man or a wonder woman by concocting some of these superhero themed recipes – and yes, including some cocktails. And I promise – none of them will make you too Thor to enjoy them yourself.

Afterall, what's a "super "party without super snacks? You can easily host a superhero party to ask guests to dress in their favorite superhero party gear or t-shirts. I hear adult Underoos are also making a comeback....but that's a column for someone else to write. But for now, whether you are hosting a party for the younger set or the older crowd, these suggestions should make you super.

For the adults:

THE DARK KNIGHT

1-1/2 oz. Sambuca
4 oz. Cola
1/2 oz. Homemade Grenadine
Maraschino Cherry Garnish

Build in a highball glass over ice, topping off with grenadine as float.
Garnish with maraschino cherry.

THE HULK

2 oz. Captain Morgan's Spiced Rum
1 tbsp Sugar
2 liter bottle of Mountain Dew

Add Captain Morgan to a glass with sugar, then add Mountain Dew until
the mix turns green.

MAN OF IRON

3 oz. Vodka
7 oz. Whiskey
5 ice cubes
Soda Water

Mix vodka and whiskey in an old-fashioned glass. Stir. Add a few ice cubes,
fill with soda water and stir gently.

SPINNING A WEB

1.0 oz. Cherry Liqueur
1.0 oz. Raspberry Liqueur

2.0 oz. Tequila
Packet of Pop Rocks

Mix cherry liqueur raspberry liqueur, and Tequila in average sized glass, add pop rocks.

MAN OF STEEL

1/3 oz. Schnapps, peach
1/3 oz. Rum, coconut
1/3 oz. Triple Sec
1 splash Grenadine

Fill with Pineapple Juice

Fill glass with ice, add equal parts rum, peach schnapps and triple sec. Fill with pineapple juice, stir. Top with grenadine.

WOMAN OF WONDER

2 oz. Midori melon liqueur
2 oz. Peach schnapps
3 oz. Orange juice
1 oz. Pineapple juice
2 oz. Cranberry juice

Fill a hurricane glass with ice. Add ingredients in order listed. Don't stir! Should have three layers; green, orange, and red. Garnish with a cherry.

WOLVERINE

1 beer
1 shot lemon rum

Pour shot into glass of beer, drink before your healing factor can reject it.

SHAZAM

1 shot Apple Schnapps
1 shot Raspberry Liqueur
3/4 oz Ice

(Fill to Top) Cranberry Juice

Add all ingredients to shaker. Shake to chill. Strain out ice and pour into glass.

And now... for the Kids:

- Even if Popeye isn't at the party, offer an iron-rich "muscle-building" spinach dip or bite-sized spanakopita. And everyone will love bacon cups filled with baked beans.
- For super X-ray vision, carrots are a must. Serve with a garlicky hummus to ward off bad spirits. Then drizzle mini black bean cakes with a sour cream sauce to resemble spider webs.
- If Superman is going to be there, kryptonite is a must. Place small bowls of rock candy and spicy bar nuts around as snacks. And no superhero will turn down meat. Set out a selection of charcuterie, cheeses, and these prosciutto rolls that are easy to enjoy in one bite.

GROOT COOKIES

Someone will have to be the "Guardian of the Cookie Jar" after these are made.

3 cups all-purpose flour
1/2 tsp cinnamon
1/2 tsp baking powder
Pinch of salt
2 sticks unsalted butter, softened
1 cup brown sugar
1 egg
Chocolate frosting

Black colored frosting
Matcha (green tea) powder

In a medium bowl whisk together the flour, cinnamon, baking powder and salt. Set aside. In the bowl of an electric mixer beat the butter and brown sugar until combined. Add the egg. Slowly add in the flour mixture until it is incorporated. The dough will form quickly, and when it starts to pull away from the bowl, it's done!

Split the dough into two and wrap in plastic wrap. Chill until you are ready to use.

Preheat the oven to 350 degrees. Prep baking sheets. Roll the dough to about 1/4 inch thick. Cut out random tree looking shapes about 4 inches tall and transfer onto the cookie sheet. Bake for 10 minutes then let cool on a wire rack.

Using a #2 tip and chocolate frosting, pipe lines to resemble tree bark.

With the black frosting and a #3 tip add the details of two eyes and a line for Groot's mouth.

For the final touch, use a pastry paintbrush dipped in Matcha (green tea) powder and add some hints of green to the top of Groot's head.

Once the frosting has set, the cookies are ready to serve

Captain America Snack Mix

1 cup milk chocolate chips
4 cups Rice Chex cereal
1 1/4 cups powdered sugar
Peanut M&M's in red, white, and blue
Whoppers Candy

Line a large baking sheet with wax paper or parchment. Put 4 cups of cereal in a large mixing bowl. Set both aside. Put the milk chocolate chips into a microwave-safe bowl. Microwave on high for 30 seconds. Stir. Repeat in 30 second intervals until the chocolate is fully melted. Use a large spoon to drizzle the melted chocolate over the cereal. Gently mix as you drizzle, making sure to coat the cereal evenly. Place the powdered sugar in a 1 gallon zip-top bag. Carefully scoop the chocolate-coated cereal into the bag with the powdered sugar. Seal the bag and shake it to cover the cereal with the powdered sugar. Let sit for 1-2 minutes, then spread it out onto the prepared baking sheet. Let dry for 1 hour. Put your cereal back in the large bowl and gently mix in the Whoppers and M&Ms.

THOR HAMMERS

One bag of mini pretzel sticks
Cheddar cheese cubes

(It's this easy) Cut cheese into trapezoid sized pieces. Stick pretzels into cheese cubes to look like hammers. You are now worthy!

SPIDER MAN STRAWBERRIES

Peter Parker approved!

Large Strawberries
Dark and White chocolate
Cocktail stirrers/or skewer sticks

Insert sticks into strawberries. Paint eyes with a brush and melted white chocolate. Border the eyes with a line of melted dark chocolate. Make three vertical lines from the nose to the forehead and the nose to the chin. Touch up with brush. Place on wax paper to dry. Chill under ready to serve

How You'd Like A Nice Hawaiian Punch?

Bring the Islands to your Home This July

For more years than I am ever going to admit – the month of July has reminded me of Hawaii. I know while most people have thoughts of fireworks and family, I remember the July right after my senior year in high school. I had finished basic training and was stationed with the U.S. Navy in Pearl Harbor in Hawaii. Barely 18 and stationed among the palm trees and coconuts – who could have asked for a better assignment? It was in Hawaii that I would spend the majority of my military service, learning to cook in the mess hall of a Destroyer.

That summer, I also attended more than one authentic Hawaiian luau. And let me tell you, a traditional Hawaiian luau feast is an event – not just a feast but a celebration, with dancing and entertainment. Among people from Hawaii, the concepts of "luau" and "party" are often blended, resulting in graduation luaus, wedding luaus, birthday luaus, and yes, even Independence Day luaus.

So put on your grass skirt, put a lei around your neck, kick off your shoes, join me in a very awkward hula and let's try out some foods the folks in our 50th state are cooking up right about now.

Coconut Shrimp With Orange Marmalade

2 cups shredded sweetened coconut
2 cups bread crumbs
Salt and freshly ground black pepper
2 cups all-purpose flour
4 large eggs, beaten
24 large shrimp, peeled and deveined
Vegetable oil, for frying

Dipping Sauce:

1/2 cup orange marmalade
1 to 2 tbsp dark rum

In a large bowl, combine coconut and bread crumbs and season with salt and pepper. Place flour, eggs, and bread crumb mixture into 3 separate bowls. Dredge the shrimp in flour and shake off excess. Next, dip the shrimp thoroughly in the egg and rub against the side of the bowl to lightly remove excess. Finally, coat the shrimp thoroughly with the bread crumb mixture. Lay out the shrimp so they do not touch on a parchment-lined baking sheet or platter until ready to fry. In a large Dutch oven, heat several inches of oil to 350 degrees F. Fry the shrimp in batches until golden brown and cooked through, about 3 to 4 minutes per batch. Be careful not to overcrowd shrimp in the oil while frying. Drain on paper towels.

For the Dipping Sauce: heat the marmalade in a small saucepan over low heat. Thin with rum as desired.

Grilled Pork Tenderloin with Grilled Pineapple Salsa

2 (1-pound) pork tenderloins, trimmed of fat and silver skin
6 tbsp olive oil
1 tbsp ground chipotle chili powder
2 tsp salt, plus a pinch
1 tsp ground black pepper

1 tsp dried oregano, crumbled
1 1/2 tbsp minced garlic
3 tbsp fresh lime juice
1 pineapple, peeled and cut crosswise into 1/2-inch slices
1/4 cup finely chopped red onion
2 jalapeno peppers, seeded and minced
2 tbsp minced red bell pepper
1 tbsp finely chopped fresh cilantro leaves
Fresh cilantro sprigs, for garnishing
Cilantro Oil, for drizzling

Preheat a grill to high. Rub the pork tenderloins all over with 3 tablespoons of the olive oil, then sprinkle evenly with the chipotle chili powder, 2 teaspoons of the salt, the pepper, and the oregano. Rub the tenderloins well with the garlic and drizzle the lime juice over all. Allow the tenderloins to sit, refrigerated, for 45 minutes before cooking. Brush the pineapple slices lightly with 1 tablespoon of the olive oil, then place the pineapple slices on the grill and cook, turning occasionally, until softened slightly and nicely marked by the grill, 2 to 3 minutes per side. Remove from the grill and allow to cool to room temperature. Dice the pineapple slices (discard the tough core portions) and place in a medium non-reactive bowl. Add the red onion, remaining 2 tablespoons of lime juice, remaining 2 tablespoons of olive oil, remaining pinch of salt, jalapeno peppers, red bell pepper, and chopped cilantro and stir to combine. Set aside while you grill the pork. Place the tenderloins on the hottest part of the grill and cook, turning occasionally, until well browned on all sides, about 10 minutes. Reduce the grill temperature to low and continue to cook, turning occasionally, until a thermometer inserted into the center registers 145 degrees F. Remove the tenderloins from the grill and allow to sit, loosely covered, for 5 to 10 minutes before serving. Slice the tenderloins on the diagonal and serve with the grilled pineapple salsa and fresh cilantro sprigs. Drizzle with Cilantro Oil.

CILANTRO OIL:

1/4 cup fresh cilantro leaves
2 tbsp fresh mint leaves

1/2 cup extra-virgin olive oil
Salt
Pepper

Place herbs in a mini-chopper and blend. Slowly add oil to emulsify. Season with salt and pepper.

Hawaiian Chicken

2-1/2 (2 to 3 pound) whole chicken, cut into pieces
2 tbsp and 1-1/4 tsp all-purpose flour
1 tbsp and 1-3/4 tsp salt
2-1/2 pinches ground white pepper
1/2 cup and 1 tbsp and 2 tsp vegetable oil
1-1/4 onion, thinly sliced
2-1/2 green bell pepper, thinly sliced
2-1/2 (8 ounce) cans crushed pineapple with juice
1 tbsp and 1-3/4 tsp soy sauce
1 tbsp and 1-3/4 tsp brown sugar
1 tbsp and 1-3/4 tsp cornstarch
1 tbsp and 1-3/4 tsp chicken stock

Preheat oven to 350 degrees. Mix flour, salt and pepper in a resealable plastic bag. One at a time, put chicken pieces in bag, seal and shake to coat. In a large skillet, heat oil over medium heat and sauté chicken pieces until brown on all sides. Place chicken in a lightly greased 9x13 inch baking dish and bake covered in the preheated oven for 45 minutes.

To Make Sauce (while chicken bakes): In the same large skillet, sauté onion and green bell pepper for about 5 minutes, until translucent. Add the pineapple, soy sauce and brown sugar. Mix together cornstarch and chicken stock and add to skillet. Stir all together and let simmer for 3 minutes until thick and clear. Pour sauce over chicken and bake 10 more minutes until tender.

Hawaiian Pineapple Beef

1 1/2 lb. London broil steak
2 green onion, finely minced
1 tsp ground ginger
1 tbsp honey
1/2 cup fresh pineapple, cut into small pieces
Cooking spray

Lightly coat the grill with cooking spray and preheat for 5 minutes. Remove any visible fat from the steak and grill the steak for 2 minutes. In a small bowl, combine the green onion, ginger, honey and mix well. Spoon the sauce over the steak and grill for 3 minutes. Add the pineapple pieces on top of and around the steak and grill for 2-4 minutes. To serve, slice the steak thinly across the grain and serve with the warm pineapple.

Macadamia Nut Crusted Mahi Mahi

1/4 pound macadamia nuts
1/2 pound plain bread crumbs
12 (6 ounce) mahi mahi fillets
1/2 pound butter
1/4 pound shallots, diced
8 cups chicken stock
1/2 pound pineapple, rough chopped
5 ounces papaya, rough chopped
6 ounces mango, rough chopped
2 tbsp shredded coconut
4 habanero peppers, seeded
salt and pepper to taste
white sugar to taste

Preheat oven to 375. In a food processor or blender, pulse together macadamia nuts and breadcrumbs until finely ground. Pour nut mixture onto a plate, and coat fish fillets on both sides. Heat butter in a large skillet over medium heat. Fry fillets on both sides until nuts are golden brown. Remove to a baking pan. Add shallots to skillet, and cook until translucent.

Stir in chicken stock. Mix in pineapple, papaya, mango, coconut, and habanero peppers. Season with salt, pepper, and sugar to taste. Simmer until sauce is thick, about 30 minutes. Strain to remove peppers, fruit, and shallots. Reserve sauce in a pan over low heat. Bake mahi mahi in preheated oven about 10 minutes, until internal temperature reaches 140 degrees. Remove fish, and lightly coat with sauce.

TRADITIONAL MAI TAI COCKTAIL

3 ounces light rum
1 1/2 ounces dark rum
1-ounce Orange Curacao
2 ounces fresh pineapple juice
1-ounce fresh orange juice
1/2-ounce fresh lime juice
Dash grenadine
Cracked ice
4 maraschino cherries, garnish
2 paper umbrellas, garnish

Fill a cocktail shaker half way with ice cubes. Add the remaining ingredients, except the cherries and shake until cold and frothy, 30 to 45 seconds. Strain into 2 tall glasses with cracked ice. Garnish each with 2 maraschino cherries and paper umbrellas. Serve immediately

TROPICAL MUDDLE PUDDLE

3 pieces fresh pineapple, plus more for garnish
4 orange slices, plus more for garnish
Ice
2 ounces coconut banana rum
4 ounces sweet and sour mix
2 ounces lemon-lime soda
1-ounce dark rum

In a large pint glass muddle the pineapple and orange. Fill glass full with ice, then add coconut banana rum, sweet and sour mix, splash of lemon lime, and float dark rum. Garnish with a wedge of pineapple and orange

Celebrating Chefs

July is National Culinary Arts Month
And Finally…. The "Rules" for Dining Out

It's July – the month of picnics and celebrating our Independence….but did you also know July is National Culinary Arts Month? It's the month that promotes the awareness of professional cooks and chefs, as well as their contributions to the new culinary trends and the world of dining. It's a month where you can dine out and say thanks to chefs and cooks at some of your favorite local restaurants.

And yes, we have them. Part of my former life as the lab coordinator for a small community college in the mountains of Maryland was not only to "manage the kitchen of a lab" but also to impart in the students some knowledge and skills they needed to go out boldly into the culinary world. I hope for the nearly 16 years I spent as a teacher I was able to inspire future chefs to love what they do as much as I do.

And let me just take a moment and proudly post that I can't dine out within a 30 mile radius of my home and not run into at least one former student at a restaurant. Some of my students chose to stay close and others spread their wings and have done everything from open their own wine bars to join professional catering businesses that serve fine food at the White House.

Sure, there are times when students join a culinary program because they are fans of the cooking competition shows on the Food Network – and I had students who walked in the first day of class and wanted to be the next Rachael Ray—and maybe one of them will be. But the students I worked with over the years soon learned that being a chef and being a line cook at a restaurant is hard work.

If you want to choose this profession you have to have a passion for it. Your clothes will forever smell like whatever cuisine your restaurant offers. Most restaurant employees work at night. You will work every Christmas, every Thanksgiving, every Mother's Day (especially Mother's Day), Valentine's Day and Easter. You will learn to celebrate your holidays with family and friends the day after the rest of the world.

My love of cooking is genetic. Two of my grandmothers had been Home Economics teachers and they instilled in me a love of culinary arts. I cooked when I was in the Navy – where I learned how to prepare meals for thousands. I also once worked for the Fox Television Studio lots in Los Angeles and served Madonna and Sean Penn burgers just before they left the county to film the movie "Shanghai Surprise." Ever hear of an actress named Ida Lupino? How about horror movie director Wes Craven? I used to cater dinner parties at their homes in Beverly Hills. I'm sure you have heard of the Cheesecake Factory – I worked at the very first one. My "bosses" were the folks that started the franchise!

I have been very fortunate to have made a career out of a passion and I sometimes forget how lucky I am to be doing what I do for a living. It's a job that is both hot and cool at the same time. And it's one that will always be in demand – people will always need to eat.

Now… all of this being said….I do have 12 general rules for how the rest of you can celebrate National Culinary Arts Month….just some tips to keep in mind while dining out – there are actually more than 12 but these are the ones I thought maybe it was time to address.

Don't harass your server

When your server brings you a dish and warns you that it's hot, don't reply with a comment like "so am I." Being harassed on the job is the number one thing servers have always complained about when they come back to the kitchen.

Never snap your fingers.

Unless you're choking, trying to wake someone up, or about to entertain the dining room with a Flamenco dance, there is never any reason to snap your fingers in a restaurant. Ever.

Respect your reservation

If you are heading to the restaurant and you know you are running late because someone took longer to get ready or you hit traffic, call the restaurant and tell them. You can't get mad when they give your table away because you did not have the courtesy to let them know you were late.

It's okay to send something back

Chefs are not personally offended if you don't like something. It's perfectly acceptable to send a dish back because the meat is not cooked to your liking. And no, no one spits in your food when you do that. So stop thinking that happens.

It's also okay to ask to speak to the chef

In most restaurants, if you enjoy a meal, you tell the server to tell the chef and the server forgets because he or she gets busy. Ask to meet the chef in person. If the chef is not busy with a table for 10, he or she will probably come out to meet someone who has been so nice.

You don't really need to ask for a booth

If you arrive as a couple and want to sit in a booth, the host or hostess already knows you want a booth. Trust me. If the restaurant has one, you will get one. If you really want to make sure you get one, reserve one.

Children can be seen and heard

Kids are kids and they are going to be fussy. Bring along activities for them to do at the table. But you can't reasonably think everyone will find it adorable when your kid runs through the dining room wearing nothing but a loose fitted diaper. And if precocious little Trevor is throwing a category-five hissy fit, he needs to leave the dining room because now he's becoming everyone's problem.

Put your cell phone away

Unless you know you're expecting an emergency phone call – say someone is in surgery or giving birth and you know you will have to take a call – keep the phone off the table. And by no means at all should you make your server wait to take your order while you finish a call. By the way, yes, it's great if you want to take a picture of a beautiful presentation for social media. Or hand your phone to a server for a group shot. But don't turn dining out into your own private photo session.

Splitting the Check

It's fine between four or six people but do not ask your server to split the check 15 ways. Figure that out among your group before you sit down if you think it's going to become an issue on who pays and how.

"Fibbing" to get free food is never Okay

Don't try to manipulate your server with a story, a fake birthday, or worse, cause a scene or an argument over your meal just because you want something for nothing.

If the restaurant is busy, don't linger.

You should never feel rushed or hurried in a restaurant and if you do feel that way, speak to a manager. But it also works the other way around. If you have already paid your bill, there is no reason to still sit there for another two hours without ordering and chat about the Real Housewives of Atlanta.

Tip

I cannot stress this enough. Tip. Tip. Tip. It's not change you have left over in your pocket or a handwritten note on the bill about the server's hair color. It's money. If you can't afford to add at least 20 percent to your bill for the server at the end of your meal, you simply can't afford to eat out. That tip is the server's bread and butter, pun intended. Here is how you calculate a standard tip. Double your bill. Then move the decimal point. If your bill was $40, double it to $80. Take that decimal point to the left and $8 is your "standard" (yes, I said 20 percent is standard) tip. You can always tip more. But never tip less

AUGUST

The Flavorful month
of August

A Taste of Every Single Summer Day

Did you know the month of August is the month in which most people take their vacations? I would have thought it was June but it's not. It happens to August and I think there is a good reason for that. I think it's because the summer is "coming to a close" and it's the last chance for families to hit the road and enjoy some quality time together. For teachers, August is usually a prep month – with faculty heading back to work a couple of weeks before students show. And for students, it's the last month to enjoy some freedom before hitting the books. And while there are no official national holidays in August (isn't that interesting?) August is a great month to celebrate culinary treats and delights — nearly every single day of this month gives foodies a chance to taste one last bite of summer. Here are a few "national observances" and a handful of recipes to complete your season eatings.

August 1

National Raspberry Cream Pie Day

25 Oreo cookies
4 tbsp butter, melted
1 generous cup raspberries, plus more for serving
3 tbsp sugar
Two 6-ounce containers raspberry yogurt
One 3.4-ounce package instant vanilla pudding mix
1 cup heavy cream
Whipped cream, for serving

Preheat the oven to 350 degrees F. To make the crust, place the cookies in a plastic bag, seal the top and smash with a rolling pin. Stir in the melted butter until combined. Pour into a regular pie pan and press the crumbs all over the pan and up the sides. Bake just long enough for it to set, 3 to 4 minutes. Let cool completely. Put the raspberries on a plate or in an empty pan. Smash them with a fork, then sprinkle on the sugar. Stir together and allow to sit for 15 minutes. Then, in the bowl of an electric mixer, combine the raspberry yogurt with the instant vanilla pudding mix (just the powder itself). Beat on low until combined, about 1 minute. Pour in the heavy cream and whip on low for 30 seconds. Stop the mixer and scrape down the bowl with a rubber spatula. Turn the mixer on medium-high speed and beat until thick, about 2 minutes. Turn off the mixer, then fold in the raspberries until just combined. Pour into the cooled crust and spread evenly. Freeze until very firm, about 2 hours. Cut into slices and top each slice with cookie crumbs, dollops of whipped cream and extra raspberries.

August 2

National Ice Cream Sandwich Day

AUGUST 3

National Watermelon Day

Instant Watermelon Pops. Cut a 1-inch slit into the rind of a just-cut watermelon wedge, and insert a wooden stick. Serve pops a variety of ways: Sprinkle with flavored salts and freshly ground pepper, drizzle with local honey and fresh lime juice, dust with red pepper, or add a splash of Schnapps.

AUGUST 4

National Chocolate Chip Day

AUGUST 5

National Mustard Day

AUGUST 6

National Root Beer Float Day

AUGUST 7

Raspberries 'n Cream Day

AUGUST 8

National Frozen Custard Day

August 9

National Rice Pudding Day

2 1/2 cups whole milk
1/3 cup uncooked short grain white rice
Pinch of salt
1 egg
1/4 cup dark brown sugar
1 tsp vanilla extract
1/4 tsp cinnamon
1/3 cup raisins

Cook the rice in milk: In a medium-sized, heavy-bottomed saucepan, bring the milk, rice and salt to a boil over high heat. Reduce heat to low and simmer until the rice is tender, about 20-25 minutes. Stir frequently to prevent the rice from sticking to the bottom of the pan. Mix egg and brown sugar, temper with rice mixture: In a small mixing bowl, whisk together egg and brown sugar until well mixed. Add a half cup of the hot rice mixture to the egg mixture, a tablespoon at a time, vigorously whisking to incorporate. Whisk eggs and brown sugar to make rice pudding temper eggs with hot rice pudding mixture. Add tempered egg mixture back to rice mixture: Add egg mixture back into the saucepan of rice and milk and stir, on low heat, for 5 to 10 minutes, until thick. Add tempered eggs back into rice pudding mixture to make rice pudding. Be careful not to have the mixture come to a boil at this point or it will curdle. Stir in the vanilla. Remove from heat and stir in the raisins and cinnamon. Serve warm or cold.

August 10

National S'mores Day

August 11

National Raspberry Bombe Day

1 pound raspberries
3 ounces lightly crushed meringues
3 ounces sugar
½ pint whipping cream

Simmer fruit until just cooked Cool, then sieve using juice for coulis. Puree remaining fruit. Whip cream. Fold meringue into cream Lightly fold puree into this mix giving marbled effect. Put into a foil lined bowl. Freeze overnight. Once frozen, serve.

August 12

National Julienne Fries Day

August 13

National Fillet Mignon Day

August 14

National Creamsicle Day

August 15

National Lemon Meringue Pie Day

1 pre-baked pie crust
1 ½ cup sugar
½ cup cornstarch
¼ tsp salt

2 ¼ cups water
1 tbsp grated lemon peel
4 egg yolks
3 tbsp butter
½ cup lemon juice
For the Meringue:
5-6 egg whites at room temperature
¼ tsp cream of tartar
½ cup sugar

In a medium-sized saucepot, bring sugar, cornstarch, salt, water, and lemon peel to a boil, stirring constantly. Remove from heat and mix in with wire whip 4 egg yolks. Return to heat for 1 minute stirring constantly. Remove from heat and whisk in 3 T. butter, then ½ c. lemon juice. Pour into pie crust and cool. Meringue topping: In a mixing bowl, beat egg whites and cream of tartar until foamy. Gradually add ½ c. sugar beating until stiff peaks form. Top pie with meringue and bake at 325 about 10 minutes or until meringue is lightly browned. Chill until set.

AUGUST 16

National Rum Day

AUGUST 17

National Vanilla Custard Day

AUGUST 18

National Ice Cream Pie Day

AUGUST 19

National Hot & Spicy Food Day

August 20

National Chocolate Pecan Pie Day

1/2 cup margarine, melted
1 cup light corn syrup
1 cup white sugar
1/4 cup unsweetened cocoa powder
1 tsp vanilla extract
1/4 tsp salt
4 eggs
1 cup chopped pecans
1 9 inch single crust pie shell – premade

Preheat oven to 325 degrees. In a heavy saucepan combine melted margarine, corn syrup, white sugar and cocoa. Cook over low heat, stirring constantly, until sugar dissolves. Add vanilla, salt and eggs, stirring well. Stir in 1/2 cup pecans. Mix well. Pour filling into unbaked pastry shell and top with remaining 1/2 cup pecans. Bake at 325 degrees. Let cool and serve.

August 21

National Spumoni Day

August 22

National Pecan Torte Day

August 23

National Sponge cake Day

August 24

National Peach Pie Day

August 25

National Banana Split Day

August 26

National Cherry Popsicle Day

August 27

National Pots de Creme Day

2 cups whipping cream
1/2 cup whole milk
5 ounces bittersweet chocolate, chopped
6 large egg yolks
1/3 cup sugar

Preheat oven to 325°F. Bring cream and milk just to simmer in heavy medium saucepan over medium heat. Remove from heat. Add chocolate; whisk until melted and smooth. Whisk yolks and sugar in large bowl to blend. Gradually whisk in hot chocolate mixture. Strain mixture into another bowl. Cool 10 minutes, skimming any foam from surface. Divide custard mixture among six 3/4-cup custard cups or soufflé dishes. Cover each with foil. Place cups in large baking pan. Add enough hot water to pan to come halfway up sides of cups. Bake until custards are set but centers still move slightly when gently shaken, about 55 minutes. Remove from water. Remove foil. Chill custards until cold and serve.

August 28

National Cherry Turnovers Day

August 29

National Whiskey Sour Day

August 30

National Toasted Marshmallow Day

August 31

National Trail Mix Day

Foam Sweet Foam

If you don't drink it, what can you do with beer?

I don't drink. I know that sometimes strikes people as weird coming from a chef who is around alcohol all the time in kitchens. People ask me "aren't you ever tempted to take a sip as you cook?" And the answer is – no, not really. Been there done that. Trust me, I'm a much better chef when I have my wits about me. Besides, once I started working with college students, I heard their horror stories and I was able to live – or re-live – vicariously through their horror stories.

But I do have uses for beer. I cook with it. And you can do.

Cooking with beer actually has a very colorful and one might even say – foamy history that comes to a head. See what I did there? The history of using beer in recipes is rich and fascinating. Beer can add an earthy flavor to soups and stews. A beer with a sweet or nutty taste can bring a surprising layer to desserts. And don't worry about getting drunk – or betraying your sobriety – virtually all of the alcohol evaporates during the cooking process. The alcohol is burned off but the taste remains. And did you know that some recipes that call for wine can actually be prepared with a cold brew? Dishes will come out with a malty and toasty flavor.

But here's a tip from you to me – never cook with a beer that you wouldn't like the taste of on its own. If you think a peanut butter and chocolate beer sounds disgusting, why would you pour it into your cooking? If you don't like the flavor in a cup, chances are you're not going to like that same taste on your plate.

Here's a few recipes for cooking, baking and using beer that I have found over the years work for me. They are great surprising treats for company.

And with the end of summer just right around the corner, a great way to empty the fridge or cooler. But I can't guarantee that either way, you'll keep your six pack.

Beer Muffins

3 cups buttermilk baking mix
2 tbsp white sugar
1 cup chopped raisins
1 cup beer

Preheat oven to 350 degrees. Lightly grease 10 muffin cups. In a large bowl, combine baking mix, sugar, raisins and beer; stir until smooth. Pour batter into prepared muffin cups. Bake in preheated oven until golden brown, about 15 minutes.

Beer Syrup

2 (12 fluid ounce) bottles any flavor beer, preferably not light beer
1 tbsp butter

Heat the beer in a saucepan over medium-high heat, stirring constantly, until it comes to a boil; allow to boil until the beer thickens to almost the consistency of a glaze, about 15 minutes. Stir the butter into the beer until the butter melts. Use immediately.

Beer Batter

1 cup all-purpose flour
1 egg, beaten
1 tsp garlic powder
1/2 tsp ground black pepper
1 1/2 cups beer

In a small mixing bowl add flour, egg, garlic powder, and black pepper. Stir in the beer.

Authentic Kentucky Beer Spread

1 cup beer
1 pound extra-sharp Cheddar cheese, shredded
2 cloves garlic, minced
1 tsp dry mustard powder
1/2 tsp freshly ground black pepper
1/2 tsp cayenne pepper
1/4 tsp salt
1/4 tsp hot pepper sauce
1/4 tsp Worcestershire sauce
1 pinch cayenne pepper, or to taste

Pour beer into a bowl and whisk until beer loses its carbonation, about 30 seconds. Set aside. Place shredded cheese into the work bowl of a food processor; add garlic, dry mustard powder, black pepper, 1/2 teaspoon cayenne pepper, salt, hot sauce, Worcestershire sauce, and flat beer. Process until smooth and creamy, pulsing a few times, scraping the sides, and blending for about 2 total minutes. Taste and adjust seasoning. If adding more seasoning, pulse a few times to mix. Transfer cheese spread to a bowl and sprinkle with a pinch of cayenne pepper. Spread tastes best when refrigerated overnight to blend flavors, but it can be served right away if needed.

Bill Hand's Beer Cheese Soup

Yup....this is my own unique creation. You're welcome, America!

4 onions (chopped)
1/2 pound bacon (chopped)
4 cups chicken stock
1 1/2 quarts beer
2 quarts heavy cream
1 block "meltable" cheese – the brand product starts with a V.
2 tbsp hot sauce
2 tsp dry mustard
1/4 cup Worcestershire sauce

1 tsp thyme

1 tsp black pepper

In a large stockpot, heat bacon and onions until the bacon browns. Add chicken stock, heavy cream, cheese and all dry seasonings. Bring up the temperature on soup until simmering. Then add beer. Strain. Serve

Grin and Beer It

The production of beer possibly dates back as early as 9500 B.C. It appears as a beverage in several references in the written history of ancient Iraq and ancient Egypt. Archaeologists speculate that beer was instrumental in the formation of civilizations. Beer was spread through Europe by Germanic and Celtic tribes as far back as 3000 BC. In 1516, William IV, Duke of Bavaria, adopted "purity laws" that regulated that beer should be defined as "purely" fermented hops, barley and distilled water. And could only be sold as such. During the Industrial Revolution, the production of beer moved from artisanal manufacturing to industrial manufacturing and commercial breweries went into production with great success. It is estimated that today, 35 billion gallons of beer are consumed annually all over the world. The top four nations for beer consumption are: 1) China 2)United States 3)Germany 4)France. Cheers!

Celebrity Cooking

"I'm a Little Bit Hungry..."
How's about cooking something up with me?

They say music is the universal language.

But I have to disagree.

I think food is.

Food speaks every language. You don't have to know how to speak French to enjoy French food. You don't have to be fluent in Italian or Greek or Japanese to savor the flavors of those parts of our world. For thousands of years, the preparation of a meal for a guest has been a display of welcome and affection. It's only after the meal that the music begins. And food and music actually go hand in hand, from minstrels who stroll from table to table with violins and guitars, to dinner theatre. And that got me to thinking – has music ever inspired recipes or vice versa? For this column, I thought it might be fun to match up some of my favorite musicians with some dishes you can make at home while rocking out (or country-ing out) to your favorite tunes.

PS: I remember meeting Donny Osmond backstage at a show in Cleveland. While the entire area was swarming around him to meet him, I stay seated at a table. Eventually, he came to me and said "so, you want to get up and say hi?" And then when we posed for pictures, he put rabbit ears behind my head. About ten years later, a friend of mine took that photo to Vegas and asked Donny to sign it for me and Mr. Osmond looked at the picture of us together and said, "I know this guy! He doesn't get up!"

And when I met his famous sister, Marie Osmond, I was told "say something nice. Compliment her. Open the conversation up with flattery." Now, I could have said how wonderful her voice was, how great she looked, how talented she is (and all of those are true) but what did I say? I said "Wow…I love your shoes!"

Probably not what she was expecting but she did tell me a story about how her daughter "blinged them out for her."

I also remember while living in Los Angeles, I shared an afternoon with a young aspiring songwriter named Sheryl Crow at a bar that faces a giant car wash. And a few years later, I was taken aback to hear her sing the lyrics "He says his name is William but I think it's Bill…Billy…Mack or Buddy."

But I digress. Those stories are for another book. You came to this book to eat. And so I'm matching up a famous artist or song with a dish you can make for your own musical night at home. I want to rock and roll all night…and cook food everyday!

MEATLOAF

The kids will flock like a "bat out of..." well, you know, when you make this easy and tasty Meatloaf recipe. When they tell you how delicious it is, just reply "I would do anything for love..." If you eat this dish by the dashboard lights, it's paradise.

1 1/2 pounds ground beef
1 egg
1 onion, chopped
1 cup milk
1 cup dried bread crumbs
salt and pepper to taste
2 tbsp brown sugar
2 tbsp mustard
1/3 cup ketchup

Preheat oven to 350 degrees F. In a large mixing bowl, combine the beef, egg, onion, milk and bread crumbs. Season with salt and pepper to taste and place in a lightly greased 5x9 inch loaf pan, or hand form into a loaf and place in a lightly greased 9x13 inch baking dish. In a separate small bowl, combine the brown sugar, mustard and ketchup. Mix well and pour over the top of the meatloaf. Bake for 1 hour.

GREAT BALLS OF FIRE

Jerry Lee Lewis would be downright delighted to encounter these appetizers based on his hit song. Goodness gracious!

For meatballs:

1 pound ground beef
1 pound ground pork
3/4 cup breadcrumbs
1/2 cup freshly grated Parmesan
1/2 cup ricotta cheese
1/4 cup fresh flat-leaf parsley, minced

1/2 tsp crushed red pepper
1/4 tsp salt
3 cloves garlic, grated.
2 whole eggs
Splash of milk
Freshly ground black pepper
1/2 cup olive oil, for frying

Sauce:

3 cloves garlic, minced
1 onion, diced
Two 28-ounce cans tomato sauce
1/4 cup fresh flat-leaf parsley, minced
3 tbsp tomato paste
2 tbsp sugar
1/4 tsp salt
Crushed red pepper
Freshly ground black pepper

For the meatballs: Combine the ground beef, pork, breadcrumbs, Parmesan, ricotta, parsley, crushed red pepper, salt, garlic, eggs, milk and black pepper in a bowl. Mash with your hands until thoroughly combined. Form into small balls and place on a baking sheet. Set in the fridge for an hour to set. Heat the oil in a large skillet over medium-high heat. Brown the meatballs in batches until nice and deep golden, then move them to a plate.

For the sauce: Into the same skillet, add the garlic and onions and cook for 2 to 3 minutes. Add the tomato sauce, parsley, tomato paste, sugar, salt, crushed red pepper and black pepper. Reduce the heat to medium low and cook for 15 to 20 minutes.

Add the meatballs back to the skillet and simmer another 15 minutes. Keep warm until serving.

Strawberry Fields Forever

John, Paul, George and Ringo would be downright pleased by this refreshing summer dessert based on their hit song. "Imagine" the compliments you'll receive. You will wish you made this "Yesterday."

1 unbaked pastry shell (9 inches)
3/4 cup sugar
2 tbsp cornstarch
1 cup water
1 package (3 ounces) strawberry gelatin
4 cups freshly sliced fresh locally grown strawberries

Line unpricked pastry shell with a double thickness of heavy-duty foil and bake for 8 minutes at 450°. Then remove the foil and bake 5 minutes longer. Cool on a wire rack. In a small saucepan, combine the sugar, cornstarch and water until smooth. Bring to a boil; cook and stir for 2 minutes or until thickened. Remove from the heat; stir in gelatin until dissolved. Refrigerate for 15-20 minutes or until slightly cooled. Meanwhile, arrange strawberries in the crust. Pour gelatin mixture over berries. Refrigerate until set.

Little Bit Country Fried Steak

Nothing says Southern front porch sittin' like country fried steak. It's a little bit of Memphis and Nashville...even if it's not on the Nutra-System plan. And she really does wear great shoes!

6 (4-oz.) cubed steaks (1 1/2 lb.)
1/2 tsp salt
1/2 tsp pepper
1/4 cup all-purpose flour
1/2 cup egg
45 saltine crackers, crushed
Vegetable cooking spray

Sprinkle steaks with salt and pepper. Dredge steaks in flour; dip in egg, and then dredge in crushed crackers. Lightly coat steaks on each side with cooking spray. Cook steaks, in batches, in a hot nonstick skillet over medium heat 3 to 4 minutes on each side or until golden, turning twice. Serve with gravy if desired.

ELVIS INSPIRED PANINI

It's a sandwich fit for a King. It was often said that Elvis Presley loved peanut butter and banana sandwiches. This is the updated version. Are you "hungry" tonight?

2 slices wheat bread – sliced thick
2 tbsp peanut butter
1 banana, sliced
2 tbsp salted butter, softened
Powdered sugar

Lay out the bread slices and spread them both with peanut butter. Lay the banana slices on one piece of bread. Press the 2 slices together. Butter one side of the sandwich and put it on a hot panini maker butter-side down. Butter the other side, close the lid and cook until it's toasted and warmed through. Sprinkle with powdered sugar, cut in half and serve!

WHAT A WONDERFUL WORLD RED BEANS AND RICE

True story. In 1971, an ailing Louis Armstrong surprised a Washington, DC, awards ceremony audience with what would be one of his final jazz performances. The legendary trumpeter and singer was a famously intense food lover, so when a recording of the impromptu concert appeared the following year, it saluted Armstrong's favorite dishes. It was called Red Beans and Rice-ly Yours—a sign-off that Armstrong actually used when he wrote letters to friends. And the recorded album liner notes contain this recipe, a favorite of Armstrong's – originated by his personal chef, Christopher Blake, of New Orleans.

1 quart red beans.

Enough water to cover.

1/2 pound pickled pork, diced, or commercial jar of pickled ham hocks, diced.

2 cups lean ham, diced, or one ham bone.

1 medium-sized onion, chopped.

1 cup tomato ketchup.

1 tbsp vinegar.

Salt and pepper to taste.

1 tsp Tabasco pepper sauce.

Sprig of thyme or pinch of fresh thyme.

Pick over beans. Wash and soak red beans overnight. When ready to cook, drain off all the water. In a heavy pot, brown the diced pickled pork and add the chopped onions. Cook for about ten minutes. Add the beans, the tomato ketchup, salt and pepper, vinegar, thyme and Tabasco pepper sauce. Cover with fresh cold water, making sure that there is enough water as the beans must cook thoroughly. After water has come to a boil, reduce heat and simmer until beans are semi-cooked. Mash about a cupful of the beans and return to the pot. Add the diced ham or the ham bone and cook slowly for two or three hours or until the beans are thoroughly cooked and the sauce is rich and creamy. Serve on a plate over a mountain of white rice with a slice of fresh bread.

Celebrity Dish

Rubbing Shoulders and Swapping Recipes

Dear Bill,

Your bio every issue says you used to work for the Fox Studio lot and that you were a caterer in Los Angeles at one time. Ever meet any celebrities and did they swap recipes with you?

Patricia King

Dear Patricia,

Yes, I spent a few years out in Hollywood, catering and operating what is called the craft service table. I actually do like collecting recipes from the kitchens of the rich and famous…so if you know any, or you are one, send me what you got and we can do a whole second volume to this book. Here are a few I have already…

DONNY OSMOND'S SAUSAGE SALAD

Boiled potatoes, cubed
1 large can Vienna sausage, cut into pieces
Cucumbers
Green onions
Celery
Green pepper
Radishes
Hard-boiled eggs

1 can peas, drained
Pimentos

Mix all the ingredients together. Toss with salad dressing and chill overnight.

KATHIE LEE GIFFORD'S TRIFLE

2 cups eggnog
16 to 20 Ladyfingers
¾ cup sweet sherry
2 ounces slivered almonds, toasted
1 cup raspberry preserves
2 cups fruit cocktail, drained
1 to 2 cups heavy cream
1 ½ tbsp. granulated sugar
And enough crushed amaretti cookies to cover the surface

Pour the eggnog into the bottom of a 2-½ quart serving bowl. Arrange the ladyfingers over the eggnog and against the sides of the dish. Moisten the ladyfingers with the sherry. Sprinkle the almonds evenly over the ladyfingers. Spoon the preserves evenly over the surface. Distribute the mixed fruit over the top. Sprinkle the surface with the crushed cookies. Cover and refrigerate until ready to serve.

In a large bowl, using an electric mixer beat the cream and the sugar until soft peaks start to form. Using a pastry bag, pipe a decorative top on the trifle, or simply spoon the whipped cream over the top.

PHYLLIS DILLER'S FRIED CUCUMBERS

2 cucumbers
1/3 cup flour
Bacon fat
Salt and pepper to taste

Pare cucumbers. Cut in half crosswise and slice lengthwise into ½ inch thick slices. Dredge in flour. Fry in bacon fat in skillet until golden brown and tender. Season to taste.

CAROL BURNETT'S LAZY COOKS MEATLOAF

½ cup milk
2 eggs
2/3 cups breadcrumbs
1-tbsp garlic salt
1-tsp pepper
½ cup finely chopped onion
½ cup finely chopped green pepper
2 pounds of ground round
1 can tomato sauce

Preheat oven to 350 degrees. Beat milk and eggs together in a large mixing bowl. Add remainder of ingredients in order except for tomato sauce. Add ½ cup tomato sauce to the mix. Combine meat mixture well. Shape into loaf. Place in greased baking pan. Pour remaining sauce over meat loaf. Bake 1 ¼ to 1-½ hours or until done.

VINCENT PRICE'S PEPPER STEAK

3 cloves garlic, minced
1 tbsp olive oil
½ tsp meat tenderizer
1 tbsp ground pepper
1 steak (approximately 2 pounds of it)
1 tbsp oil
1 tbsp butter
1 cup dry white wine
¼ cup butter
½ tsp salt

Combine garlic, oil, tenderizer and pepper. Rub mixture into both sides of steak. Marinate at least two hours at room temperature or overnight in a refrigerator. When ready to cook, heat heavy iron skillet. Add oil and butter. Pan fry steak five minutes on each side for rare, seven minutes each side for medium and nine minutes each side for well done. Add wine to skillet and bring to a boil. Add butter and salt. Serve over steak.

August is National Sandwich Appreciation Month

So how about a few "Earls" of wisdom?

Once upon a time, many years ago, in a land far far away, there was a kingdom. It was a place of kings and queens and dukes and duchesses. And when they drove through McDonald's and Burger King or stopped in at Subway, the menu was verily sparse.

This is eighteenth-century England and as the carriage pulled into Wendy's, the meat came to the window on a plate all by itself. Oh sure, you might get a slice of cheese or a hunk of bread but it was all separated. Chicken nuggets? Forget about it. You got a huge turkey leg and maybe a carrot if you were lucky.

That is, until a bloomer wearing and wig sporting very proper gent named John Montagu came along. Johnny, you see, was the 5th Earl of Sandwich and he had grown quite weary of parking his horse by the speaker at Sonic and not being able to balance that tray on the pony's head.

Actually, I made up all of that – except the part about John Montagu. He really was the 5th Earl of Sandwich and he really did have something to do with inventing what we know as the sandwich.

The very first written usage of the English word "sandwich" as a culinary concoction appears in writings by Edward Gibbon around 1765. He infers in his journals that Montagu (again he's the Earl of Sandwich) was an 18th-century English aristocrat. And he ordered his "manservant" to bring him meat tucked between two pieces of bread. He liked the invention so much he started asking for it when he played cards with his friends and the friends began to request it as well – stating "I'll have the same as Sandwich."

The food item caught on because the men could play cards and not get the cards sticky from the food they were snacking. Of course, grease from a turkey leg left on the Queen of Diamonds could give one's hand away next round as well.

Another writer – a Frenchman named Pierre-Jean Grosley's Londres contends that the Earl of Sandwich not only wanted a snack he could hold while playing cards, he wanted a meal he could easily eat at his desk while continuing to work.

In that regard, not much has changed.

However, while Montagu might get the credit, he may not have actually been the first to stick two pieces of meat between bread and call it lunch.

The ancient Jewish sage known as Hillel the Elder is said to have wrapped lamb meat and bitter herbs between two pieces of soft matzah in order to make the Passover meal portable. If true, this means the Gyro predates the Sandwich.

Initially the sandwich was seen as a quick food that men shared while gaming and drinking, but it soon became accepted as a novelty in polite society and later was adapted as a fashionable late night meal among the rich. Just think, when you fix a PB&J for a midnight snack, you're downright aristocratic.

But whatever the reason and whatever the history, the sandwich has become a staple in the culinary world as a portable, delicious, and creative meal. Since August is National Sandwich Appreciation Month (it really is), I thought I'd offer some creative suggestions to help celebrate!

GRILLED MAC AND CHEESE

4 slices of sandwich bread
2 tbsp butter spread
4 slices of cheddar cheese
1 serving boxed macaroni and cheese (leftovers work)

Make macaroni and cheese according to directions on box. Spread about 1/2 tbsp butter on one side of each slice of bread. Place a slice of cheese on top of each un-buttered side of bread. Spread half of the macaroni cheese on one piece of bread and the other half on another piece of bread. Place remaining slices of bread on top, to form two sandwiches. Place frying pan on stove and turn to medium heat. Once hot, place both sandwiches in the frying pan, cooking the buttered sides until golden and toasty and the center of the sandwiches are melty.

ITALIAN GRILLED CHEESE

Ciabatta bread
Mozzarella slices
Butter
Spicy Salami sliced
Roasted Red Bell Peppers
Pasta Sauce (for dipping)

Cut a ciabatta roll into two, butter each inner side and grill on pan until golden brown. With browned inner sides of the rolls facing up, layer slices of mozzarella, Salami, and finally roasted red bell peppers on top of bread. Place in the oven with broiler on high until cheese is melted.

Combine the two sides, cut and serve with pasta sauce for dipping.

Note: This recipe is great if you have a Panini press!

Slow Cooker Buffalo Chicken Sandwiches

1 skinless, boneless chicken breast halves
1 large bottle buffalo wing sauce, divided
1/2 (1 ounce) package dry ranch salad dressing mix
2 tbsp butter
6 hoagie rolls, split lengthwise
Jar of taco sauce - Medium

Place the chicken breasts into a slow cooker, and pour in 3/4 of the wing sauce and the ranch dressing mix. Cover, and cook on the low setting for 6 to 7 hours.

Once the chicken has cooked, add the butter, and shred the meat finely with two forks. Pile the meat onto the hoagie rolls, and splash with the remaining buffalo wing sauce to serve.

Tuna Nicoise Sandwich

3 tbsp extra-virgin olive oil
2 tbsp white-wine vinegar
1 tbsp Dijon mustard
Coarse salt and ground pepper
2 cans oil-packed tuna (6 ounces each), drained
1/4 cucumber, thinly sliced
1/2 small red onion, halved and thinly sliced
1 8-inch round loaf country-style bread
3 tbsp jarred olive tapenade
1 cup fresh basil leaves
2 large eggs, hard-cooked and sliced

In a medium bowl, whisk together oil, vinegar, and mustard; season with salt and pepper. Transfer 2 tablespoons dressing to another bowl; toss with tuna. To remaining dressing, add cucumber and onion; toss to combine.

Cut bread in half horizontally; remove most of soft interior crumb. Spread tapenade on bottom half. Top with basil leaves, then egg slices; season with salt and pepper. Top with tuna, then cucumber mixture; close sandwich.

Wrap sandwich tightly in plastic and place between two baking sheets. Weight with a heavy skillet. Let stand 1 hour (or refrigerate, up to overnight). To serve, cut into quarters.

PORTOBELLO PICNIC SANDWICH

2-3 grilled or oven-roasted Portobello mushrooms, sliced
4 slices sourdough bread
Sliced red onion
Sliced tomato
Fresh baby spinach
1/4 cup feta cheese
2 tablespoons cream cheese, softened at room temperature
Balsamic dressing

In a small bowl mix the feta cheese and cream cheese. Divide the cheese mixture among the 4 slices of bread and spread over the tops. Add the sliced mushrooms, the red onions, tomato and fresh baby spinach. Drizzle with balsamic dressing. Eat as is or lightly toast to melt the cheese and warm the veggies.

HAWAIIAN HAM SANDWICH WITH
PINEAPPLE APRICOT SPREAD

1/4 pound thinly sliced honey or brown sugar style ham, divided
4 slices of baby Swiss cheese
Romaine leaves
Grilled pineapple slices
2 tbsp mayonnaise
1 tbsp apricot preserves
4 slices whole wheat Hawaiian-style bread

In a small bowl combine the mayonnaise and the fruit preserves, mixing well. Spread each slice of bread with the mixture. On a slice of bread, spread the fruit spread and add one slice of Swiss cheese. Add the ham, grilled pineapple and romaine. Top with the remaining slice of Swiss cheese and bread, repeat for second sandwich and serve.

OMELET SANDWICH

1 tsp oil
1 link sausage, about 2oz, thinly sliced
1/2 red pepper, diced
1 tsp oil
2 eggs, beaten
1/4 tsp salt
1/8 tsp pepper
2 tbsp shredded cheddar
2-inch section cucumber, thinly sliced
2 slices bread

Heat a teaspoon of oil on medium heat. Stir fry sausage and diced red peppers until peppers are cooked but not soft. Remove everything from the pan.

Heat up another teaspoon of oil on low. Whisk salt and pepper into the beaten eggs, and then pour onto the heated oil. Let the eggs cook enough so that the bottom is solid but the top is a little runny still. Spoon sausage and peppers into the middle of the omelet and sprinkle shredded cheddar on top. Fold up the four sides of the omelet.

Transfer omelet onto a slice of bread and create a sandwich. Toast sandwich on both sides in the pan. When the sandwich is well-toasted, add thinly sliced cucumbers into the sandwich.

Be a Weekend Warrior

"Smart Stockpiling for the Back to School Season"

Did you know that you can actually plan your meals ahead? With a little strategizing you can easily turn one meal into three, each with its own distinct flavor. No one really likes leftovers – especially when we have no choice but to stay at home (Spring of 2020 everyone). But when you already have cooked pork or chicken or a tenderloin on hand, you're ahead of the game. Making dinner will be a snap.

Roast chicken can easily do triple-duty. On the first night, roast it with some potatoes and rosemary — the whole house will smell like heaven. The next day, slice up some of the breast, lay it across some hearts of romaine, top with Caesar salad dressing and parmesan shavings and you have an uptown, tasty lunch right from your fridge. That night, use soft tortillas to make a chicken quesadilla with the last of the chicken. Throw in canned black beans from your pantry, and top with salsa and sour cream. Take a bite and savor your genius.

A big steak, like a London Broil, can be reinvented over several meals. On the first night, rub it with a spice mix, pop it in the broiler or on the grill and delight in slices of juicy steak.

The next day, layer some slices on a ciabatta roll, add blue cheese and sliced tomato and enjoy a hearty, big-flavor lunch that would cost a fortune at a restaurant. That night, sauté the last of the steak with sliced onions, peppers, and Mexican seasonings and serve on warm tortillas: you have fajitas.

Cook a pork tenderloin and then go international. For your next three meals, enjoy a southern-style Pulled Pork Sandwich, Asian Pork Chow Mein and Cuban Style Pork with Papaya Mango Salsa.

Another key to delicious two and three day suppers is making dishes that taste better the next day. Soups, stews and chilis all benefit from sitting a day or two in the fridge; their flavors marry and become more intense. So don't think of yesterday's beef stew as leftovers — think of it as a meal that's just about to hit its prime.

Here are some other recipes that are good for summer stockpiling – or anytime of the year. With each of these recipes, they either keep in the refrigerator well overnight for a day or two or you can use the leftovers (if there are any) and put them into dishes – like salads, sandwiches, stews, quesadillas, and fajitas for the next few days.

DRY RUBBED LONDON BROIL

1 (2-pound) London broil
2 tbsp olive oil
Rub (Recipe below)

Rub London broil with olive oil and then coat generously with the dry rub. Let stand for about 15 minutes at room temperature. Preheat a grill pan over medium-high heat. Place meat on grill and grill for about 5 minutes on each side for medium-rare. Remove from heat and let rest for 5 to 10 minutes before slicing on the bias.

Rub:

2 tbsp chili powder
1 tbsp dried oregano
1 tbsp sweet paprika
2 tsp garlic powder
4 pinches salt
15 grinds black pepper

Mix all ingredients together thoroughly in a small bowl.

Lemon & Herb Roasted Chicken With Baby Potatoes

1 (4 to 5 pound) free-range chicken
Salt and freshly ground black pepper
1 lemon, halved
1 head garlic, halved
1/4 bunch each fresh rosemary, thyme, and parsley
1/4 cup olive oil
11/2 pounds red new potatoes

Preheat the oven to 400 degrees F. Rinse the chicken with cool water, inside and out, then pat it dry with paper towels. Season the cavity with salt and pepper, and then stuff the lemon, garlic, and herbs inside. Place the chicken, breast-side up, in a roasting pan. Tie the legs of the chicken together with kitchen twine to help hold its shape. Toss the potatoes around the chicken. Season the whole thing with a fair amount of salt and pepper and drizzle with olive oil. Roast the chicken and potatoes for 1 to 1 1/2 hours. Don't forget to baste the chicken with the drippings and rotate the pan every 20 minutes or so to insure a golden crispy skin. The chicken is done when an instant-read thermometer says 165 degrees F when inserted into the thickest part of the thigh (the legs of the chicken should wiggle easily from the sockets too.) Remove the chicken to a platter and let stand for 10 minutes, so the juices settle back into the meat before carving. Serve with the roasted potatoes on the side.

Roast Pork Loin

1 tbsp vegetable oil
1 boneless center-cut pork loin roast (about 2 pounds), trimmed and tied (see below)
Salt and freshly ground pepper
2 tbsp mustard
2 tbsp cider vinegar

Preheat the oven to 375 degrees. Heat the oil in a large ovenproof skillet over high heat. Season the pork with salt and pepper and sear on all sides until golden brown. Combine the mustard and vinegar and brush over the pork. Transfer to the oven and roast the pork until a thermometer inserted in the center reads 145 degrees, about 35 minutes. Transfer the pork to a cutting board and tent with foil for 10 minutes. Remove strings, slice and serve.

APPLE SMOKED BACON, WHITE CHEDDAR AND POTATO OMELET

2 tbsp unsalted butter
1 large Idaho potatoes, peeled and grated
Salt
Freshly ground white pepper
6 large eggs
1/2 pound Apple Smoked Bacon, cooked until crispy
3 ounces White Cheddar cheese, grated
2 tbsp chopped chives

Preheat a stove top or electric griddle, over medium high heat. Using a hand grater, grate the potato onto a clean cloth towel. Squeeze out any liquid into a bowl. Melt the butter on the griddle. Place an even layer of the potatoes over the griddle. Season with salt and pepper. Using a metal spatula, flip the potatoes over occasionally until the potatoes are crispy and golden, about 2 to 3 minutes. Meanwhile, place the eggs in a blender. Season with salt and pepper. Blend until the eggs are frothy. Pour the eggs over the potatoes. Cook for about 1 minute. Sprinkle the bacon and cheese over the egg potato mixture and continue to cook for about 1 minute. Using the metal spatula, fold the omelet into thirds. Continue to cook for about 30 seconds on both sides. Remove from the griddle. Slice the omelet in half and place on serving plates. Garnish with chives.

GREEN BEAN CASSEROLE

1/3 stick butter
1/2 cup diced onions
1/2 cup sliced fresh mushrooms

2 cups sliced green beans
3 cups chicken broth
1 (10 3/4-ounce) can cream of mushroom soup
1 (2.8-ounce) can French-fried onion rings
1 cup grated Cheddar

Preheat the oven to 350 degrees F. Melt the butter in a large skillet. Sauté the onions and mushrooms in the butter. Boil green beans in chicken broth for 10 minutes and drain. Add the green beans, mushroom soup, and onion rings to taste, to the onion mixture. Stir well. Pour into a greased 1 1/2-quart baking dish. Bake for 20 minutes, then top the casserole with the Cheddar and bake for 10 minutes longer, or until the casserole is hot and cheese is melted.

SALAD WITH POACHED EGGS AND BACON DRESSING

2 tsp extra-virgin olive oil
1 piece bacon, cut crosswise into 1/2 inch thick strips
1 tsp aged sherry or red wine vinegar
Salt and freshly ground black pepper
1 tbsp distilled vinegar
1 to 2 large eggs
1-1/2 cups mixed greens, washed and spun dried
1 or 2 (1/2-inch) thick slices of a baguette or sourdough bread, lightly toasted

Heat the oil in a small sauté pan over medium heat. Sauté the bacon strips until golden and crispy. Remove the bacon with a slotted spoon to a paper towel to drain and reserve. Pour off the oil and bacon fat, and reserve. Return the pan to the heat and add the vinegar and stir with a wooden spoon, scraping up any browned bits from the bottom of the pan. Whisk in about 4 teaspoons of the reserved pan drippings to make a dressing. Season with salt and pepper to taste and set aside. Fill a small sauce pan with 3 inches of water. Add the distilled vinegar. Bring to a gentle simmer over medium heat, adjust heat to so the water is just under a simmer. Break the egg(s) into the water and poach to desired doneness, about 3 to 5 minutes. Meanwhile toss the salad with the reserved bacon and the dressing. Season with salt and pepper. Put the salad on a plate and place the toasts on the salad. Remove eggs from the water with a slotted spoon and pat the back of the spoon with paper towels. Place egg on toast and serve immediately.

Fennel, Orange, and Pomegranate salad

Fresh Orange juice (about 6 Tablespoons)
2 tbsp Balsamic vinegar
¼ cup olive oil
½ medium fennel bulb cored and sliced thinly
¼ cup pomegranate seeds
Orange segments
Watercress

Make dressing by whisking together the orange juice, vinegar, and oil. Add salt and pepper to taste. Combine fennel, pomegranate, and orange sections in bowl. Pour dressing over them and let marinate at room temperature for 20 minutes. Drain the dressing form the items and put back into remaining dressing. Toss watercress with dressing and serve with orange fennel and pomegranate on top.

SEPTEMBER

Take a "wok" on the wild side

Learning to appreciate the flavors of China

One of my favorite classes to teach to adults is "A Taste of China." And it's also one of the most popular. And I think that is for good reason. When most of us think of Chinese Food, we think of cute cardboard containers with wire handles, and chopsticks, or noodles and rice. And fortune cookies. I once opened a fortune cookie and it was empty. I still think that was a bad sign.

Many of us never think of it as a "home cooked" meal – or something you can make yourself.

But you can. After all, in China, this is home cooked. And that begs the question, in China, is Chinese Take Out just called "Take Out?"

The first food people associate with Chinese food is probably rice. And that's for a good reason. Rice was the first grain that people farmed in China. There is archaeological evidence of rice farming along the Yang-tse River as early as about 5000 BC. People cooked rice by boiling it in water, the way they do today. Or they made it into wine. Rice wine has been popular in China since prehistory.

During ancient times – around 3000 BC, meat – mostly chicken and pork – was added to rice, but only on special occasions – like weddings. But keep in mind, most people in China didn't eat meat anyway for a long time because of religious reasons. Since meat was so expensive and because Buddhists didn't eat meat, starting around the Sung Dynasty (about 1000 AD) people of China began using tofu (or bean curd) in their food as a source of protein.

Because China doesn't have big forests, it was always hard to find fuel to cook with. So the Chinese people learned to cut up their food into very small pieces so it would cook quickly on a very small fire – and the wok and stir fry as we know it today was born.

The odd thing (if you can call it odd) about China and Chinese food is the lack of a lot of starch. Marco Polo, who may have visited China from Venice, noted as early as the days of Kublai Khan (1200 A.D) that Chinese people did not bake or eat bread. And they still don't.

But they do eat a lot of pretty good – and healthy – foods. Here are a few recipes I have found that keep coursing through my cooking courses.

CHINESE DONUTS

1 can refrigerated biscuits
1/3 cup sugar
oil, to deep fry in

Use either a deep fryer, or a large deep skillet. Be sure to add enough of oil to line the bottom of the pan a couple of inches deep. Heat oil to 350 degrees. Remove biscuits from can and fry a few at a time in the fryer. When browned on one side, turn over. When golden brown on both sides remove from oil, and drain on paper towels. Pour sugar into a small container, and once the doughnuts have cooled slightly toss the doughnut into the sugar, and coat on both sides. Be sure to fry only a couple at a time.

FRIED RICE

2 cups uncooked basmati rice
2 cups water
1/2-3/4 cup chicken stock
1 ham steak (cut into cubes)
1/2 cup frozen peas
2 eggs
3 tsp canola oil (or peanut oil)
1/4 tsp salt
2 tbsp soy sauce

Cook your rice. You want to leave it a little on the crunchy side. Don't overcook it. Let your rice cool completely. Heat a wok over high heat with 1 tbs. of oil. Add eggs and scramble until cooked. Add ham and peas and fry for about a minute. Remove from wok. Add remaining oil to the wok and heat over high heat until it is very hot. Add your cold rice to the wok and stir to coat every grain. Add the chicken stock to the rice; do it a little bit at a time to give the rice a chance to soak up the liquid. Stir until there is no liquid left, then chop up your cooked egg and add it, along with the soy sauce and salt. Stir. Serve

GENERAL TSO'S CHICKEN

1 lb. chicken boneless, skinless and cubed
3 eggs, beaten
1/2 cup cornstarch, plus
2 tsp cornstarch
5 dried chili pods
1 1/2 tbsp rice vinegar
2 tbsp rice wine
3 tbsp sugar
3 tbsp soy sauce

In a large bowl, thoroughly blend the 1/2 cup of cornstarch and the eggs; add the chicken and toss to coat. If the mixture is too thick, add some vegetable oil to separate the pieces. In a small bowl, prepare the sauce mixture by combining the 2 tsp cornstarch with the wine, vinegar, sugar and soy sauce. Heat 1-2 inches of peanut oil in a wok to medium-high heat. Fry the chicken in small batches, just long enough to cook the chicken through. Remove the chicken to absorbent paper and allow to stand. Leave a tablespoon or two of the oil in the wok. Add the pepper pods to the oil and stir-fry briefly, awakening the aroma but not burning them. Return the chicken to the wok and stir-fry until the pieces are crispy brown. Add the sauce-mixture to the wok, tossing over the heat until the sauce caramelizes into a glaze. Serve immediately.

BEEF AND BROCCOLI STIR FRY

3 tbsp cornstarch, divided
1/2 cup water, plus
2 tbsp water, divided
1/2 tsp garlic powder
1 lb. boneless round steak or 1 lb. charcoal chuck steak, cut into thin 3-inch strips
2 tbsp vegetable oil, divided
4 cups broccoli florets
1 small onion, cut into wedges
1/3 cup reduced sodium soy sauce

2 tbsp brown sugar
1 tsp ground ginger
hot cooked rice

In a bowl, combine 2 tablespoons cornstarch, 2 tablespoons water and garlic powder until smooth. Add beef and toss. In a large skillet or wok over medium high heat, stir-fry beef in 1 tablespoon oil until beef reaches desired doneness; remove and keep warm. Stir-fry broccoli and onion in remaining oil for 4-5 minutes. Return beef to pan. Combine soy sauce, brown sugar, ginger and remaining cornstarch and water until smooth; add to the pan. Cook and stir for 2 minutes.

THE RED LOTUS

1 1/2 ounces vodka
1 1/2 ounces lychee liqueur
1 ounce cranberry juice

Pour the ingredients into a cocktail shaker with ice. Shake well. Strain into a chilled "old fashioned" glass filled with ice

Where is the heart and warmth of your home?

How to make the kitchen everyone's favorite room of the house

People often ask me "Is your favorite room of your house really your kitchen? Or do you get sick of being in the kitchen when you get home from working in a kitchen all day?"

And the answer is – it depends on what kind of day I've had at work. There are honestly days when the last thing I want to do when I get home is cook. But there are also times – on weekends and holidays and when friends and family are coming over – when all I want to do is find something to make for dinner. I love being creative in my own kitchen and preparing meals for friends. They say a chef shows his or her appreciation and love through cooking. So please don't tell someone who loves to cook "not to bother." It's like telling someone to stop loving you. Just let a cook cook and a baker bake.

I especially love it when I can cook for large groups of people at parties. I catered my own birthday party earlier this year and I loved it. When a nephew and his wife were planning their rehearsal dinner, I jumped in to volunteer my services. It ended up being a lot less expensive – and a lot more personal.

I often notice that people want to congregate and visit in the kitchen anyway. I used to make the mistake of having all the food ready for a big gathering so when guests arrived, all I had to do was serve and then clean. But one time, I was running late and my guests wanted to help me get food ready, and wanted to hang out in the kitchen so now, I include my company in the process.

I have conducted mini-cooking classes in my kitchen just with friends. I've asked guests to slice meat and cheese, to plate dishes, and once, I even showed a good friend how to prepare an entire tenderloin – she always wanted to learn and so I taught her. So, if you're coming to my house for dinner, don't be surprised if we stand around in the kitchen, talk, and cook. It's one of my favorite ways to spend an evening in my house.

That said, if you're going to have this type of dinner party – where you want your guests involved – make sure they all have something to do. Ask someone to set and decorate the table; someone else can make mixed drinks or open the wine. For meals, I'd suggest things like tacos, fajitas, or tossed salads. How about you make your own pizzas? You provide the toppings, everyone arranges their own creations? Or bruschetta? And ask your guests to cut up different ingredients!

Whether you're having close friends over or expecting a large family gathering, I thought I would offer some uncomplicated and easy to prepare meals that should keep everyone well-fed and happy. Get everyone involved and make your kitchen the favorite room of your house too.

Spinach Lasagna

1 lb. part-skim ricotta cheese
10 oz. frozen chopped spinach, thawed and squeezed dry
2 cups shredded mozzarella cheese, divided
1 large egg
1/4 tsp. salt
32 oz. jar marinara sauce
9 oz. box no-boil lasagna noodles

Stir together ricotta, spinach, 1 cup mozzarella, egg, and salt. In slow cooker bowl, layer marinara sauce, lasagna noodles, and ricotta mixture, starting and ending with marinara sauce and breaking noodles to fit. Top with 1 cup mozzarella. Cover and cook on low 4 hours or until noodles are tender.

Korean Pork Lettuce Wraps

1/4 cup miso
1/4 cup soy sauce
3 tbsp Sriracha, plus more for serving
1 tbsp toasted sesame oil
1 tsp pepper
1 boneless pork shoulder (about 4 lb.), trimmed of excess fat and quartered
Lettuce leaves, for serving
Radishes, for serving
Cucumbers, for serving
Green onions, for serving

Whisk miso, soy sauce, Sriracha, sesame oil, and pepper. In slow cooker bowl, combine pork shoulder with soy mixture (marinate in refrigerator overnight if desired). Cover and cook on High 6 to 7 hours or on Low 8 to 10 hours until pork is tender. Shred pork and serve with lettuce leaves, radishes, cucumbers, green onions, and additional Sriracha.

Spicy Bánh Mì Sandwiches

1 Roasted Chicken
6 Sandwich rolls, split and lightly toasted
1 cup mayonnaise
1 cucumber, thinly sliced
3/4 cups shredded carrots
1/2 cup fresh cilantro leaves

Sriracha hot sauce, to taste

Cut meat from Chicken, discarding skin and bones; thinly slice. Spread mayonnaise on rolls; top with chicken, cucumber, carrots and cilantro. Drizzle with Sriracha if desired.

CIOPPINO

3 tbsp oil
1 medium onion, finely chopped
2 cloves garlic, minced
1/2 tsp salt
1 28 oz. can crushed tomatoes
2 8 oz. bottles clam juice
2 tbsp butter
1 pound shelled, deveined shrimp
2 pounds mussels, scrubbed
1 pound boneless cod fillet, cut into 3-in. chunks
Chopped parsley, for serving
Crusty bread, for serving

In 7-to 8-quart saucepot, heat oil on medium. Add onion, garlic, salt and cook 8 minutes, stirring. Add tomatoes, clam juice and butter. Heat to simmering on high. Add shrimp, mussels, and cod fillet. Cover; simmer 10 to 12 minutes or until most mussels have opened. Discard any unopened mussels. Sprinkle with parsley; serve in bowls with crusty bread.

SPANAKOPITA PENNE BAKE

1 pound penne
2 10-oz. boxes frozen chopped spinach
1 cup crumbled feta cheese
1/4 cup loosely packed dill, chopped
15 oz. part-skim ricotta
1/2 tsp salt
8 oz. part-skim mozzarella, shredded

Cook penne for half of time label directs, adding spinach and reserving 1/2 cup cooking water just before draining. Combine feta, dill, ricotta, and salt. Combine penne, cheese mixture and reserved cooking water; spread evenly in 3-quart baking dish. Top with mozzarella. Cover with foil; bake at 400 degrees F 25 minutes. Uncover and bake 10 minutes more.

GLAZED MEATLOAF

1 c. quick-cooking oats
½ c. fat-free (skim) milk
1 medium onion
salt
pepper
1 large red pepper
3 clove garlic
2 tsp. lower-sodium soy sauce
¼ c. ketchup
2 tbsp. ketchup
2 lb. ground beef
3 medium carrots
2 tbsp. spicy brown mustard

Directions: Heat oven to 400 degrees F. Line meatloaf or bread pan with foil; lightly coat with nonstick cooking spray. In medium bowl, stir together oats and milk until combined. Coat bottom of 12-inch skillet with nonstick cooking spray; heat on medium. Add onion and pinch salt; cook 2 to 4 minutes or until onion softens, stirring occasionally. Add red pepper and garlic; cook 4 to 6 minutes or until pepper softens, stirring often. Transfer to medium bowl; refrigerate to cool. Meanwhile, in small bowl, whisk together soy sauce and 1/4 cup ketchup. In large bowl, with hands, combine beef, turkey, carrots, oat mixture, cooled vegetable mixture, mustard, 2 tablespoons ketchup, pinch salt, and 1/4 teaspoon freshly ground black pepper until mixed. Form mixture into 8-inch by 4-inch loaf on prepared pan. Brush top and sides with soy ketchup. Bake 45 to 50 minutes

So...what should I have in my Kitchen Pantry?

Every kitchen of every home should contain the following staples for your pantry, refrigerator or freezer. These are your "go to" items. How many are on your list?

In your pantry or cupboard you should always have "on hand": baking powder, baking soda, bread, brown sugar, canned beans, cereal, chicken, beef, or vegetable broth, cider or white vinegar, cocoa powder, coffee and/ or tea and condiments (ketchup, mustard, mayonnaise, barbecue sauce, soy sauce, pickles), cornstarch, dried herbs (like basil, bay leaves, oregano, rosemary, tarragon, thyme, and parsley), flour, granulated sugar, ground spices (like black pepper, cayenne pepper, chili powder, cinnamon, cumin, curry powder, ginger, dry mustard, nutmeg, and paprika), jam, jelly, or preserves, pancake syrup, pasta, peanut butter, rice, salt, tomato sauce, paste, and canned tomatoes, vanilla extract, and vegetable oil.

In your refrigerator, you should take a look and see if you have plenty of: butter, cheeses, eggs, fresh fruit, fresh vegetables, meat (meat like beef, fish and poultry should not be in the fridge longer than three days), milk, sour cream, yogurt.

In your freezer, always have at the ready: fruit, vegetables, ice, ice cream (or frozen yogurt), meat (beef, poultry or fish – enough supply to last a week)

The Heart of Every Home needs a healthy pulse

Family recipes from my own Grandma's kitchen

The kitchen is indeed the heart of every home. That's what they say. I didn't come up with that. Someone wiser than me said it. Probably someone's grandmother – because grandmothers just happen to be the wisest people walking the face of the earth.

That was certainly true in my grandmother's house. Interestingly enough, Esther Braman of Atlantic, Iowa was a home-education teacher and taught cooking. I like to think I come from a long line of family members whose favorite room of the house is the kitchen.

Recently, while cleaning out my own kitchen for an extensive and long overdue renovation, I came across some of my Grandma Braman's recipes and I thought I would share them with all of you. She taught home economics for an astounding 55 years so you can imagine the personal handwritten collection she had. Maybe that will be my next book!

The kitchen is that part of the home where most of us gather to not only eat but to laugh and to love. September is also the month of Grandparents' Day. And so, these recipes are from her kitchen to my kitchen, to yours… now let's get cooking! It's not nice to keep your grandmother waiting.

BAKED MACARONI AND CHEESE

1 (8 ounce) packages macaroni
4 tbsp butter
4 tbsp flour
1 cup milk
1 cup cream
1/2 tsp salt
fresh ground black pepper, to taste
2 cups cheddar cheese, shredded good quality
1/2 cup breadcrumbs, buttered

Preheat oven to 400. Cook and drain macaroni according to package directions; set aside. In a large saucepan melt butter. Add flour mixed with salt and pepper, using a whisk to stir until well blended. Pour milk and cream in gradually; stirring constantly. Bring to boiling point and boil 2 minutes (stirring constantly). Reduce heat and cook (stirring constantly) 10 minutes. Add shredded cheddar little by little and simmer an additional 5 minutes, or until cheese melts. Turn off flame. Add macaroni to the saucepan and toss to coat with the cheese sauce. Transfer macaroni to a buttered baking dish. Sprinkle with breadcrumbs. Bake 20 minutes until the top is golden brown.

BROCCOLI AND CHEESE SOUP

3 tbsp room temperature unsalted butter
2 tbsp cold unsalted butter, cut into pieces
1 cup yellow onions or sliced leeks (white parts only, well rinsed)
1/2 tsp salt
1/4 tsp freshly ground white pepper
1/2 tsp minced garlic
1/2 tsp chopped fresh thyme leaves
3 tbsp all-purpose flour
3 cups chicken stock
1 (16-ounce) package frozen broccoli, thawed and separated
1/2 cup heavy cream
1 1/4 cups shredded medium Cheddar

In a medium pot, melt the 3 tablespoons butter over medium-high heat. Add the onions, salt, pepper, and nutmeg and cook, stirring, until soft, 3 minutes. Add the garlic and thyme cook, stirring, until fragrant, for 20 seconds. Add the flour and cook, stirring until the mixture is well blended and smells fragrant, 2 minutes. Slowly add the chicken stock, whisking constantly, and bring to a boil. Reduce the heat and simmer until thickened, about 5 minutes. Add the broccoli and cook, stirring, until tender, for 10 minutes. Add the cream and bring to bare simmer to heat through. Add the cheese and cook over low heat, stirring, until melted. Add the remaining 2 tablespoons cold butter, stirring to blend serve immediately.

CHICKEN PARMESAN

1/4 cup extra-virgin olive oil, plus 3 tablespoons
1 medium onion, chopped
2 garlic cloves, minced
2 bay leaves
1/2 bunch fresh basil leaves
2 (28-ounce) cans whole peeled tomatoes, drained and hand-crushed
Pinch sugar
Salt and pepper
4 skinless, boneless, chicken breasts (about 11/2 pounds)
1/2 cup all-purpose flour
2 large eggs, lightly beaten
1 tbsp water
1 cup dried bread crumbs
1 (8-ounce) ball fresh buffalo mozzarella, water drained
Freshly grated Parmesan
1 pound spaghetti pasta, cooked al dente

Coat a sauté pan with olive oil and place over medium heat. When the oil gets hazy, add the onions, garlic, and bay leaves; cook and stir for 5 minutes until fragrant and soft. Add the olives and some hand-torn basil. Carefully add the tomatoes, cook and stir until the liquid is cooked down and the sauce is thick, about 15 minutes; season with sugar, salt and pepper. Lower the heat, cover, and keep warm. Preheat the oven to 450 degrees F. Get the ingredients together for the chicken so you have a little assembly line. Put the chicken breasts side by side on a cutting board and lay a piece of plastic wrap over them. Pound the chicken breasts with a flat meat mallet, until they are about 1/2-inch thick. Put the flour in a shallow platter and season with a fair amount of salt and pepper; mix with a fork to distribute evenly. In a wide bowl, combine the eggs and water, beat until frothy. Put the bread crumbs on a plate, season with salt and pepper. Heat 3 tablespoons of olive oil over medium-high flame in a large oven-proof skillet. Lightly dredge both sides of the chicken cutlets in the seasoned flour, and then dip them in the egg wash to coat completely, letting the excess drip off, then dredge in the bread crumbs. When the oil is nice and hot, add the cutlets and fry for 4 minutes on each side until golden and crusty, turning once. Ladle the tomato-olive sauce over the chicken and sprinkle with mozzarella, Parmesan, and basil. Bake the Chicken Parmesan for 15 minutes or until the cheese is bubbly. Serve hot on the spaghetti.

GREEN BEAN CASSEROLE

1/3 stick butter
1/2 cup diced onions
1/2 cup sliced fresh mushrooms
2 cups sliced green beans
3 cups chicken broth
1 large can cream of mushroom soup
1 small can French-fried onion rings
1 cup grated Cheddar

Preheat the oven to 350 degrees. Melt the butter in a large skillet. Sauté the onions and mushrooms in the butter. Boil green beans in chicken broth for 10 minutes and drain. Add the green beans, mushroom soup, onion rings, and House Seasoning, to taste, to the onion mixture. Stir well. Pour into a greased 1 1/2-quart baking dish. Bake for 20 minutes, then top the casserole with the Cheddar and bake for 10 minutes longer, or until the casserole is hot and cheese is melted.

Roasted Potatoes, Carrots, Parsnips and Brussels Sprout

1/3 cup extra-virgin olive oil
3 medium carrots, cut into 1 1/2-inch thick circles
1 1/2 cups Brussels sprouts, halved
4 cups red bliss potatoes, cut into 1 1/2-inch thick slices
3 medium parsnips, cut into 1 1/2-inch thick slices
1 cup sweet potatoes, cut into 1 1/2-inch thick slices
1 tbsp dried oregano
1 tbsp dried rosemary
1 tsp dried thyme
1 tsp dried basil
1/4 tsp sea salt
2 tbsp freshly ground black pepper

Preheat oven to 400 degrees F. Grease an 11 by 17-inch baking sheet pan with extra-virgin olive oil. Place vegetables in baking sheet and add the dried herbs, salt and pepper. Toss well, evenly coating all the vegetables with the seasonings and oil. Add more oil if the vegetables seem dry. Spread the vegetables evenly on a large baking sheet. Place on middle rack in oven and bake for 35 to 40 minutes.

Ultimate Shrimp and Grits

For the grits:

3 cups milk
3 cups heavy cream
1 cup stone-ground white cornmeal
2 tbsp unsalted butter
Salt
Freshly ground black pepper

For the shrimp:

2 tbsp extra-virgin olive oil
1 medium white onion, minced
1 garlic clove, minced
1 pound andouille or spicy Italian spicy sausage, cut in chunks
1/4 cup all-purpose flour
2 cups chicken stock
2 to 3 bay leaves
2 pounds large shrimp, peeled and deveined, tails on
Pinch cayenne pepper, adjust to personal preference
1/2 lemon, juiced
salt
Freshly ground black pepper
2 tbsp finely chopped fresh flat-leaf parsley
4 green onions, sliced

For the grits: Place a 3-quart pot over medium-high heat. Add the milk and cream. Slowly whisk in the cornmeal. When the grits begin to bubble, turn the heat down to medium low and simmer, stirring frequently with a wooden spoon. Allow to cook for 10 to 15 minutes, until the mixture is smooth and thick. Remove from heat and stir in the butter, thin it out with a little extra cream. Season with salt and pepper.

For the shrimp: Place a deep skillet over medium heat and coat with the olive oil. Add the onion and garlic; sauté for 2 minutes to soften. Add the sausage and cook, stirring, until there is a fair amount of fat in the pan and the sausage is brown. Sprinkle in the flour and stir with a wooden spoon to create a roux. Slowly pour in the chicken stock and continue to stir to avoid lumps. Toss in the bay leaves. When the liquid comes to a simmer, add the shrimp. Poach the shrimp in the stock for 2 to 3 minutes, until they are firm and pink and the gravy is smooth and thick. Add the cayenne pepper, Tabasco and lemon juice. Season with salt and pepper; stir in the parsley and green onion. Spoon the grits into a serving bowl. Add the shrimp mixture and mix well. Serve Immediately

Re-Inventing the TV Dinner

The popular living room meal has evolved over the years. And here is how you can re-create it.

Admit it. You have had at least one.

Either as a kid in front of the television set—or in the college dorm – or maybe even at work. A TV dinner. An invention of a meal specifically tailored to sit on a tray while you sit in front of the television. When the foiled lined frozen meal was invited in the early 1950s by Swanson Foods, no one knew would a remarkable innovation this would be. Swanson only sold 5000 of them in its first year. But the idea quickly caught on – because families could now move their meals from the formal dining room and right into the living room to sit near that new status symbol of the day called a TV. You didn't have to choose between dessert or *Uncle Miltie*.

The first Swanson-branded TV Dinner was introduced in November, 1953 and contained a "sad man's" Thanksgiving meal of turkey, cornbread dressing, frozen peas and sweet potatoes. The original aluminum tray was modeled after the meal plates served on major airlines at the time. Each item had its own compartment.

Over the next nearly 70 years, the TV dinner – like the TV itself – has evolved. And now the meals (still made by Swanson by the way) are in microwavable containers. And other food companies like Banquet, Morton and Stouffers jumped on the chuck wagon and invented their own. Even popcorn has gone from the days of shaking Jiffy Pop over the stove to allowing a preset button to determine how many kernels will pop inside that brown paper bag.

The traditional TV dinner usually consists of a cut of meat – beef, chicken or turkey; a vegetable, such as peas, carrots, corn, or potatoes; and sometimes a dessert, such as a brownie or apple crisp. The main dish could also be pasta with a meatball or a common type of fish. Today, a wider variety of frozen complete meals are available. Companies have now added fried chicken, Salisbury steak, Chinese food and Mexican cuisine.

And now, the tray itself has been re-invented. Today, a complete frozen pre-cooked ready meal can come in an almost-pretty serving tray, ready to be put on the table. Or in a bag that needs to be emptied into a bowl. There is everything from the stand-by traditional turkey to a variety of stir frys. But hardcore TV Dinner enthusiasts – the ones that yearn for the days of Howdy Doody and Huckleberry Hound, will tell you, if it doesn't burn a layer of skin peeling back a layer of tin foil – and if it doesn't have those three of four compartments – it's not a true TV dinner.

That said, here are some recipes inspired by TV dinners that you can make at home. Adjust the rabbit ears, put on an *I Love Lucy* rerun and enjoy.

SALISBURY STEAK

Salisbury steak was invented by an American physician, Dr. J. H. Salisbury in 1897.

1 can condensed French onion soup
1 1/2 pounds ground beef
1/2 cup dry bread crumbs
1 egg
1/4 tsp salt
1/8 tsp black pepper
1 tbsp flour
1/4 cup ketchup
1/4 cup water
1 tbsp Worcestershire sauce
1/2 tsp mustard powder

In a large bowl, mix together 1/3 cup condensed French onion soup with ground beef, bread crumbs, egg, salt and black pepper. Shape into 6 oval patties. In a large skillet over medium-high heat, brown both sides of patties. Pour off excess fat. In a small bowl, blend flour and remaining soup until smooth. Mix in ketchup, water, Worcestershire sauce and mustard powder. Pour over meat in skillet. Cover, and cook for 20 minutes, stirring occasionally.

EASY MEATLOAF

A variation of meatloaf dates back to the Romans in the 5th century.

1½ lbs. lean ground beef
3 eggs
1½ sleeves crushed Ritz crackers
½ cup finely chopped onion
4 oz shredded sharp cheddar cheese
½ cup milk
1 tsp salt
¼ tsp pepper

Topping:

½ cup ketchup
½ cup brown sugar
1 tsp mustard

Preheat oven to 350 °F. Line a baking sheet with parchment or aluminum foil. Mix all the topping ingredients in a small bowl; set aside. In a separate large bowl, beat the eggs then add the cracker crumbs, onion, green pepper, milk, salt, pepper and cheese; stir to combine. Add the ground beef and mix well. Turn out the meatloaf mixture onto the prepared pan; shape into a loaf. Bake for 30 minutes then spread topping on the meatloaf. Bake for an additional 30 minutes. Let stand for 5-10 minutes to rest, then slice and serve.

BEER BATTERED FISH

Fish and chips is mentioned in Charles Dickens' 1859 classic A Tale of Two Cities.

One or two cups of vegetable oil
12-ounce bottle beer
2 cups all-purpose flour
1 1/2 pounds cod fillets, skinned with bones removed, and cut diagonally.

For Seasoning:

1 cup salt
1/4 cup black pepper
1/4 cup garlic powder

In a Dutch oven, heat oil to 375 degrees. In a small bowl, mix together ingredients for seasoning. Set aside. Then, in a large bowl, pour in the bottle of beer. Sift 1 1/2 cups flour into the bowl, whisking in gently until just combined, then stir in seasoning from the small bowl. Pat fish dry and season on both sides with salt and pepper and coat the fish in the beer batter. Dredge the pieces of fish in 1/2 cup of remaining flour and slide into oil as coated. Fry fish, turning over frequently, until deep golden and cooked through. Transfer to a paper towel-lined baking sheet and keep warm in oven (225 degrees) until all the pieces have been fried.

APPLE CRISP

A distant cousin of apple pie and apple tarts, apple crisp is first referenced in an 1886 cookbook.

4 medium tart cooking apples, sliced
¾ cups packed brown sugar
½ cup all-purpose flour
½ cup quick-cooking or old-fashioned oats
1/3 cup butter or margarine, softened
¾ tsp cinnamon
¾ tsp nutmeg

Heat oven to 375°F. Grease bottom and sides of 8-inch square pan with shortening. Spread apples in pan. In medium bowl, stir remaining ingredients except cream until well mixed; sprinkle over apples. Bake about 30 minutes or until topping is golden brown and apples are tender when pierced with a fork.

EASY BROWNIES

Betty Crocker and Fannie Farmer both take credit for publishing the first recipe for Brownies in 1905.

2 1/2 cups granulated sugar
1 1/4 cups unsalted butter
1 3/4 cups unsweetened cocoa powder
1/2 tsp salt
4 large eggs
1 cup all-purpose flour
2 tsp baking powder
1 tsp vanilla extract

Preheat the oven to 325 degrees and mist an 8 by 8-inch pan with non-stick spray. Line with parchment. Place the sugar, butter, cocoa, and salt in a large microwave-safe bowl, and microwave in one-minute increments, stirring, until the butter is completely melted and the mixture feels very warm to the touch. Add the eggs, one at a time, stirring after each addition. Stir in the flour and baking powder. Stir in the vanilla. Transfer the batter to the prepared pan, and bake for 45-60 minutes, or until set around the edges but still soft towards the middle. Cool and cut into squares.

The Most Important Meal of the Day?

And why you shouldn't start your day without doing this one thing!

For years, you have probably been told that breakfast is the most important meal of the day. And it was true when you heard it from the cafeteria ladies in school just as much as it is coming from me reminding you of it now. It still is the most important meal – for physical as well as psychological reasons.

Studies have shown that children who have breakfast are less likely to participate in "risky behavior" or succumb to peer pressure at school. Breakfast is also said to improve work and school performance. If you skip breakfast, you're likely to have trouble staying on task later in the day, resulting in being tired or even irritable long before you get a break for lunch. Breakfast skippers usually don't make up for the nutrients they missed at breakfast—and they actually overeat later when hungry – and usually it's not healthy foods. Eating breakfast everyday will actually help you lose weight, make better diet decisions, give you better energy, improve your work, school or home performance and better your mood.

So, what's the best breakfast? Start with a protein packed morning meal. Have a glass of milk, a cup of yogurt, a piece of cheese, peanut butter on toast or just one egg. If nothing else, grab a slice of pizza left over from the night before and finish that off.

To remind yourself not to skip breakfast and to get into the "habit of healthy eating," try getting all the supplies out the night before. Put the cereal or bread in a place where you can see it when you pass through the kitchen. Just having the items out will remind you to eat.

You can also write yourself a note and stick it on the coffee pot. A simple "Eat" will do. Or you could cut this article out and put it on the fridge – allowing me to remind you every morning to eat your breakfast – but I'm not going to nag you. If you skip breakfast, your body will do all the reminding you need.

Why is it called Breakfast anyway?

Now that we've established why you should have breakfast every morning, how did this meal get its name? It's not what you might think. It does not mean take a quick break, grab what you can and hit the road. It actually means the opposite. When you are asleep for six to eight hours a night, you are going the most you will go in your day without eating – without refueling your body. Your body is fasting. When you wake up and eat your first meal of the day – refueling your body for the day ahead – you are *breaking* the *fast*.

September 26 is National Breakfast Awareness Day

WHOLE-WHEAT MUFFINS

It'll be like your own coffeeshop experience. You can even misspell your name on your cup.

½ cup margarine or butter
½ cup granulated sugar
½ cup light brown sugar
1 tsp baking soda
1 egg
¼ tsp vanilla
1 cup milk
2 cups whole-wheat flour

Preheat oven to 400 F. Let ingredients get to room temperature and line a muffin tin using paper baking cups. You could also use a mist of a cooking spray. With electric mixer (or by hand), cream margarine, granulated sugar, brown sugar and baking soda together, scraping bowl with spatula. In a small bowl, using a fork, beat together the egg and vanilla; add to creamed mixture. Beat until light and fluffy. Add milk to creamed mixture. Gradually add whole-wheat flour and lightly stir ingredients together so dry ingredients are barely moistened. Fill the tins two-thirds full and bake 15 to 17 minutes, or until browned. Remove and cool.

BREAKFAST FRUIT BOWL

3 tbsp orange juice
2 medium apples, diced
1 orange, peeled and diced
1 banana, peeled and sliced
1 cup diced cantaloupe (or any other fruit that is in season)

Pour juice in a medium bowl. As you slice and dice the fruits add to the bowl and toss lightly, covering with juice (like it's a salad dressing). Chill and serve.

Cinnamon French Toast

2 eggs
4 egg whites
1 cup milk
1/8 tsp cinnamon
8 pieces toast, cut thick

In a bowl, blend together the eggs, egg whites, milk and cinnamon. Dip each piece of bread into the egg mixture and coat thoroughly. Place on a greased, preheated skillet and cook for about two minutes per side. Top with yogurt, fruit or syrup.

English Muffin Breakfast Pizzas

1 English muffin, split
1 small tomato, seeded and diced
1 tsp extra-virgin olive oil
1 thin slice Canadian bacon, diced
1/4 cup shredded mozzarella

Preheat the oven to 450 degrees. Line a small baking sheet with foil. Place the English muffin halves cut-side up on the baking sheet. Top each with tomato and drizzle with the olive oil. Sprinkle the Canadian bacon over the tomatoes, then top with the mozzarella. Bake for 10 to 12 minutes, or until the cheese is melted and beginning to brown.

Homemade Granola

3 cups rolled oats
1 cup slivered almonds
1 cup cashews
3/4 cup shredded sweet coconut
1/4 cup plus 2 tablespoons dark brown sugar
1/4 cup plus 2 tablespoons maple syrup
1/4 cup vegetable oil

1/4 tsp salt
1 cup raisins

Preheat oven to 250. In a large bowl, combine the oats, nuts, coconut, and brown sugar. In a separate bowl, combine maple syrup, oil, and salt. Combine both mixtures and pour onto 2 sheet pans. Cook for 1 hour and 15 minutes, stirring every 15 minutes to achieve an even color. Remove from oven and transfer into a large bowl. Add raisins and mix until evenly distributed.

OCTOBER

Falling for Fall

Savoring the Flavoring of Autumn

Fall is one of my favorite times of the year in the kitchen. It's the season of soups and seasonings. It's the time when you don't feel guilty if the kitchen is getting too hot. You've packed the barbecue grill away and it's time to enjoy a new harvest. One of the more popular requests I have received in recent months has been for pumpkin soup. Someone asked me last year for a recipe for pumpkin soup and to be honest, I had never made it before so I didn't want to make a recommendation. This year, I can. I tried a few variations and finally found one I liked. Not only that, but I am taking the suggestion a step further and providing a use for the leftover pumpkin seeds once the pumpkin "meat "is used. And, just because it's that time of year, I have also included a unique recipe I recently discovered for sweet potato and apple soup. Yes, you read that right…. Sweet potato and apple soup. You're going to love it.

Sweet potato and apple soup

1 3/4 pounds sweet potatoes, peeled and cut into 1-inch dice
1 small parsnip, peeled and cut into 1-inch dice
2 garlic cloves, coarsely chopped
2 tbsp extra-virgin olive oil
6 cups vegetable stock
1-cup apple cider
1 tsp Tabasco sauce

Finely diced Granny Smith apple and minced parsley

Preheat the oven to 375°. On a baking sheet, toss the sweet potatoes with the parsnip, garlic, olive oil and salt. Bake for 45 minutes, or until tender. In a blender, puree half of the vegetables with 3 cups of the stock; transfer to a large saucepan. Repeat with the remaining vegetables and stock. Add the apple cider and Tabasco and heat through. Serve with the diced apple and garnish with the parsley.

Pumpkin Sage Soup

3 tbsp butter
3 onions, chopped
3 cloves garlic, chopped
4 pounds pumpkin, peeled and cut into 2-inch pieces
3 cups chicken stock or canned low-sodium chicken broth
1 tsp salt
1 tbsp chopped fresh sage
2 cups cream
¼ tsp fresh-ground black pepper

In a large pot, heat the butter over moderately low heat. Add the onion and garlic and cook, stirring occasionally, until translucent, about 5 minutes. Add the pumpkin and stock. Bring to a boil. Reduce the heat and simmer, covered, for about 30 minutes. Stir in 1 tablespoon of the fresh sage and simmer 5 minutes longer. Puree the soup in a blender or food processor until smooth. Strain the puree back into the pot and add the cream. Stir in pepper. Simmer over low heat for 5 minutes. Top with the remaining 1 tablespoon chopped fresh sage. For fun, you could serve it individually in hollowed out pumpkin shells or place on the table in one giant hollowed shell.

Pumpkin Seed Brittle

1/3-cup sugar
2 tbsp light corn syrup
2 tbsp water
1/4 cup and two side tbsp of pumpkin seeds
1/8-tsp baking soda dissolved in 1-tsp water

Line a baking sheet with parchment paper and butter the paper. In a medium saucepan, combine the sugar, corn syrup and water and bring to a boil over moderately high heat, stirring just until the sugar dissolves. Continue to cook, undisturbed, until a caramel forms or 8 to 9 minutes. Remove from heat. Add the pumpkin seeds and the dissolved baking soda and stir until combined, then quickly pour the mixture onto the baking sheet, spreading it into a thin layer with a spatula. Let cool until hardened. Break into pieces and serve. The brittle can be kept in an airtight container for up to a week.

Bowl Me Over

Welcome to Soups 101

Fall is here. One of my favorite times of the year. And it's the perfect season to enjoy something that I really do love making in the kitchen. Soup! I love cooking soups and stews on the stove and having it handy as we go into these cool shorter nights that lie ahead.

Soups are one of the most versatile dishes ever. I promise you – unless you completely omit something or allow it to burn, making soup is pretty fool proof. You just follow the steps, let it simmer, and enjoy. When I make soup, I usually begin the morning or even the day before I want to serve it. This allows time for all the ingredients to marry and marinate and for the flavors to burst upon your taste buds upon impact. And does nothing smell better from the kitchen that a pot of soup cooking on the stove?

Served with chunks of fresh bread or a grilled cheese, to me, nothing says cuddle up and get cozy than a bowl or even a big oversized mug of soup. The following recipes are actually all mine – some were inspired by well known techniques but I modified them to make them by own and so if you have ever had one of my soups while dining out, this is what you've had – step by step – from my kitchen to yours. And a few of these remain the recipes most people ask me for.

You might say it's the ideal time of year to "fall" for soup!

Prep carrots, celery and onions. Make mirepoix by chopping these to a fine texture in the food processor. Place large soup pot over heat and melt butter. Add mirepoix. Sweat mirepoix for about 15 minutes. Add flour to pot while stirring to make roux. Add chicken and crab base, garlic and thyme. Allow mixture to cook for about 15 minutes to heat through. Add heavy cream and crabmeat. Allow soup to cook for about 30 minutes to heat through. Be careful not to boil. Add seasonings and flavor ingredients listed. Simmer and allow all the flavors to develop before eating.

BILL HAND'S FAMOUS CREAM OF CRAB

2 large onions, peeled and quartered
2 carrots, peeled and cut into one inch sections
8 stocks of celery, cut into one-inch sections
½ pound butter
1 cup all purpose flour
8 tbsp crab base
2 tbsp chicken base
2 quarts water
2 quarts heavy cream
2 pounds crabmeat

Seasonings:

1/8 cup Cabernet or Burgundy
3 tbsp of garlic
1/8 cup hot sauce
Old Bay seasoning, to taste
4 pinches of chopped parsley
4 pinches of chopped cilantro
1 cup Sherry
1 tbsp Thyme
1 tbsp white pepper
Worcestershire sauce – to taste

Prep carrots, celery and onions. Make mirepoix by chopping these to a fine texture in the food processor. Place large soup pot over heat and melt butter. Add mirepoix. Sweat mirepoix for about 15 minutes. Add flour to pot while stirring to make roux. Add chicken and crab base, garlic and thyme. Allow mixture to cook for about 15 minutes to heat through. Add heavy cream and crabmeat. Allow soup to cook for about 30 minutes to heat through. Be careful not to boil. Add seasonings and flavor ingredients listed. Simmer and allow all the flavors to develop before eating.

THE HAND FAMILY ROASTED ROOT VEGETABLE SOUP

2 parsnips, peeled and roughly chopped
1/2 medium celeriac, peeled and roughly chopped
3 carrots, peeled and roughly chopped
1/4 medium swede, peeled and roughly chopped
2 medium potatoes, peeled and roughly chopped
1 tbsp virgin olive oil
2 stalks celery, sliced
1 medium onion, roughly chopped
1 slice butter
4 7/8 cup vegetable stock (Marigold vegetable bouillon)
Sea salt
coarse-ground black pepper
1 pinch dried rosemary or 1 sprig fresh rosemary
1 pinch dried sage
2 bay leaves

Heat the oven to 425. Place the parsnip, celeriac, swede and half the chopped carrot on a roasting tray and mix it with the olive oil. Roast for about 15-20 minutes until brown. In a large saucepan, gently fry the onion, celery and the rest of the carrots in the butter until soft (around 10 minutes). Add the vegetable stock, potato, bay leaves, sage and rosemary and simmer for 20 minutes until the potatoes are soft. Remove the bay leaves and blend until smooth. Stir in the roasted root vegetables and season with the salt and pepper.

SENATE BEAN SOUP

2 pounds Michigan navy beans
4 quarts water
1 thick slice leftover spiral ham, cut into small pieces (not country ham, which is too salty

1/4 cup (1/2 stick) butter
1 medium onion, chopped
Salt and pepper
1/4 cup fresh parsley leaves

Rinse the beans in hot water until they are white. Place them in a stockpot, add the water, and bring to a boil. Reduce the heat and simmer for 3 hours. Heat the butter in a small skillet over medium heat. Sauté the onion until lightly browned. Add the onion to the pot of beans. Remove 2 cups of the bean mixture, puree in a blender, and return to the soup. Add to ham to soup mixture. Just before serving, season the soup with salt and pepper, to taste. Garnish with parsley.

BEEF STEW

1 tbsp Essence, recipe below
1 tbsp all-purpose flour
1 pound beef stew meat, cut into 1-inch cubes
1 tbsp olive oil
1 medium yellow onion, cut into medium dice
2 stalks celery, cut into medium dice
1/4 tsp salt
1/4 tsp ground black pepper
1 cup button mushrooms, quartered
1 tbsp chopped garlic
1 bay leaf
1 tsp chopped fresh thyme leaves
1 tsp chopped fresh rosemary leaves
1 cup dry red wine
2 1/2 cups beef broth
3 parsnips, peeled and cubed
2 turnips, peeled and cut into 1/2-inch cubes
2 cups chopped collard greens
2 tbsp chopped fresh parsley leaves
Rice, for serving

Essence Recipe:

Combine the following thoroughly: 2 1/2 tablespoons paprika, 2 tablespoons salt, 2 tablespoons garlic powder, 1 tablespoon black pepper,1 tablespoon onion powder, 1 tablespoon cayenne pepper

1 tablespoon dried oregano, and 1 tablespoon dried thyme.

Place unused combined seasonings in a jar or shaker and use in stews and other meats as needed at a later time.

Combine the Essence, flour, and beef cubes in a bowl. Toss to coat well. Add the oil to a pressure cooker and heat over medium-high heat until hot. Add the meat and cook, turning occasionally, until evenly brown, about 5 minutes. Transfer the meat to a plate and set aside. Add the onion, celery, salt, pepper, and mushrooms and cook, stirring, until the vegetables are wilted, about 3 minutes. Add the browned meat, garlic, bay leaf, thyme, rosemary, red wine, and broth. Cover the pressure cooker and cook for 20 minutes, turning down heat once a steady stream of steam is emitted from the valve.

Add the parsnips, turnips, and collard greens, stir well, and replace lid. Cook an additional 20 minutes. Garnish with chopped parsley and serve over rice.

CARROT GINGER SOUP

2 tbsp butter
1 tbsp olive oil
1 cup diced onions
1/2 cup diced celery
1/4 cup minced ginger
1 tbsp minced garlic
1/2 pound carrots peeled and roughly chopped
4 to 6 cups chicken stock
1 tsp salt
1/2 tsp freshly ground white pepper

1 bay leaf
1/2 cup heavy cream
1/4 cup sour cream
Chopped chives, for garnish

Set a 4-quart stock pot over medium-high heat. Add the butter and olive oil to the pot. Once the butter is melted, place the onions and celery in the pot. Sweat the vegetables until the onions are translucent, about 3 to 4 minutes. Add the ginger and garlic to the pot and cook for 30 seconds. Place all of the carrots in the pot and cook, stirring occasionally, until the carrots are lightly caramelized and start to soften, about 7 to 8 minutes. Add the stock, salt, pepper and bay leaf to the pot and bring to a boil, then reduce to a simmer. Cook the soup until the carrots are tender, about 20 to 25 minutes.

Remove the bay leaf from the pot and using an immersion blender puree the soup directly in the pot or in batches in a bar blender. Adjust the seasoning; add the heavy cream to the pot. To serve, garnish with 1 tablespoon of sour cream per serving and a sprinkling of fresh chives.

The Soup-er History of Soup

The word soup comes from French soupe ("broth") which comes through Vulgar Latin suppa ("bread soaked in broth"), which originally comes from a Germanic source, from which also comes the word "Sop," a piece of bread used to soak up soup or a thick stew.

Interestingly, the word restaurant was first associated with soup. The word itself "restaurant" loosely translated means "something restoring" and was first used in France in the 16th century, to refer to a highly concentrated, inexpensive soup, sold by street vendors, that was advertised as a quick cure for physical exhaustion.

In 1765, a Parisian entrepreneur opened a permanent shop specializing in soup. He stuck the word restaurant on the shingle and we have been calling them that ever since.

Bacon Bacon Bacon!

The return of the forbidden "B" word to the kitchen table

What is up with bacon? It's everywhere. On everything. It used to really only be the "B" word in a classic BLT. The headliner if you will.

And sometimes it got some credit as a side dish for eggs in a hearty country breakfast.

But (drum roll please) did you know that before peanut butter teamed up with jelly, it was first served on a sandwich with bacon? Peanut butter and bacon sandwiches were served to soldiers in both world wars. They could be wrapped and transported; they didn't spoil easily and they were quick energy providers for war fatigued fighters. Then somewhere along the line, bacon – which once served its patriotic duty – got this nasty reputation that it could kill you (or at the very least give you acne) and we cut out the bacon and went leaner – anyone remember that soy bacon substitute that already had the bacon lines "baked on."

Then, like anything that comes and goes, bacon came back with a vengeance. And with good reason. Bacon tastes pretty darn good. And we started coming up with creative ways to use it. It is now not only a side dish but a star. It has made a triumphant comeback to the spotlight and to the plate. It still makes appearances with lettuce and tomato and on top of cheeseburgers but now it's showing up in recipes that make us sit up and think "you put bacon in ….what?"

Bacon has become so "in demand" that there are actual culinary classes being taught on alternate and tasty uses for it. I know that because I have actually taught a couple of them myself.

So please curl up and enjoy these savory suggestions – maybe with a side of bacon?

Easy Bacon Dogs

1 (16 ounce) package hot dogs
16 slices bacon (cut into thirds)
2 cups packed brown sugar

Preheat the oven to 350 degrees. Next, spread about 1/3 of the brown sugar in the bottom of a 9x13 inch baking dish. Slice each hot dog into six pieces and wrap each piece with 1/3 slice of bacon. Secure with toothpicks. Arrange half of the bacon wrapped dogs in a single layer over the sugar in the baking dish. Sprinkle another 1/3 of the sugar over them. Top with another layer of bacon dogs, followed by the remaining sugar. Cover the dish with aluminum foil. Bake all of this for 45-60 minutes in a preheated oven. Be sure to stir a few times. Once you have checked it and the bacon looks crisp, remove the dish from the oven and transfer the contents to a slow cooker. Set on high for about 10 minutes, then set to low to keep warm while serving.

Pork Bacon Tenderloin

Cooking spray
8 slices smoked maple bacon
3 tbsp apple butter
2 tbsp honey
1/3 tsp allspice
¼ tsp chili powder
1 (3 pound) pork tenderloin

Preheat oven to 325 degrees. Spray a broiler pan with cooking spray. Place bacon in a large skillet and cook over medium heat, turning occasionally, until bacon begins to brown but is still flexible, about 5 minutes. Mix apple butter, honey, allspice, and chili powder in a small bowl. Wrap tenderloin in 4 slices of partially-cooked bacon and secure with toothpicks. Brush half the apple butter mixture over bacon and wrap the tenderloin with remaining slices of bacon. Brush remaining apple butter mixture over the meat. Place tenderloin on prepared broiling pan. Bake in the preheated oven until apple butter mixture has baked into a glaze and an instant-read meat thermometer inserted into the thickest part of the tenderloin reads at least 145 degrees, about 30 minutes.

Bacon & Hazelnut Napoleons

1 lb. Bacon
1 pound cake
1 jar of Chocolate Hazelnut Spread
sea salt

Cut the strips of bacon into quarters. Sizzle in a skillet until reddish-brown and mostly crisp. Cut a pound cake into 1/4 inch slices. Then use a 1 - 1 1/2 inch cookie cutter to cut small circles of cake. You end up with about 60-70 circles, depending on the size of your pound cake. Place some hazelnut spread in a piping bag (or a regular plastic bag with the corner snipped off) and layer the pound cake, hazelnut spread, and bacon strips, three pound cake slices high. Drizzle a little extra hazelnut on top and sprinkle with a touch of sea salt.

The Original Bacon Martini

Fry three strips of bacon until crisp. Try to use the heartiest hickory smoked bacon you can find. Massage the bacon into a bottle of vodka and let it sit for two days (that's 48 whole hours). Pour the bacon infused vodka into a cocktail shaker with ice and shake well. Then strain into a chilled martini glass and serve with olive garnishes. It's that easy!

Makin' Bacon

Did you know...

Kermit's Cologne: The formula for a cologne using bacon as an ingredient was patented in Paris, France in 1920.

Six degrees of delicious: There actually is a statue of actor Kevin Bacon... made entirely out of bacon.

Hard Habit to Break: Bacon and eggs are eaten together 71 % of the time.

Advice for Moms to Be: A chemical found in bacon has been shown to help with fetal brain development.

Bellies Up: The price of pork bellies is the highest it has been since 1988.

Made in China: The Chinese may have discovered bacon as we know. The earliest recipe of it dates back to China, circa 1500 B.C.

Better Than Lipo: a 250 pound pig can yield about 23 pounds of bacon!

What do you like in your coffee?

Cream and sugar? Steak and lady fingers?
Cooking with Coffee 101

Two Sweet and Lows and enough heavy cream to make it blonde. That's how I like my coffee, thanks for asking. If you're talking coffee specialty drinks, I'll never turn down a caramel macchiato with a splash of hazelnut with two extra shots of espresso poured in there.

I like my coffee sweet – almost dessert-like. I know people who like it dark, rich and bitter and other people who put so much milk or cream in it that you can hardly tell there's any grounds in there at all.

As the October weather brings a bit more of the cold, this is the time of year you'll start seeing your local and favorite coffee shops bustling with business.

As the thermometer decreases, it seems everyone needs a hot cup of high octane.

But did you know there is much more to coffee than just swallowing it? You can use it in main dishes and desserts. And the flavor can be a welcomed and hearty addition.

It can be a great ingredient in things like rubs for beef and chicken. It can end up in sweet treats to finish a meal. If you're a connoisseur, you probably already know the many ways coffee can be manipulated into your menu.

So...whether you call it coffee, liquid gold, Java, or a cup of Joe, coffee just isn't for breakfast anymore!

Coffee Rub Prime Rib

1/3 cup finely ground coffee
2 tbsp salt
1 tbsp ground black pepper
1/4 vanilla bean, split and seeds scraped
One 12-pound, bone-in prime rib roast

In a bowl, thoroughly blend the coffee with the salt, pepper and vanilla bean seeds. Set the rib roast in a roasting pan and rub it all over with the coffee mixture, concentrating most of the rub on the fatty part of the meat. Turn the roast bone side down and let stand at room temperature for 30 minutes. Preheat the oven to 450°. Roast the meat for 15 minutes. Reduce the oven temperature to 325° and roast for about 2 1/2 hours longer. Transfer the roast to a carving board and let rest for 20 minutes. Scrape off any excess coffee rub. Carve the meat in 1/2-inch-thick slices and serve. Here's a tip: The coffee-rubbed roast can be refrigerated overnight. Just be sure to bring the meat to room temperature before roasting.

Coffee Glazed Pork Chops

1 cup cool strong coffee
6 ounces molasses
2 tbsp apple cider vinegar
1 tbsp Dijon mustard
2 cloves garlic, minced
1 tsp salt
1/2 tsp ginger
6 to 8 sprigs fresh thyme
1/2 tsp ground black pepper
4 (6 to 8-ounce) bone-in pork chops

Place all of the ingredients into a 1-gallon zip top bag, seal, and shake to combine. Place in the refrigerator to marinate for at least 2 hours or up to overnight. Preheat grill to medium-high. Remove the chops from the marinade. Transfer the marinade to a small saucepan and place over high heat. Bring to a boil, reduce heat to medium-high, and boil gently, stirring often, until reduced to about 1/2 cup liquid, 12 to 15 minutes. Remove the thyme stems after the glaze has reduced. Meanwhile, grill pork chops 3 to 4 minutes per side. Allow the pork chops to rest 4 to 5 minutes before serving with the glaze.

FIVE LAYER MOCHA CHOCOLATE ICE BOX CAKE

2 cups cold heavy cream
12 ounces Italian mascarpone cheese
1/2 cup sugar
1/4 cup coffee liqueur
2 tbsp unsweetened cocoa powder.
1 tsp instant espresso powder
1 tsp pure vanilla extract
24 ounces of packaged chocolate chip cookies

Using a whisk, combine the heavy cream, mascarpone, sugar, coffee liqueur, cocoa powder, espresso powder, and vanilla. Continue to whisk until the mixture forms firm peaks. Then arrange chocolate chip cookies flat in an 8-inch springform pan, covering the bottom as much as possible. You can break up the cookies to fill in the pieces. Spread a fifth of the mocha whipped cream evenly over the cookies. Place another layer of cookies on top, lying flat and touching, followed by another fifth of the cream. Continue layering cookies and cream until there are five layers of each, ending with a layer of cream. Smooth the top, cover with plastic wrap, and refrigerate overnight. Sprinkle the top with the chocolate, cut in wedges, and serve cold.

POTS DE CREME

12 ounces semisweet chocolate chips
2 tsp brandy
1 tsp vanilla extract
1 pinch salt
4 eggs, at room temperature
8 ounces very hot strong coffee

Brandy Whipped Cream
Chocolate bar shavings
For the Brandy Whipped Cream:
1 cup heavy cream
1/4 cup powdered sugar
1 tbsp brandy

Add the heavy cream and sugar to the bowl of an electric mixer fitted with a whisk attachment and whip until it forms soft peaks. Refrigerate and set aside.

Place the chocolate chips in a blender. Add the brandy, vanilla, salt and eggs and turn on the blender. While it is blending, remove the circular disk from the blender lid and very slowly pour in the coffee. It is essential that the coffee be extremely hot in order for the final product to be the right consistency and texture. Blend until the mixture is smooth and fairly free of visible bits of chocolate. Pour the mixture into 3 large glasses or dessert cups, leaving plenty of room to add a heap of whipped cream later. Place in the refrigerator for at least 3 to 4 hours so the mixture has a chance to set. Before serving, spoon in the Brandy Whipped Cream and decorate with shaved chocolate.

Tiramisu

2 cups boiling-hot water
3 tbsp instant-espresso powder
1/2 cup plus 1 tablespoon sugar, divided
3 tbsp coffee liqueur (or just coffee if you want the NA version)
4 large egg yolks
1/3 cup dry Marsala
2 1/2 cups mascarpone
1 cup chilled heavy cream
36 Italian ladyfingers cookies
Unsweetened cocoa powder for dusting

Stir together water, espresso powder, 1 tablespoon sugar, and coffee mixture in a shallow bowl until sugar has dissolved, then cool. Beat egg yolks, Marsala, and remaining 1/2 cup sugar in a metal bowl set over a saucepan of barely simmering water using a whisk and beat for 5 to 8 minutes or until the volume looks like it has tripled. Remove bowl from heat. Beat in mascarpone until just combined. Beat cream in a large bowl until it holds stiff peaks. Fold mascarpone mixture into whipped cream gently but thoroughly. Dipping both sides of each ladyfinger into coffee mixture, line bottom of a 13 x 9-x 3" baking pan with 18 ladyfingers in 3 rows, trimming edges to fit if necessary. Spread half of mascarpone filling on top. Dip remaining 18 ladyfingers in coffee and arrange over filling in pan. Spread remaining mascarpone filling on top and dust with cocoa. Chill, covered, at least 6 hours. Let tiramisu stand at room temperature 30 minutes before serving, then dust with more cocoa

O que está cozinhando

Um pouco de sabor do Brasil
U Receitas com Classe para uma Classe de
Receitasm pouco de sabor do Brasil

No final de outubro de 2018, lembro-me de dar a um delicioso grupo de pessoas uma classe chamada "Celebrate Brazil". Foi tão divertido que pensei em compartilhar alguns desses pratos com todos vocês nesta coleção. Amo os sabores do Brasil e amo vocês. Não importa quem você é - estudante atual, futuro ou atual - todos vocês são pessoas bonitas!

Any idea what I just wrote?

Well, if you were ever a student in one of my "Celebrate Brazil" classes you would already know.

Brazilian cuisine is influenced by Europe, Africa, and yes, even the Americas. Brazil is a nation rich in tradition and fused with all sorts of delicious foods. Brazilian cuisine varies greatly determine on which region of the nation is represented. And did you know Brazil is the largest country in both South America and the Latin American region? It is actually the world's fifth largest country, both by geographical area and by population, with over 202 million people.

Por favor, aproveite as opções de comida brasileira que podem ou não fazer parte de algumas das minhas aulas favoritas. Espero um dia ensinar todos vocês novamente e espero vê-los todos muito em breve. E lembre-se, eu ainda te amo. Feliz outubro!

CAIPIRINHA

Brazil's national cocktail – it's refreshing and delicious! But you might have to ask the local liquor store to order Cachaca for you if they don't stock it because there is no substitute.

1/2 lime, quartered
1 tsp white sugar
2 1/2 fluid ounces cachaca
1 cup crushed ice

In a large rocks glass squeeze and drop in 2 eighths of lime. Add sugar, crush and mix with a spoon. Pour in the cachaca and plenty of ice. Stir well.

BRIGADEIRO

Chewy, fudgy, addictive. These little chocolate fudge bon-bons are as common and as loved in Brazil as cookies and brownies are in the United States.

2 (14-ounce) cans sweetened condensed milk
4 tbsp unsalted butter
2 tbsp heavy cream
2 tsp light corn syrup
3 ounces semisweet chocolate, chopped
2 tsp unsweetened cocoa powder
1 cup chocolate sprinkles

In a medium heavy-bottomed saucepan, place the condensed milk, butter, heavy cream, and corn syrup and bring to a boil over medium heat. When the mixture starts to bubble, add the chocolate and the cocoa powder. Whisk well, making sure there are no pockets of cocoa powder. Reduce the heat to low and cook, whisking constantly, until it is the consistency of a dense fudgy batter, 8 to 10 minutes. You want the mixture to bubble toward the end, so it's important to use low heat or the sides of the pan will burn the fudge. If you undercook it, the brigadeiro will be too soft; if you overcook it, it will be too chewy. It is done when you swirl the pan and the mixture slides as one soft piece, leaving a thick burnt residue on the bottom. Slide the mixture into a bowl (without scraping the bottom) and let cool at room temperature. Cover the bowl with plastic wrap and chill in the refrigerator for at least 4 hours. Scoop the mixture by the teaspoonful and, using your hands, roll each into a little ball. Place the sprinkles in a bowl. Roll one at a time through the sprinkles, making sure they cover the entire surface.

Feijoada

1 (12 ounce) package dry black beans, soaked overnight
1 1/2 cups chopped onion, divided
1/2 cup green onions, chopped
1 clove garlic, chopped
2 smoked ham hocks
8 ounces diced ham
1/2 pound thickly sliced bacon, diced
1 tbsp olive oil
2 bay leaves
1/8 tsp coriander
Salt and pepper to taste

Heat the oil in a large pot or Dutch oven. Add 3/4 cup of chopped onion, green onions, and garlic; cook and stir until softened, about 4 minutes. Pour in the soaked beans and fill with enough water to cover beans by 3 inches. Bring to a boil, then reduce heat to medium-low, and simmer uncovered for 2 hours, or until tender. While beans are cooking, place ham hocks in smaller pot with 1/4 cup of the chopped onion. Cover with water and simmer, until meat pulls off of the bone easily, about 1 hour. Drain and add to the beans. Preheat oven to 375 degrees. Place ham, bacon, and remaining onion in a baking dish. Bake 15 minutes or until mixture is crispy. Drain the bacon and ham mixture, and add to the beans. Season with bay leaves, coriander, salt and pepper. Simmer uncovered 30 minutes more.

TURKEY VATAPA

Vatapa is a rustic Brazilian stew, a fiery blend with beer, coconut milk, and ground peanuts as its base. Made with leftover turkey, it's easy to prepare.

1 tsp peanut oil
1/2 cup finely chopped onion
3 garlic cloves, minced
1 tbsp minced
Fresh ginger
1 jalapeño pepper, minced
1 cup water
1 (28-ounce) can no-salt-added diced tomatoes, undrained
1 (12-ounce) can light beer
1/4 cup unsalted, dry-roasted peanuts
3 cups chopped and skinned cooked turkey
1/2 cup light coconut milk
1/2 cup finely chopped fresh parsley
1/2 cup finely chopped fresh cilantro
1 tbsp fresh lime juice
1/2 tsp salt
1/2 tsp black pepper

Heat oil in a Dutch oven over medium-high heat. Add onion and garlic; sauté 2 minutes. Add ginger and jalapeño; sauté 30 seconds. Stir in water, tomatoes, and beer; bring to a boil. Cover, reduce heat, and simmer 20 minutes. Place peanuts in a spice or coffee grinder; process until finely ground. Add ground peanuts, turkey, and coconut milk to pan, stirring to combine. Increase heat to medium. Bring mixture to a simmer; cook 5 minutes, stirring occasionally. Stir in parsley, cilantro, juice, salt, and black pepper. Garnish with cilantro sprigs, if desired.

Brazilian Misto

A Brazilian Twist on the Classic Grilled Cheese

2 slices bread (whole wheat or white)
2 tsp butter
2 slices lean ham
2 slices mozzarella or Muenster cheese

Spread butter on the outside of bread slices and layer cheese and ham on one unbuttered slice. Cover with remaining slice of bread, butter on the outside, and add oregano to top if desired. Use a sandwich maker or put in oven at 300 F until cheese and melted and bread is toasted.

Cuscuz Branco

2 cups milk
1 and 1/4 cups raw shredded coconut
2 tbsp condensed sweetened milk
1 and 1/2 cups pearl tapioca
1/2 cup coconut milk
1/4 cup granulated sugar
1 tbsp coconut shreds for covering

In a large serving bowl, add the 1 and 1/4 cup coconut shreds, the pearl tapioca, and sugar and mix well. Add the milk, coconut milk, and condensed milk to a saucepan on medium heat until it boils. Once boiling, pour this liquid over the dry ingredients in the bowl and mix well. Once well mixed, cover with the tablespoon of coconut shreds and then place the bowl in the refrigerator. Let it cool for 2-3 hours.

GALINHADA

6 chicken breasts, cut into chunks
2 cubes of chicken bouillon, diluted in 1/2 cup water
Juice of one lemon
5 tbsp oil
2 scallions, finely chopped
2 garlic cloves, pressed
2 cups rice, washed and drained
2 tomatoes, peeled, cored and diced
1 green pepper, deseeded and diced
4 tbsp peas
A few saffron threads
1 tbsp parsley, finely chopped
1 tbsp cilantro, finely chopped
Salt
Pepper

Mix the chicken, chicken bouillon, parsley, cilantro and lemon juice. Marinate for 2 hours. In a large pot, heat oil and brown the chicken pieces and the marinade for 3 minutes at high heat, stirring constantly. Add onion and garlic and cook for 5 minutes over high heat, stirring constantly. Add the rice, saffron, tomatoes, peppers, and peas. Mix well and cover with 3 cups of boiling water. Stir well and cook covered for 15 minutes over low/medium heat, stirring gently so that the rice does not stick to the bottom of the pot

Viva Las Vegan

Vibrant, Flavorful…delicious

I will admit that I am not a vegan. I know people who are and I respect and even admire their fortitude and their lifestyle. That said, I get asked many times if I have any healthy and tasty (and not bland) recipes for Vegan dishes. And I actually do. Veganism is the practice of abstaining from the use of animal products, particularly in diet, as well as an associated philosophy that rejects the commodity status of sentient animals. The difference between vegetarian and Vegan is that Vegan tends to be a way of life – avoiding all products that come from an animal – not just the meat and protein of an animal but products like egg, milk and cheese as well. I thought for this chapter, I would explore some vegan recipes and debunk the myth that all vegan food is tasteless and boring. In fact vegan food can be vibrant and flavorful. In my time practicing with animal free cooking I have realized that there are some important things to remember when cooking vegan: Proper seasoning, taste, and texture. And some vegan recipes are quite capable of leaving your taste buds tingling.

BUTTERNUT SQUASH SOUP

3 quarts vegetable stock
4 lbs. butternut squash
2 cups carrots, diced 1/2 inch dice
2 cups celery, diced 1/2 inch dice
1 cup onion, diced 1/2 inch dice
1/2 cup dry sherry
2 tbsp olive oil
2 tsp salt
1 bay leaf
1 pinch white pepper
1/2 tsp nutmeg, freshly ground
2 tsp parsley, finely chopped
1/4 tsp paprika

Cut butternut squash in half lengthwise and remove seeds. Place squash cut side down on a parchment lined sheet pan and roast in a 350 degree oven for 30-40 minutes or until squash is soft to the touch, and the skin begins to pull away from the flesh. Remove from oven and let cool. Spoon roasted squash out of the skin and pass it through a ricer or food mill to remove any of the stringy fibers. Heat olive oil in a large stockpot and "sweat" the carrots, celery and onions, until the onions and carrots just start to caramelize. Deglaze the pot with sherry. Add the vegetable stock, salt, pepper, nutmeg and bay leaf and bring to a boil. Add the squash, reduce to a simmer and cook for 45 minutes. Remove the by leaf, and puree the soup in the pot with an immersion blender until it reaches a smooth creamy consistency. Garnish with chopped parsley and paprika and serve.

FAJITAS WITH ROASTED CORN AND BLACK
BEAN SALAD WITH SALSA VERDE

Ingredients for Fajitas: Red bell pepper Julienned; Green Bell Julienned; Red Onion Sliced thin; Mushrooms (any kind); Carrots; Chili powder; Cumin; Cayenne Pepper

Ingredients for Salad: Canned Black Beans; Super Sweet Corn (Frozen or fresh); Garlic clove diced; Onion diced; Red pepper diced; Jalapeno Diced; Cumin; Chili powder.

Ingredients for salsa Verde: 6 tomatillos Husked and cut in half; Garlic Cloves; Red onion quartered; Jalapeno pepper; Cilantro; Cumin;Salt and pepper; 2 tablespoons of vinegar; Lime Juice

Simmer Chopped garlic, peppers, and onion on medium low heat to extract the most flavor from the garlic without burning it. Add frozen corn and turn heat to high, add salt pepper and all of the other seasonings. Sautee until corn is cooked. Add canned black beans (drained) and toss around in pan, serve alongside or inside of the fajitas.

For Salsa Verde: Cut tomatillos in half and place on greased baking sheet with garlic cloves, onion, and pepper and roast in 475 degree oven until charred. Combine the roasted vegetables along with the other remaining ingredients in the food processor and let cool. Serve on top of fajitas

ASIAN VEGETABLE STIR FRY WITH QUINOA

Any vegetables can be substituted for this recipe

Bok Choy
Shitake mushrooms
Red bell peppers
Fresh ginger grated
Red pepper flakes
Carrots
Green onions
Garlic
Sesame oil
Broccoli
Water chestnuts
2 cups Quinoa
4 cups water
Soy Sauce

Orange juice
Sweet chili sauce
Brown sugar

Place quinoa in pot with water salt and garlic bring to boil and cook like rice 15-20 minutes. While that is cooking turn on wok and place 2 tablespoons of sesame oil inside. Throw all of the veggies into the wok and season with salt in pepper. Let cook for a couple of minutes and add about a cup of orange juice to deglaze the wok and reduce. Once juice is almost cooked out add 1/2 cup brown sugar, soy sauce and sweet Thai chili. Remove from wok and serve over quinoa.

BRUSCHETTA AND OLIVE TAPENADE CROSTINI

10 Roma Tomatoes diced
Fresh basil
Garlic Cloves
Balsamic vinegar
Sun dried tomatoes diced
Salt & pepper
Diced Onion
Baguette Bread cut into slices

Combine all ingredients in bowl and let sit for 10 minutes. Coat bread in garlic butter and toast in oven until brown, top bread with bruschetta mix and serve.

TAPENADE

1/2 pound pitted mixed olives (Kalamata)
1 small clove garlic, minced
2 tbsp capers
2 to 3 fresh basil leaves
1 tbsp freshly squeezed lemon juice
2 tbsp extra-virgin olive oil

Thoroughly rinse the olives in cool water. Place all ingredients in the bowl of a food processor. Process to combine, stopping to scrape down the sides of the bowl, until the mixture becomes a coarse paste, approximately 1 to 2 minutes total. Transfer to a bowl and serve on toast points.

West African Groundnut Stew

1 Large onion chopped
2 tbsp. vegetable oil
1 tsp cayenne powder
2 garlic cloves, chopped
2 tsp ginger, minced
1 green bell pepper, chopped
3 sweet potato, peeled, cubed
3 cups tomato juice
1 cup apple juice
1 tsp salt
2-16 oz. cans diced tomatoes in juice
2 okra, chopped
1/2 cup crunchy peanut butter
Cilantro for garnish

In a large pot, sauté onions in oil for about 8 minutes. Stir in cayenne, garlic and ginger and sauté for 3-4 minutes. Add cabbage, green pepper and cubed sweet potatoes and then cover for 3-4 minutes. Mix in tomato juice, apple juice, salt and tomatoes. Cover and simmer on medium-low heat for about 15 minutes until sweet potatoes are tender. Stir in okra and peanut butter, whisk Peanut butter vigorously. Simmer on low-heat until ready to serve. If stew is too thick, add water or more juice if desired. Garnish with cilantro

Fennel, Orange, and Pomegranate salad

Fresh Oranges juice (about 6 Tablespoons)
2 tbsp Balsamic vinegar
¼ cup olive oil

½ medium fennel bulb cored and sliced thinly
¼ cup pomegranate seeds
Orange segments
Watercress

Make dressing by whisking together the orange juice, vinegar, and oil. Add salt and pepper to taste. Combine fennel, pomegranate, and orange sections in bowl. Pour dressing over them and let marinate at room temperature for 20 minutes. Drain the dressing form the items and put back into remaining dressing. Toss watercress with dressing and serve with orange fennel and pomegranate on top.

ROASTED CAULIFLOWER WITH KALAMATA VINAIGRETTE

1 large head cauliflower – chopped
1/4 cup extra-virgin olive oil, divided
1 small garlic clove
1 to 2 tbsp fresh lemon juice (to taste)
1/4 cup pitted Kalamata olives, finely chopped

Preheat oven to 450°F with rack in lower third. Cut cauliflower lengthwise into 3/4-inch-thick slices. Put in a large 4-sided sheet pan and toss with 2 tablespoon oil and 1/2 teaspoon each of salt and pepper. Roast, turning once or twice, until golden and just tender, about 25 minutes. While cauliflower roasts, mince and mash garlic to a paste with a pinch of salt, then whisk together with lemon juice, remaining 2 tablespoons oil, olives, 1/8 teaspoon salt, and 1/2 teaspoon pepper. Serve cauliflower drizzled with Kalamata vinaigrette.

VEGAN BANANA CHOCOLATE CHIP BREAD PUDDING

6 cups 1" cubed stale bread (about 1 lb.)
1 cup chocolate chips
3 ripe bananas, sliced ½" thick
2-2¼ cups rice milk, almond milk or soy
3 tbsp arrowroot powder or tapioca flour

½ cup maple syrup
1 tsp vanilla extract
½ tsp cinnamon
¼ tsp nutmeg

Preheat oven to 350 degrees and grease a 9 x 5 loaf pan. Place cubed bread in a large bowl. In a small bowl whisk together ½ cup soy milk and the arrowroot powder till no lumps remain. Add 1½ cups soy milk, maple syrup, vanilla, cinnamon and nutmeg and whisk to combine. Pour over cubed bread and stir to coat every piece. Allow to sit for at least 15 minutes for liquid to soak into bread. Depending on what kind of bread you use and how stale it is, add more soy milk (¼ cup at a time) and allow more soaking time till every piece of bread is saturated and there's a little bit of extra liquid. Mixture should look mushy and wet. Fold in chocolate chips and bananas (using hands is the easiest for this), mashing up a little bit of the bananas. Pour mixture into loaf pan, patting down to make an even top. Bake 28-35 minutes till top is puffed, slightly browned and feels firm. Allow to cool slightly before slicing and serving. Also pudding can be scooped with an ice cream scoop when slightly cooled.

SAMOAN PANIKEKE

3 1/2 cups all-purpose flour
1 1/3 cups white sugar
2 tsp baking powder
2 very ripe bananas, mashed
1 tablespoon vanilla extract
1 1/2 cups water
6 cups vegetable oil for frying

Combine the flour, sugar, and baking powder in a bowl until thoroughly mixed, and stir in the bananas, vanilla extract, and water to make a smooth, sticky dough. Heat oil in a deep-fryer or large saucepan to 350 degrees. The oil should be deep enough to completely cover the panikekes while frying, or at last 3 inches deep. Scoop up a scant 1/4 cup of batter with a large spoon, and use another spoon to push it off into the oil. Fry in small batches of 4 or 5 until they float to the top and turn golden brown, about

3 minutes, then flip them to fry the other side. Remove from the fryer and let drain on paper towels. Can be served with Nutella, melted chocolate, fresh fruit, or peanut butter.

ITALIAN LEMONADE

2 cups lemon juice, about 12 to 15 lemons
2 cups Basil Simple Syrup, recipe follows
2 cups cold or sparkling water
Ice
Lemon twists, for garnish
Basil Simple Syrup:
1 bunch fresh basil, washed and stemmed
2 cups sugar
1 cup water

Mix lemon juice, Basil Simple Syrup, and water together in a pitcher. Store in the refrigerator until ready to serve. Pour over ice filled glasses and garnish with a lemon twist.

Basil Simple Syrup: In a saucepan combine basil, sugar, and water and simmer until the sugar is dissolved, 5 minutes. Cool, strain the simple syrup, and store in the refrigerator.

BELLINI COCKTAIL

4 tbsp white peach puree

1 bottle Prosecco or Champagne, chilled (use sparkling juice or seltzer for a non-alcoholic cocktail

Place 1 tablespoon white peach puree into the bottom of a Champagne flute. Fill the glass with Prosecco or Champagne

Celebrating the Sweetest Day of the Year

Dinner for Two? No problem.

October 17. I love Sweetest Day. The day holds special meaning to me. I have a wonderful memory connected to this date. For the last 21 years it has been, for me personally, one of the sweetest days of the year. October really is a sweet month for many reasons, but the most being the fact that I get to celebrate what has always been a special day to me with everyone else.

Sweetest Day actually has quite an interesting history dating back to 1922. That was when Herbert Birch Kingston, a candy employee and philanthropist, decided he wanted to cheer up the local orphans, elderly, and poor people in his hometown of Cleveland (wow, Cleveland comes into play in this story too huh? And the circle tightens!) And because he worked in the candy industry, Kingston started handing out sweet treats to the less fortunate.

Following his lead, other local candy makers began to do the same—and eventually the third Saturday in October was proclaimed as the "sweetest day of the year." As time passed, "Sweetest Day" became more and more romantically inclined. In fact, today the Fall Foliage filled day is considered a romantic book end with Valentine's Day.

For this reason, Sweetest Day is also becoming a very popular day to get married. In fact, they're saying "October is the new June" for weddings.

So whether you are already married, about to get married, or just one of those people who likes – like me – to observe Sweetest Day, here are some suggested easy recipes sure to set the proper music. Some assembly required. Luther Vandross and candlelight not included.

Chocolate Covered Strawberries

6 ounces semi-sweet chocolate, chopped
3 ounces white chocolate, chopped
1 pound strawberries with stems (about 20), washed and dried very well.

Put the semisweet and white chocolates into two heatproof medium bowls. Fill two medium saucepans with a couple inches of water and bring to a simmer over medium heat. Turn off the heat; set the bowls of chocolate over the water to melt. Stir until smooth. (Alternatively, melt the chocolates in a microwave at half power, for one minute, stir and then heat for another minute or until melted.) Once the chocolates are melted and smooth, remove from the heat. Line a sheet pan with parchment or waxed paper. Holding the strawberry by the stem, dip them one at a time into the dark chocolate, lift and twist slightly, letting any excess chocolate fall back into the bowl. Set strawberries on the parchment paper. Repeat with the rest of the strawberries. Dip a fork in the white chocolate and drizzle the white chocolate over the dipped strawberries. Set the strawberries aside until the chocolate hardens, or at least 30 minutes.

Surf and Turf Main Course

2 tsp finely chopped onion
1 garlic clove, minced
1 tbsp olive oil, divided
1 tbsp butter, divided
2 tbsp beef broth
8 uncooked medium shrimp, peeled and deveined
2 nice beef tenderloin steaks

In a small skillet, sauté the onion and garlic in 1-1/2 teaspoons oil and 1-1/2 teaspoons butter until tender. Add broth; cook and stir for 1 minute. Add the shrimp; cook and stir until shrimp turn pink, about 3-5 minutes. Cut a pocket in each steak; place three shrimp in each pocket. Cover remaining shrimp and broth mixture; keep warm. Then, in a large skillet, heat remaining oil and butter over medium-high heat. Add steaks; cook until meat reaches desired doneness, turning once. Top with reserved shrimp and broth mixture.

Seasoned Fan Potatoes

2 medium baking potatoes
1 tsp Italian seasoning
1/2 tsp salt
1 tbsp butter, melted
2 tbsp finely shredded cheddar cheese
1 tbsp grated Parmesan cheese

With a sharp knife, slice potatoes thinly but not all the way through, leaving slices attached at the bottom. Fan potatoes slightly. Place in an ungreased 8-in. square baking dish. Sprinkle with Italian seasoning and salt. Drizzle with butter. Bake, uncovered, at 425° for 50 minutes. Sprinkle with cheeses; bake until lightly browned.

Peach Melba Dessert

2 individual round sponge cakes
2 canned peach halves in syrup
2 scoops vanilla or peach ice cream
1 tbsp raspberry jam, warmed
2 tsp chopped nuts

Place cakes on dessert plates. Drain peaches, reserving 1 tablespoon syrup; spoon 1-1/2 teaspoons syrup over each cake. Place peach halves hollow sides up on cakes. Top with ice cream. Drizzle with jam and sprinkle with nuts.

Chocolate Espresso Martini

4 ounces semisweet chocolate, finely chopped
2/3 cup brewed espresso, chilled
2/3 cup coffee liqueur
2/3 cup vanilla-flavored vodka
Ice

Combine the chocolate and 1/4 cup water in a small bowl and place over a pan of barely simmering water. Stir until the chocolate is completely melted and the mixture is smooth, 2 minutes. Set aside to cool slightly. Dip the rims of 4 martini glasses into the melted chocolate, allowing any excess chocolate to drip back into the bowl. Chill the glasses in the freezer for 10 minutes. In a pitcher, mix together the espresso, coffee liqueur and vodka. Fill a cocktail shaker with ice. In batches, add the vodka mixture and shake for 10 seconds. Strain the mixture into the prepared glasses and serve

Your Gourmet Guide to a Spook-tacular Season

Recipes that will help you get in the "spirit" of Halloween

Boo, it's October! Did I scare you?

This really is a fun month – or should be – it's the month where the leaves in the east coast and in the mountains – particularly here in Maryland where I live – are at their best. Fall foliage is at its most spectacular. And Halloween is here.

Not only is this season the month of Trick or Treat and Masquerade Parties but it can also be the month where your creative and culinary skills can shine.

Imagine going to your friends' party with a plate of spider cookies or a platter of witches' hats! Decorating for Halloween doesn't have to be limited to your front porch or your face. You can bring it into the kitchen and out of the oven and impress your favorite boys and ghouls. This is Halloween... just like dear ol' Mummy used to make.

Caramel Apples

The caramel coating here can be very gooey, so refrigerate the apples for about 15 minutes, or until the caramel has firmed up.

6 apples
14 ounces individually wrapped caramels, unwrapped
2 tbsp milk
Six to 10 skewers or craft sticks

Remove the stem from each apple and press a craft stick into the top. Butter a baking sheet. Place caramels and milk in a microwave safe bowl, and microwave 2 minutes, stirring once. Allow to cool briefly. Roll each apple quickly in caramel sauce until well coated. Place on prepared sheet to set.

Rice Krispy Mummies

One of the easiest desserts you might make.

As many prepared Rice Krispy treats as you want. Pre cut into squares or rectangles. Cooled.

Place white chocolate chips in a microwave-safe bowl and microwave on half power for 2 minutes. Stir and return to microwave for 20 seconds at a time stirring after each until chocolate is completely melted and smooth. Dip rice Krispy treats in the chocolate being sure to coat the front and sides (the back side can remain uncovered). Place uncovered-side-down on a foil-lined plate or small baking sheet. Repeat process with remaining rice Krispy treats. Transfer plate/baking sheet to fridge or freezer to cool for 2-3 minutes. While treats are cooling, spoon melted white chocolate into a small zip lock bag. Remove treats from fridge/freezer. Use scissors to snip off a tiny bit of one bottom corner of the chocolate-filled bag, then drizzle chocolate in a random pattern over the treats to create the look of mummy wrapping. Return treats to fridge or freezer for 1-2 minutes. Pipe two dots onto each rice Krispy treat to create mummy eyes. Store in airtight container up to 1 week.

BLACK MAGIC CAKE

1 3/4 cups all-purpose flour
2 cups white sugar
3/4 cup unsweetened cocoa powder
2 tsp baking soda
1 tsp baking powder
1 tsp salt
2 eggs
1 cup strong brewed coffee
1 cup buttermilk
1/2 cup vegetable oil
1 tsp vanilla extract

Preheat oven to 350 degrees. Grease and flour two 9 inch round cake pans or one 9x13 inch pan. In large bowl combine flour, sugar, cocoa, baking soda, baking powder and salt. Make a well in the center. Add eggs, coffee, buttermilk, oil and vanilla. Beat for 2 minutes on medium speed. Batter will be thin. Pour into prepared pans. Bake at 350 degrees for 30 to 40 minutes, or until toothpick inserted into center of cake comes out clean. Cool for 10 minutes, then remove from pans and finish cooling on a wire rack. Fill and frost as desired.

PEANUT BUTTER SPIDER COOKIES

1/2 cup shortening
1/2 cup peanut butter
1/2 cup packed brown sugar
1/2 cup white sugar
1 egg, beaten
2 tbsp milk
1 tsp vanilla extract
1 3/4 cups all-purpose flour
1 tsp baking soda
1/2 tsp salt
1/4 cup white sugar for rolling

24 chocolate candy spheres with smooth chocolate filling, refrigerated until cold
48 decorative candy eyeballs
1/2 cup prepared chocolate frosting

Preheat oven to 375 degrees. Line baking sheets with baking parchment. Beat shortening, peanut butter, brown sugar, and 1/2 cup white sugar together with an electric mixer in a large bowl until smooth. Beat egg into the creamy mixture until fully incorporated. Stir milk and vanilla extract into the mixture until smooth. Mix flour, baking soda, and salt together in a small bowl; add to the wet mixture in the large bowl and stir until completely incorporated into a dough. Divide and shape dough into 48 balls. Spread 1/4 cup white sugar into a wide, shallow bowl. Roll dough balls in sugar to coat and arrange about 2 inches apart onto prepared baking sheets. Bake in preheated oven until golden brown, 10 to 12 minutes. Remove cookies from oven and quickly press a dimple into the middle of each cookie using the blunt end of a wooden spoon. Cool cookies on sheets for 10 minutes before transferring to a wire cooling rack to cool completely. Cut each chocolate sphere into two hemispheres. Put one piece atop each cookie with the rounded side facing upwards. Spoon frosting into a pastry bag with a small round tip or a plastic freezer bag with one end snipped off. Dab a small amount of frosting onto the back of each candy eyeball and stick two onto each chocolate candy to resemble eyes. Then pipe frosting in four thin lines, starting at the base of the candy, on each side atop the cookie to resemble spider legs. Let frosting harden at room temperature, about 30 minutes. Store cookies in an airtight container.

WITCHES' HATS

2 (16 ounce) packages fudge stripe cookies
1/4 cup honey
9 ounce bag of milk chocolate candy kisses, unwrapped
1 tube decorating gel

Place a fudge stripe cookie with bottom side up onto a work surface. Smear a small dab (about 1/8 teaspoon) of honey onto the bottom of a chocolate kiss, and secure the candy piece to the center of the cookie, covering the hole. Use decorating gel to pipe a small bow onto the cookie at the base of the candy piece. Repeat with remaining ingredients.

BLOODY BROKEN GLASS CUPCAKES

For the Cake:

1 (18.25 ounce) package white cake mix
1 cup water
1/3 cup vegetable oil
3 eggs
1 can white frosting

For the Sugar Glass:

2 cups water
1 cup light corn syrup
3 1/2 cups white sugar
1/4 tsp cream of tartar

For the Edible Blood:

1/2 cup light corn syrup
1 tbsp cornstarch
1/4 cup water, or more as needed
red food coloring
blue food coloring

Preheat an oven to 350 degrees Line 2, 12-cupcake tins with paper cupcake liners. Blend cake mix, 1 cup water, vegetable oil, and eggs in a large bowl. Beat with a mixer on low speed for 2 minutes. Divide cake batter between lined cupcake tins. Bake cupcakes in preheated oven until a toothpick inserted in the center comes out clean, 18 to 22 minutes. Cool completely. Frost cupcakes with white frosting.

Make the sugar glass: Mix 2 cups water, 1 cup corn syrup, white sugar, and cream of tartar in a large saucepan; bring to a boil. Use a candy thermometer and boil sugar syrup until temperature reaches 300 degrees, stirring constantly. The mixture will thicken as water evaporates. When sugar reaches 300 degrees, quickly pour onto a metal baking pan. Cool until completely hardened. Break into "shards" using a meat mallet.

Make the edible blood: Mix together 1/2 cup corn syrup and cornstarch in a large bowl. Slowly stir in the 1/4 cup of water, adding more if necessary, until the corn syrup mixture has thickened to the consistency of blood. Stir in the red and blue food coloring.

Stab each frosted cupcake with a few shards of broken sugar glass. Drizzle on drops of "blood" to complete the effect.

WITCHES' BREW

Great for parties. A fake hand is frozen in a disposable glove and then slipped into the punch bowl!

1 package frozen raspberries, thawed
2 1/2 cups cranberry juice
2 envelopes unflavored gelatin
2 liters ginger ale
2 liters sparkling apple cider
6 gummi snakes candy

To make the frozen hand: Wash and rinse the outside of a rubber glove. Turn glove inside out and set aside. In a 4 cup measuring cup, combine the thawed raspberries and cranberry juice. Pour 2 cups of the raspberry mixture into a small saucepan. Sprinkle the gelatin over and let stand 2 minutes. Warm over low heat, stirring constantly, just until gelatin dissolves. Mix back into the reserved raspberry mixture in the measuring cup. Pour raspberry mixture into the inverted glove. Gather up the top of the glove and tie securely with kitchen twine. Freeze until solid, or several days if possible.

To serve: Carefully cut glove away from frozen hand. Place frozen hand, palm side up, leaning against side of a large punch bowl. Pour in ginger ale and sparkling cider. Garnish with gummy snakes.

NOVEMBER

Bringing dinner back
to its "roots"

One Potato, Two Potato, Three Potato, Sweet Potato

I love potatoes – just regular white from the ground potatoes – in any form. But lately, I've become hooked on the sweet potato. Because I have learned how versatile a root vegetable it is. And how very nutritious. There is so much more to it than serving it with butter and brown sugar. It really is a much underappreciated staple.

Yes, the lowly and humble sweet potato.

It never really gets its due.

Only during Thanksgiving do we even really pay attention to it.

And when we do, we throw it in a casserole dish, douse it with marshmallow cream and bake it dead in the oven.

But did you know the sweet potato is more closely related to a flower than a regular potato? It's true. A sweet potato shares its DNA with Morning Glories. So really….treat it like the edible flower it is!

The first Europeans to taste sweet potatoes are said to be members of Christopher Columbus' expedition in 1492. And they've been eating sweet potatoes in Central America for 5,000 years.

Besides simple starches, sweet potatoes are rich in complex carbohydrates, dietary fiber and beta-carotene and are high in vitamin B5, vitamin B6 and manganese. Once cooked, for some unexplained reason, their Vitamin

C content is also increased. A cooked sweet potato can actually give you 24-percent of your daily Vitamin C requirement.

Commonly – and especially this time of year – candied sweet potatoes are a side dish consisting mainly of sweet potatoes prepared with brown sugar, marshmallows, maple syrup, and molasses. You're bound to see one sweet potato casserole this Thanksgiving.

But what else can you do with the humble but mighty sweet potato? You might be pleasantly surprised…

Spiced Sweet Potato Hummus

1 large sweet potato, cubed
2 cups cooked chickpeas
4 tbsp tahini
2 tbsp olive oil
2 garlic cloves, minced
Lemon juice (equal to squeezing ½ the lemon)
1 tbsp cumin
1 tsp sriracha
A dash of nutmeg
A dash of cinnamon
Salt/Pepper to taste

Bring a large pot of water to a boil. Lower to medium low and add in the sweet potatoes. Cook until softened. Strain and let cool. Once at room temperature, in a large blender blend all the ingredients together until a desired consistency is reached. Taste and add more olive oil if dry. Serve with baked pita chips.

Savory Sweet Potato Stackers

2 tbsp organic butter, melted
2 tbsp coconut oil, melted
2 tbsp grated parmesan cheese, plus extra for garnish
1 tsp fresh rosemary, chopped, plus extra for garnish
Sea salt and pepper
5-6 large sweet potatoes, thinly sliced

Preheat oven to 375 degrees. Spray 12 muffin cups with nonstick cooking spray.

In a large bowl whisk together butter, coconut oil, parmesan, chopped rosemary, salt, and pepper.

Add sweet potatoes and toss to coat evenly. Layer potatoes slices into muffin pan and fill to the top. They will shrink down once they are cooking. Bake for about 45-50 minutes and edges and tops are golden brown and center in tender. Let cool and carefully remove with a spoon. Place on serving tray and top with extra parmesan cheese and fresh chopped fresh rosemary. Serve immediately.

SWEET POTATO SOUP

5 medium sized sweet potatoes, peeled and cubed
1/4 cup plus 3 tablespoons olive oil
2 carrots, peeled and thinly sliced
2 leeks, cleaned and thinly sliced
6 cups water
2 cups chicken or vegetable stock
1 bay leaf
2-3 tsp salt
Sherry vinegar, to taste

Heat 1/4 cup of the olive oil in a small saucepan until hot, but not boiling, then take it off of the heat. Allow it to cool to room temperature. Heat the remaining olive oil in a large stockpot over medium-high heat; add the thinly sliced carrots and leeks, season with a pinch of salt, and cook until softened and the vegetables have begun to brown. Add the sweet potato and cook for a few more minutes. Add water, stock, and bay leaf, bring to a boil, and then reduce the heat to keep the soup at a simmer. Simmer for 30 minutes, or until the sweet potatoes are fork-tender.

SWEET POTATO LEFTOVER BRIE AND BACON SANDWICHES

2 tbsp unsalted butter, softened for spreading
4 slices whole grain bread
1/3 cup leftover sweet potato casserole
4 ounces brie cheese
4 slices cooked bacon

Heat a large skillet or grilled over medium-low heat. Spread the outsides of each slices with softened butter. On the insides, add a slice or two of brie, the bacon slices, a big spoonful of the sweet potatoes and some more cheese. Top it off with the remaining bread, buttered sides up. Cook the sandwiches until golden brown on both sides.

SWEET POTATO BURGERS

2 cups mashed sweet potatoes
2 bulbs of roasted garlic
1 cup cannellini beans (rinsed and drained if canned)
2 garlic cloves, minced
1/3 cup panko bread crumbs
1/3 cup flour
1 large egg, lightly beaten
1 1/2 tsp smoked paprika
1 tsp onion powder
Salt and pepper to taste
1/8 tsp cumin
2-3 tbsp olive oil
1 avocado, sliced
2/3 cup sour cream
1 tsp maple syrup
4 sandwich buns

In a large bowl, coarsely mash beans with a fork. Add in sweet potato and mash together, then add in spices, salt and pepper, minced garlic, egg, panko and flour. Mix together until combined, then place bowl in the fridge for 15-20 minutes. This helps form them into patties. While mixture is chilling, combine sour cream with 2 bulbs (squeezed out) of roasted garlic cloves, maple syrup and a sprinkle of salt and pepper in a blender or food processor. Process until smooth then set aside until ready to use. Heat a large skillet over medium heat and add 2 tablespoons olive oil. Remove mixture from fridge and form into patties, then place in the skillet once hot. Cook until golden on one side (about 5-6 minutes) and then flip very gently. And cook other side for 5-6 minutes. Place cooked patties on buns. Top with roasted garlic cream and avocado and serve

How Sweet It Is

Sweet potatoes are a Native American plant that was the main source of nourishment for early homesteaders and for soldiers during the Revolutionary War. Colonial physicians called them the "vegetable indispensable" and they were probably among the first offerings at that "first Thanksgiving." Our very first President, George Washington grew sweet potatoes on his farm at Mount Vernon, Virginia. While inventor George Washington Carver developed 118 different products from sweet potatoes, including a mucilage for postal stamps, an economic method for sizing cotton fabrics, dehydrated food and an alternative to corn syrup.

Holiday Entertaining 101

The Best Ways to Prepare Your Home For Guests

Face it. It's November. And in just a short couple of weeks, you are going to have people over – you'll be expected to not only feed them but keep them slightly entertained. This is the season for having company into your home. And it's the time of year that you also go to other people's houses – over the river and through the woods as the song would say.

The first thing you need to do is take a look at your space – you need to prep your house for company coming over for a complete meal or even cheese, crackers, and drinks. So take a look around and decide what you need to clean up. Do you have to pick up toys, vacuum cat hair off the couch, launder the lace tablecloth? Have you ever gone to an event at a hotel or a private home and marveled at how wonderfully the whole event flowed throughout the evening? That was what we in the hospitality and restaurant business call "effective preparation of public space." The way you prepare your home for company speaks volumes about your commitment to ensuring that your guests have a fantastic time.

I once taught a class called Holiday Entertaining 101. We prepared appetizers and drinks as if we were all hosting a small dinner party but I also offered some tips for those in the class on how to prepare your house before you even get started in the kitchen. Some of those tips include:

- Clean the porch and walkway. Sweep. Shovel. Whatever it takes to make a clean and clear and unobstructed path to your front door.
- Light the way. Make sure that all exterior lightbulbs are working.
- Put out a clean or new "Welcome" mat. This time of year, opt for something fun or festive. Then place a rug right inside the door too so that guests can wipe their feet.

- Designate a place for coats. If you don't have a coat rack in your front entrance, assign someone to collect coats and stash them in a bedroom until they are needed again.
- Guests probably will want to take in your decorations but make sure the location of the main party space obvious. Use all the senses to direct your guests - platters of food in visible areas, and even the mood of the music.
- Offer your guests a beverage immediately upon arrival. Or have a beverage station set up where guests can clearly help themselves. Make sure you have a variety and plenty of ice at the ready. Place tongs near the ice so folks are discouraged from digging in with their hands.
- Offer an appetizer. Or if food is already prepared, escort your guest into an area where the food is available. Either create a station-based setup where you would have your appetizers in one area, your main meal in another, and your desserts in a third area. Conversely, you could set out your food in one larger area, and perhaps scatter bowls of snack foods (chips, nuts, candies) throughout the party space.
- Select your style of food center based upon the floor plan of the party space, your menu and the timing of the event.
- Tell your guest where the restroom is. You don't want someone wandering around your home and into your bedroom looking at unwrapped gifts while they search for the facilities. And make sure the powder room is clean – fresh hand towels and use liquid soap in a dispenser if possible.
- Make sure your guests are aware where your trash containers are for the party.
- Be prepared for some type of spill. As the host, have the proper "arsenal" at the ready should someone spill a meatball on the carpet or red wine on your favorite chair. Have white towels, paper towels, dish soap and seltzer water handy for messes. And don't panic or make your guest feel even more terrible than he or she already does for the accident. Clean spills up calmly but quickly.
- Consider rearranging furniture. Look around your house. While those chairs may be great when just you or the family is home, that big easy chair may be interrupting the flow. Consider taking it out of the room for the night or moving it to a different location

to promote party flow. There should be at least 18" of clearance for pathways between furniture.

- Remember to also create "conversational groupings", (seating for 2 or 3 in fairly close proximity to one another), to allow for your guests to talk.

- Do you have valuables in your home that you are worried about someone toppling over? Do you shutter at the thought of your 6-year old niece grabbing that glass bowl from the coffee table? Just move it out of the way. If you think it could break during your party, wrap it in newspaper and put it in an empty laundry basket in a safe place until the party is over.

- Take time to enjoy the party yourself. Often times, hosts are so busy fretting about food and drink or making sure each guest is happy that the host himself or herself forgets to eat, or even sit. Work the room. Make sure you visit with each guest and that each guest is comfortable. And then take time to enjoy the evening yourself. Grab a drink, a plate and settle into a conversation. But not for long. Spend no more than 15 minutes in one small group before visiting with another. Your ice breaker as you enter a conversation is simply "Can I get anyone anything?"

Giving Thanks

A Complete Thanksgiving Day Menu…
…. Made simple

The number one question I get asked this time every year is "do you really cook your own Thanksgiving Day dinner?" And the answer is not always yes. But I do actually enjoy preparing a Thanksgiving Day dinner because believe it or not, I like to cook. Any self respecting chef that says he or she doesn't like Thanksgiving can not be trusted. Come on, it's a whole holiday centered completely around cooking and eating – the two things chefs are supposed to love to do.

And you can actually love it too. Thanksgiving is about being thankful and being grateful for your blessings. It shouldn't be about stressing out. So…along with providing a complete menu with easy recipe suggestions, I thought I'd also include some tips for enjoying a stress free and worry free Thanksgiving. You got this!

Plan Ahead: If you want your holiday meal to run smoothly, make a dinner menu. If you use this chapter, that's already done for you.

Stay Organized: Make lists of everything you need (ingredients, dishes, appliances, accessories) and then go out and get what you don't have.

Know your Guest List. Don't spend all your time stressing over a head count. Expect some changes on your guest list, and always too much rather than too little.

Prepare in Advance. It's okay to make some of your side dishes and desserts a day or two ahead of time. As long as they can keep a day or two in the fridge, you'll be fine

Ask for Help. Request that other people at your house set the table, help with clean-up, plate up special dishes. It's okay to get other people involved in the meal preparation. Thanksgiving is all about a family gathering. They can nap when it's over.

Appetizer

HOLIDAY BRIE EN CROUTE

1 egg
1 tbsp water
½ of a 17.3-ounce package of Puff Pastry Sheets (1 sheet), thawed
½ cup apricot preserves or seedless raspberry jam
1/3 cup dried cranberry
¼ cup toasted sliced almond
1 (13- to 16-ounce) Brie cheese round
1 package Crackers (your choice)

Heat the oven to 400 degrees F. Beat the egg and water in a small bowl with a fork. Unfold the pastry sheet on a lightly floured surface. Roll the pastry sheet into a 14-inch square. Spread the preserves on the pastry to within 2 inches of the edge. Sprinkle with the cranberries and almonds. Place the cheese in the center of the pastry. Fold the pastry up over the cheese to cover. Trim the excess pastry and press to seal. Brush the seam with the egg mixture. Place seam-side down onto a baking sheet. Decorate with the pastry scraps, if desired. Brush with the egg mixture. Bake for 20 minutes or until the pastry is golden brown. Let stand for 45 minutes. Serve with the crackers.

Salad

GREEN SALAD WITH CRANBERRY VINAIGRETTE

This salad is not only great at Thanksgiving but it's perfect to pack for lunch on the go. Just reduce the amount and make it just for you. Or double and triple it and serve it in a bowl for large parties.

1 cup sliced almonds
3 tbsp red wine vinegar
1/3 cup olive oil
1/4 cup fresh cranberries
1 tbsp Dijon mustard
1/2 tsp minced garlic
1/2 tsp salt
1/2 tsp ground black pepper
2 tbsp water
1/2 red onion, thinly sliced
4 ounces crumbled blue cheese
1 pound mixed salad greens

Preheat oven to 375 degrees. Arrange almonds in a single layer on a baking sheet. Toast in oven for 5 minutes, or until nuts begin to brown. In a blender or food processor, combine the vinegar, oil, cranberries, mustard, garlic, salt, pepper, and water. Process until smooth. In a large bowl, toss the almonds, onion, blue cheese, and greens with the vinegar mixture until evenly coated.

ARUGULA SALAD WITH FRIED GORGONZOLA

7 ounces Gorgonzola
1 large egg, beaten to blend
¾ cup dried Italian bread crumbs
3 tbsp fresh lemon juice
1 garlic clove, minced
½ tsp grated lemon peel
1/3 cup olive oil, plus more for deep-frying

Salt and freshly ground black pepper
12 cups coarsely torn arugula (about 10 ounces)

Blend the Gorgonzola in a food processor until smooth and creamy, scraping down the sides of the work bowl occasionally. Using 1 rounded teaspoon of cheese for each, form the cheese into 18 (1-inch) balls. Working in batches, coat the balls with the egg then with the bread crumbs. Repeat coating the balls in the egg and bread crumbs. Arrange the balls on a small baking sheet. Cover and refrigerate until cold, at least 2 hours or overnight. Whisk the lemon juice, garlic, and lemon peel in a medium bowl to blend. Gradually whisk in 1/3 cup oil. Season the dressing, to taste, with salt and pepper. Set the dressing aside. Add enough oil to a heavy small saucepan to come 2 inches up the sides of the pan. Heat the oil over medium heat. At this point, remove the refrigerated Gorgonzola balls from the refrigerator. Working in batches, add the cold balls to the hot oil and fry just until golden brown, about 20 seconds. (It is essential that the Gorgonzola balls be cold when they go into the oil, otherwise they will fall apart in the oil. If they start to warm up at any point, return them to the refrigerator to firm back up.) Using a slotted spoon, transfer the fried balls to paper towels to drain. Toss the arugula in a large bowl with enough dressing to coat. Season the salad, to taste, with salt and pepper. Mound the salad on plates. Top the salads with the hot fried Gorgonzola balls and serve immediately.

Bread

BUTTERMILK CORNBREAD

1/2 cup butter
2/3 cup white sugar
2 eggs
1 cup buttermilk
1/2 tsp baking soda
1 cup cornmeal
1 cup all-purpose flour
1/2 tsp salt

Preheat oven to 375 degrees. Grease an 8 inch square pan. Melt butter in large skillet. Remove from heat and stir in sugar. Quickly add eggs and beat until well blended. Combine buttermilk with baking soda and stir into mixture in pan. Stir in cornmeal, flour, and salt until well blended and few lumps remain. Pour batter into the prepared pan. Bake in the preheated oven for 30 to 40 minutes, or until a toothpick inserted in the center comes out clean.

Entrée

THE PERFECT TURKEY

This recipe is simple but slow….and yes, you totally can handle this..

1 (18 pound) whole turkey, neck and giblets removed
2 cups salt
1/2 cup butter, melted
2 large onions, peeled and chopped
4 carrots, peeled and chopped
4 stalks celery, chopped
2 sprigs fresh thyme
1 bay leaf
1 cup dry white wine

Rub the turkey inside and out with the kosher salt. Place the bird in a large stock pot or in one side of your kitchen sink, and cover with cold water. Allow the turkey to soak in the salt bath for at least 12 hours, if not overnight. Preheat oven to 350 degrees and toss out the brine mixture. Brush the turkey with 1/2 the melted butter. Place breast side down on a roasting rack in a shallow roasting pan. Stuff the turkey cavity with 1 onion, 1/2 the carrots, 1/2 the celery, 1 sprig of thyme, and the bay leaf. Scatter the remaining vegetables and thyme around the bottom of the roasting pan, and cover with the white wine. Roast uncovered 3 1/2 to 4 hours in the preheated oven, until the internal temperature of the thigh reaches 180 degrees. Carefully turn the turkey breast side up about 2/3 through the roasting time, and brush with the remaining butter. Allow to sit and cool for at least 30 minutes before carving.

Sides

CROCKPOT STUFFING

You can get this all together and then watch the parade.

1 cup butter or margarine
2 cups chopped onion
2 cups chopped celery
1/4 cup chopped fresh parsley
12 ounces sliced mushrooms
12 cups dry bread cubes
1 tsp poultry seasoning
1 1/2 tsp dried sage
1 tsp dried thyme
1/2 tsp dried marjoram
1 1/2 tsp salt
1/2 tsp ground black pepper
4 1/2 cups chicken broth,
2 eggs, beaten

Melt butter or margarine in a skillet over medium heat. Cook onion, celery, mushroom, and parsley in butter, stirring frequently. Spoon cooked vegetables over bread cubes in a very large mixing bowl. Season with poultry seasoning, sage, thyme, marjoram, and salt and pepper. Pour in enough broth to moisten, and mix in eggs. Transfer mixture to crockpot or slow cooker, and cover. Cook on High for 45 minutes, then reduce heat to Low, and cook for 4 to 8 hours.

BEST EVER CRANBERRY SAUCE

You can actually make this night before. Or even the night before that.

1 cup frozen cranberry juice concentrate, thawed
1/3 cup white sugar
1 (12 ounce) package fresh cranberries, rinsed
1/2 cup dried cranberries
3 tbsp orange marmalade
2 tbsp orange juice
2 tsp minced orange peel

Stir the cranberry juice concentrate and sugar together in a saucepan over medium-high heat, and bring to a boil, stirring until sugar has dissolved. Mix in the fresh and dried cranberries, reduce heat to medium, and cook until the dried cranberries soften and the fresh ones pop, 7 to 10 minutes. Remove from heat. Mix in the orange marmalade, orange juice, and orange peel until thoroughly combined. Allow the cranberry sauce to cool completely. Pour into glass serving dish, cover, and chill until cold, at least 2 hours.

EASY MASHED BAKED POTATOES

5 pounds Yukon Gold potatoes
2 (3 ounce) packages cream cheese
8 ounces sour cream
1/2 cup milk
2 tsp onion
salt ground black pepper to taste

Boil the potatoes until soft and then mash, living the skin off if desired. Combine mashed potatoes, cream cheese, sour cream, milk, onion salt, and pepper to taste. Mix well and place in a large casserole. Cover and bake at 325 degrees for 50 minutes.

Homemade Mac and Cheese

8 ounces uncooked elbow macaroni
2 cups shredded sharp Cheddar cheese
1/2 cup grated Parmesan cheese
3 cups milk
1/4 cup butter
2 1/2 tbsp flour
2 tbsp butter
1/2 cup bread crumbs
1 pinch paprika

Cook macaroni according to the package directions. Drain. In a saucepan, melt butter or margarine over medium heat. Stir in enough flour to make a roux. Add milk to roux slowly, stirring constantly. Stir in cheeses, and cook over low heat until cheese is melted and the sauce is a little thick. Put macaroni in large casserole dish, and pour sauce over macaroni. Stir well. Melt butter or margarine in a skillet over medium heat. Add breadcrumbs and brown. Spread over the macaroni and cheese to cover. Sprinkle with a little paprika. Bake at 350 degrees for 30 minutes. Serve.

Roasted Cauliflower with Broccoli and Bacon

1 pound fresh broccoli, chopped
1 pound fresh cauliflower, chopped
1/4 cup olive oil
1 tsp freshly ground pepper
1/2 tsp salt
1 pound bacon, cooked and crumbled
1/3 to 1/2 cup balsamic vinaigrette

Preheat oven to 375°. In a very large bowl, toss broccoli and cauliflower with oil, pepper and salt. Transfer to two greased 15x10x1-in. baking pans. Roast 20-25 minutes or until vegetables are tender. Transfer to a serving bowl. Just before serving, add bacon and drizzle with vinaigrette; toss to coat.

CHEESY HASH BROWN CASSEROLE

1 (32 ounce) package frozen hash brown potatoes
8 ounces cooked, diced ham
2 small cans condensed cream of potato soup
16 ounces sour cream
2 cups shredded sharp Cheddar cheese
1 1/2 cups grated Parmesan cheese

Preheat oven to 375 degrees. Lightly grease a 9x13 inch baking dish. In a large bowl, mix hash browns, ham, cream of potato soup, sour cream, and Cheddar cheese. Spread evenly into prepared dish. Sprinkle with Parmesan cheese. Bake 1 hour in the preheated oven, or until bubbly and lightly brown. Serve immediately.

Desserts

RED WINE POACHED PEARS WITH MASCARPONE FILLING

6 firm Bartlett pears
1 bottle red wine
1 vanilla bean, whole
2 cinnamon sticks
2 bay leaves
2 cups sugar
2 (8 ounce) containers mascarpone cheese, softened
½ cup heavy cream
Pinch cinnamon
½ cup powdered sugar
2 tablespoons butter

Peel pears and leave stem intact. In a large saucepan, bring wine and an equal amount of cold water to a simmer. Split vanilla bean lengthwise and add to wine and water mixture. Add cinnamon sticks, bay leaves and sugar, to taste. Add pears to liquid and simmer for about 20 minutes or until tender. Cool pears in wine mixture to room temperature. You can refrigerate them in the poaching liquid until you're ready to fill them. Remove stems from pears and set stems aside. Core pears with an apple corer, leaving pear whole. Whisk together mascarpone cheese, heavy cream, pinch cinnamon and powdered sugar until smooth. Transfer to a pastry bag, or if you do not have one, use wax paper tightly wrapped into a cone with the corner snipped off. Pipe filling into cored pears and finish by putting the stems gently into the mascarpone filling on top of the pears. Bring sauce up to a simmer and reduce by half. Add butter to reduced sauce and stir until combined. Spoon generously over pears. Cool to room temperature before serving.

EGGNOG PUMPKIN PIE

1 can (15 oz) solid pack pumpkin
1 ¼ cups commercial eggnog
2/3 cups sugar
3 eggs
1 ½ tsp pumpkin pie spice
1 unbaked pastry pie shell

In a large bowl, combine the pumpkin, eggnog, sugar, eggs, and pumpkin pie spice. Pour into the shell. Bake at 375 degrees for 60 minutes or until a knife inserted in the center comes out clean. Cool on a wire rack and serve.

The 12 Dishes of Christmas

A Complete Holiday Menu
A Stress-Free Dinner Dressed to Impress

It's beginning to smell a lot like Christmas.

The holiday season isn't just filled with the sights and sounds that can only be seen in this most wonderful time of the year but for a chef it's a great time of the calendar because it means smells of spices, baked goods, cookies, and country hams. It's the best of aromatic times.

Remember what your mother or grandmother's kitchens smelled like when you were a kid and you walked into the dining room for Christmas or holiday dinner. The smells that almost lifted you from your feet and carried you to the table?

You know they say the sense most closely related to memory is smell and I believe it. Just smelling gingerbread baking or cinnamon takes me back to being a little boy and being scooted out of the working kitchen by my grandma, the home economics teacher. More than pine, the smell of Christmas dinner cooking makes me sentimental for the holiday.

That said, I also know that for some people, preparing the holiday meal for a bunch of guests or relatives can be the most stressful thing you do all year. It doesn't have to be. You can relax and enjoy yourself. I have your holiday dinner menu all planned out for you in this issue. All you have to do is follow the directions. And some of these items can be prepared a day or two ahead of time and then just warmed up.

Some of the menu options are traditional – like glazed ham – and others are a bit daring – like the poached pears. But none of them are intimidating and they will all impress the holly berries out of your company.

After all, the only worry you should have these season is whether or not your niece is still into Doc McStuffins because you spent a fortune on that lab coat and stethoscope.

Appetizer

CHEESE SAMPLER BOARD

It's one of the easiest appetizers you will ever serve

2 (10-ounce) tins smoked almonds
1/2 pound wedge Brie with herbs
1/2 pound wedge blue cheese
1 (6-ounce) log goat cheese
1 baguette, sliced
1 pound grapes (any variety or color) separated into small bunches

Pour nuts into large snifter and set on cheese board. Arrange cheeses with baguette slices and clusters of grapes. Place a few spreaders near cheeses and set out where guests will gather.

Beverages

RASPBERRY SHERBET PUNCH

Everyone likes a holiday punch and this one is so simple, you'll be making it at every gathering. Plus, when's the last time you used that punch bowl?

1 gallon raspberry sherbet
1 gallon cranberry juice, well chilled
Two 2-liter bottles ginger ale, well chilled

Make sure all the ingredients are very cold. Scoop the sherbet into a large punch bowl, then pour in the cranberry juice and ginger ale and stir gently. That's it!

BUTTERED COFFEE

Yes, it sounds crazy but this sweet treat is actually becoming all the rage in coffee shops out west. What "butter" time than the holiday to try it?

12 Ounce coffee mug
freshly brewed strong black coffee
1 tsp butter
1 tsp coconut oil

Put the butter and oil in the mug. Slowly pour the hot coffee on top, swirling the cup as you do to melt the butter. When the mug is full, swirl with your hand. Do not stir with a spoon. Allow the cream to come to the surface on its own as you drink it.

CROCK POT HOT CHOCOLATE

1 ½ cups heavy cream
1 can sweetened condensed milk
2 cups milk chocolate chips
6 cups whole milk
1 tsp vanilla

Place all items in a crock pot over medium heat at first until chips are melted. Then stir with a wooden spoon. Turn heat to low setting to keep warm and ladle out when ready to be served.

Main Dish

OLD FASHIONED GLAZED HAM

3/4 cup Dijon mustard
1/2 cup light brown sugar, plus more for sprinkling
2 tsp chopped fresh thyme leaves
1 (14-pound) cooked and smoked cured ham, shank end
3/4 cup pineapple juice
20 canned pineapple rings
1/2 cup maraschino cherries

Preheat the oven to 350 degrees F. Put oven rack in the middle of the oven. In a small bowl, mix together the Dijon mustard, brown sugar, and thyme. Put the ham in a large roasting pan, fat side up. Rub the ham with mustard glaze. Pour the pineapple juice into the bottom of the pan. Put the ham in the oven and bake for 2 hours, brushing every 20 minutes with the pineapple juice. Remove the ham from the oven. Turn oven to 400 degrees. Using toothpicks, decoratively adhere the pineapple rings around the ham and put a cherry in the center of the pineapple ring. Sprinkle the pineapple rings lightly with brown sugar. Return to the oven, uncovered, and bake until the pineapples turn a light golden brown. Remove from the oven to a serving platter and let rest for 15 minutes before slicing.

Sides

CHEESE ENCRUSTED SQUASH

One large squash
2 minced garlic cloves
8 minced sage leaves
Zest of 1 lemon
1/2 cup grated parmesan
3 tbsp breadcrumbs
3 tbsp olive oil
salt and red pepper flakes

Mix all the ingredients listed above (with the exception of the squash itself) Cut squash into thin wedges. Pat mix ingredients into the wedges. Bake in a single layer at 450 degrees F, 15 to 20 minutes.

Scalloped Potatoes

3 tbsp butter or margarine
2 tbsp all purpose flour
3 cups milk
1 tsp salt
¼ tsp pepper
8 medium potatoes – peeled and sliced thin
2 tbsp chopped onion

Preheat oven to 350 degrees. Make white sauce of first five ingredients. Pour half the potatoes in a greased two quart casserole dish. Cover with half the onions and half the sauce. Repeat layers. Cover and bake at 350 for one hour. Uncover. Continue baking for about 10 more minutes until top is browned. Sprinkle with shredded cheddar cheese if you'd like.

Brussels Sprouts with Balsamic and Cranberries

Sweeten up a hearty side dish and give your dinner guests a taste they won't expect!

3 pounds Brussels sprouts
1/2 cup olive oil
1 cup sugar
3/4 cup balsamic vinegar
1 cup dried cranberries

Preheat the oven to 375 degrees F. Trim and clean the Brussels sprouts, then cut them in half. Arrange on 2 baking sheets and toss with the olive oil. Roast until brown, 25 to 30 minutes. Combine the balsamic vinegar and sugar in a saucepan. Bring to a boil, then reduce the heat to medium-low and reduce until very thick. Drizzle the balsamic reduction over the roasted sprouts, then sprinkle on the dried cranberries.

Holiday stuffing with bacon

8 ounces applewood-smoked bacon, chopped into 1/2-inch pieces

Rice:

4 1/2 cups low-salt chicken broth
3 tbsp chopped fresh thyme
1 1/4 cups short-grain brown rice
1 1/4 cups wild rice

Vegetables:

2 tbsp unsalted butter, at room temperature
2 tbsp extra-virgin olive oil
One 14-ounce bag frozen pearl onions, thawed
1 tsp salt
3/4 tsp freshly ground black pepper
12 ounces (3 large) portobello mushrooms, shredded or thinly sliced
8 ounces Brussels sprouts, trimmed and thinly sliced
1/2 cup hazelnuts, toasted, husked, coarsely chopped, optional

Cook the bacon like you normally would until very crisp. Drain on paper towels.

For the rice: In a heavy saucepan, bring the broth and thyme to a boil over medium-high heat. Add the brown and wild rice. Cover the saucepan and simmer until the rice is tender. Turn off the heat and allow the rice to stand for 10 minutes. Fluff with a fork.

For the vegetables: In the same skillet used to cook the bacon, heat the butter and oil over medium-high heat. Add the onions and season with 1/2 teaspoon salt and 1/4 teaspoon pepper. Cook, stirring occasionally until light golden, about 5 minutes. Add the mushrooms, 1/4 teaspoon salt and 1/4 teaspoon pepper. Cook until softened, about 8 minutes. Add the Brussels sprouts and the remaining 1/4 teaspoon salt and 1/4 teaspoon pepper. Cook for 5 minutes.

Transfer the vegetable mixture to the saucepan of cooked rice. Add the hazelnuts and cooked bacon. Toss until all the ingredients are mixed. Transfer to a large bowl and serve.

Desserts

GINGERBREAD CUPCAKES

It's a lot of ingredients but once mixed together, it's super simple.

1/4 cup dark rum (or water)
1/2 cup golden raisins
1/4 pound unsalted butter
1 cup molasses
1 cup sour cream
1 1/2 tsp grated orange zest
2 1/3 cups all-purpose flour
3/4 tsp baking soda
1 1/2 tsp ground ginger
1 tsp ground cinnamon
1/4 tsp ground cloves
1/2 tsp salt
1/3 cup minced dried crystallized ginger
For the frosting:
8 ounces cream cheese, at room temperature
1/4 pound unsalted butter, at room temperature
1/2 tsp orange zest
1/2 tsp pure vanilla extract
1/2 pound confectioners' sugar

Preheat the oven to 350 degrees. Line a muffin pan with paper liners. Place the rum and raisins in a small pan, cover, and heat until the rum boils. Turn off the heat and set aside. Place the butter and molasses in another small pan and bring to a boil over medium heat. Pour the mixture into the bowl of an electric mixer fitted with the paddle attachment. Cool for 5 minutes, then mix in the sour cream and orange zest. Meanwhile, sift the flour, baking soda, ginger, cinnamon, cloves, and salt together into a small bowl. Mix with your hand until combined. With the mixer on low speed, slowly add the flour mixture to the molasses mixture and mix only until smooth. Drain the raisins and add them and the crystallized ginger to the mixture with a spatula. Divide the batter among the muffin pan (1 rounded standard ice cream scoop per cup is the right amount). Bake on the middle rack of the oven for 25 to 30 minutes, or until a toothpick comes out clean. Cool for 10 minutes before removing from the pan.

For the frosting, mix the cream cheese, butter, orange zest and vanilla in the bowl of an electric mixer fitted with the paddle attachment until just combined. Add the sugar and mix until smooth.

When the cupcakes are cool, frost them generously.

STICKY TOFFEE PUDDING

Pudding:

2 cups pitted dates
3/4 cup dark spiced rum
1 tsp vanilla extract
3 1/2 cups all-purpose flour
1 tbsp baking powder
1/2 tsp ground cinnamon
Pinch salt
2 cups brown sugar
1 stick butter, at room temperature, plus extra for baking dish
3 eggs, separated
Toffee Sauce:
3 sticks butter
1 1/2 cups brown sugar
1/2 cup brandy

Preheat the oven to 350 degrees. Butter a 9x13-inch baking dish. In a small saucepan, combine the dates, rum and 3/4 cup water. Bring the liquid to a boil, reduce to a simmer and simmer for 5 more minutes. Remove the pan from the heat and add the vanilla extract. Let the liquid cool, and then puree the dates with their liquid in a food processor. Reserve. Sift together the flour, baking powder, cinnamon and salt. Combine the brown sugar and butter in a large mixing bowl on a medium speed. Beat the butter and sugar together. Beat in the eggs one at a time. Gently mix in the flour mixture in thirds over a low speed. Stir in the date puree. Transfer the batter to the prepared baking dish and bake in the oven for 35 minutes.

For the toffee sauce: Make this while the pudding is baking. Combine the butter, sugar, brandy and 1/4 cup water in a medium saucepan. Bring the mixture to a simmer, whisking frequently. Cook the sauce until it thickens to a sauce consistency.

To finish the pudding: Remove the pudding from the oven and let cool for about 10 minutes. Using a skewer, poke holes in the pudding about every inch or so.

Pour half the toffee sauce over the cake and let it soak in for at least 20 minutes. Serve the pudding in a warm pool of the remaining sauce.

Host or Hostess Gift

HOLIDAY GIFT OF PEANUT BRITTLE

Taking your dinner host a gift? Or maybe you want each guest at your dinner to leave with a sweet treat? Consider this clever gift of food.

1 tsp vanilla extract
1 tsp baking soda
1 tsp salt
3/4 cup butter
3 cups sugar
1 cup light corn syrup
3 cups shelled raw peanuts

Measure the vanilla into a small bowl and set aside. Combine the baking soda and salt in another small bowl and set aside. Butter a cookie sheet with 1/2 stick of the butter. Set aside. Combine the sugar, corn syrup and 1/2 cup water in a large saucepan. Bring the mixture to a boil and cook over medium-high heat until the syrup spins a thread when poured from a spoon. Stir in the peanuts and continue cooking and stirring until the candy becomes golden brown. Remove from the heat immediately and quickly add the remaining butter and the vanilla, baking soda and salt. Stir only until the butter melts, and then quickly pour the brittle onto the cookie sheet, spreading the mixture thinly. When the brittle has completely cooled, break the candy into pieces and store in a tightly covered container. When it's time to give as a gift or serve, place it in a nice collectible tin

DECEMBER

Hi Ho. Hi Ho. It's off to the Kitchen I go

Disney Classic Inspires Seven Classic Recipes

Did you know that besides all the wonderful holidays that happen in December, it's also an anniversary of animation history? December 21 is not only the Winter Solstice, it's the birthday of a movie classic that to this day remains one of my favorites. While my all-time favorite Disney movies are *Lady and the Tramp* and the *Aristocat*s, neither one of those—and none of the Disney movies ever created before or since—would have been possible had it not been for a movie that premiered in December, 1937, *Snow White and the Seven Dwarfs.*

While *Cinderella* gets much of the credit, Snow White is the original OG out of the Disney princess line. She was ruling the castle and shining her magic mirrors while Cinderella was still barefooted and talking to mice in the attic.

Disney's Snow White was the very first full length animated film. And it's a classic that still holds up this day. It's a masterpiece. In honor of the anniversary of this movie, it would have been simple to throw in a few "poison" apple recipes but I will save those for another time.

Instead, I thought it might be fun to give you seven recipes – each one inspired by one of Snow's hard working little friends. I can't guarantee any of them will make you more "Charming" but anyone of them could melt the black heart of even the most evil of queens.

For Doc

I think even the wisest of Dwarfs would approve of this healthy smooothie!

Kale and Pineapple Detox Smoothie

Ingredients

1/2 cup pineapple
2 large cucumbers
4 cups of chopped kale
1/2 lemon, squeezed
pinch of Ginger
½ cup fresh mint

Chop ingredients so they are able to fit into juicer. Juice ingredients one at a time.

For Grumpy

Want to turn that frown around? Here's a recipe that claims to jump start a good mood and please even the pickiest member of your crew

Old Fashioned Mac and Cheese

Ingredients:

10 ounces shredded sharp cheddar cheese
1 fourteen-ounce box macaroni
2 ¼ cups milk
1 tsp soy sauce
1 tsp onion powder
1/2 tsp dry mustard
1/4 tsp paprika
1/2 tsp salt
1/8 tsp ground pepper

1 tbsp cornstarch
2 tsp whipped butter (or trans-fat free margarine)

Bring a large pot of unsalted water to a boil. Add the macaroni and follow the directions on the package for al dente pasta. While the macaroni is cooking, prepare the cheese sauce: In a large saucepan, combine 2 cups of the milk with soy sauce, onion powder, dry mustard, paprika, salt, and pepper. Place over medium heat, and cook until the mixture comes to a gentle simmer. In a small bowl or cup, mix the cornstarch with remaining ¼ cup cold milk. Add the cornstarch mixture to the saucepan and stir to combine. Return sauce to a simmer and cook for 2 to 3 minutes, stirring occasionally. The mixture should thicken slightly. Remove the saucepan from the heat and add the shredded cheese. Continue stirring until the cheese is completely melted and no lumps remain. Add the butter or margarine spread to the cheese sauce and stir until it is completely melted and combined. Drain the macaroni (do not rinse it), and return it to the pot. Pour the cheese sauce over the cooked macaroni and stir until everything is coated. Transfer to a 9x13-inch baking dish coated with oil spray. Sprinkle it with ¼ cup shredded or grated parmesan cheese. Place under a preheated broiler for 4 to 7 minutes, or until top is golden brown and crispy; check often to make sure cheese does not burn.

For Happy

Nothing can make your little one at home happier than homemade Apple Crisp Oatmeal. But hurry...use those apples before your stepmother gets a hold of them.

APPLE CRISP OATMEAL

Ingredients:

1/2 cup old-fashioned oats
1 apple, chopped
2 tsp brown sugar
2 tbsp milk
1/4 tsp ground cinnamon

In a small bowl, combine the oats with 1 cup water and microwave for 2 minutes.

Add half of the chopped apple, the brown sugar, and the milk and stir thoroughly. Top the oatmeal with the rest of the chopped apple and sprinkle with the cinnamon. Microwave the oatmeal for 1 additional minute and serve.

For Sleepy

Can't rest at night? Try this herbal remedy for "Sleepy-Time" tea.

HERBAL BEDTIME TEA

Ingredients

-3 parts chamomile flowers
2 parts lemon balm
1 part catnip
1 part oat straw
1 part passionflower
¼ part hop flowers
1/4 part valerian root

Measure the parts of each of the herbs listed and mix in a large bowl until well combined. Place in a sealable container or bag. Shake and blend well. Remove from bag and place tea blend in a cool, dark place until needed. Use a teapot or single tea infuser to make tea when needed. Drink 30 minutes before bed.

For Bashful

It will put a smile on even the most shy of you.

BLUSH AND BASHFUL WHIP

Bananas
Mix & Match Ingredients:
Cocoa powder (unsweetened)
Vanilla extract
Peanut Butter
Honey
Strawberries
Raspberries

Cut bananas into thick 1-1.5 inch slices. Stick bananas in your freezer overnight. In the morning, put the slices in a food processor and blend. Then blend in any of the optional ingredients. You can even serve this as a topping on ice cream or pie.

For Sneezy

This simple recipe for a pepper garlic spice rub might get your nose to twitching.

PEPPER GARLIC SPICE RUB

3 tbsp freshly ground black pepper
1 tbsp paprika
1 tbsp chili powder
1 tbsp garlic powder
1 tbsp dark brown sugar
2 tsp ground cumin
2 tsp chopped fresh sage
1 1/2 tsp dry mustard
1 tsp ground coriander
1 tsp ground red pepper

Combine all ingredients. Rub into beef, chicken of fish.

For Dopey

Did you know that dark chocolate is a natural mood enhancer? This recipe for dark chocolate brownies should do the trick...besides, "dopey" and "brownies" historically share a connection anyway.

DARK CHOCOLATE BROWNIES

1 Cup unsalted butter
8 ounces bittersweet dark chocolate chips
2 cups sugar
1 tsp vanilla extract
5 large eggs
2/3 cup all-purpose flour
1/3 cup unsweetened Dutch cocoa
1/2 tsp salt

Preheat oven to 350 degrees. Butter and flour 13 x 9 pan. In 3 qt heavy saucepan, melt butter and chocolate over low heat, stirring until smooth. Remove from heat and allow to come to room temperature. Whisk in sugar and vanilla into chocolate/butter combination. Whisk in eggs, one at a time until thoroughly combined. Set aside. In separate bowl combine chocolate powder, flour and salt. Combine flour mixture with chocolate/butter and whisk thoroughly. Spread brownie batter in pan and bake for 25-35 minutes. Cool completely

Fruitcake's Bad Reputation

And how to dress it up, disguise it, get it drunk and avoid it

Dear Fruitcake.

Face it. No one likes you. You can sit in that fancy collectible tin and wrap yourself up in the prettiest cellophane color but you're still fruitcake. And like it or not, for some reason, you have received this nasty reputation. You're unwanted, under appreciated and regifted. If I show up at someone's holiday or New Year's Eve party with you I'm testing the limits of a host or hostess's social skills. I have to make sure I bring you on some sort of collectible porcelain plate the person can keep when the dog is finally served you because that's the only way I'll be invited to the same party next year.

Then why are you so popular this time of year? Fruitcake, you're one of those winter time staples like your distant cousin, Egg Nog. No one sits under the shade of a weeping willow in August thinking "if I just had a slice of fruitcake and some nice cold egg nog."

You are one of those items that – for good of for bad – is associated with just 25 days in December. Does anyone even think about you on Valentine's Day? Does anyone want you around come Easter? Are you doomed, Fruitcake, or are there things that can be done to make you more welcome? The answer is a surprising yes. Never fear, Fruitcake....if you follow a few of my suggestions, I'll have you back on the "Nice" list in no time.

Drunken Fruit Cake

If you're going to force it on your guests, it should at least be doused in holiday cheer. If someone has more than two slices, take their keys. Don't let your friends drive cake-faced.

For the fruit

1 cup dark rum
4 oz. dried apricots, chopped into 1/4- to 1/2-inch pieces (3/4 cup lightly packed)
3 oz. dried apples, chopped into 1/4- to 1/2-inch pieces (1 cup lightly packed)
3 oz. currants or dark raisins (3/4 cup lightly packed)
1/2 tsp. freshly grated orange zest

For the cake batter

5 oz. unsalted butter, softened; more for the pan
5 oz. unbleached all-purpose flour
1/2 tsp. ground cinnamon
1/2 tsp. ground allspice
1/4 tsp. ground cardamom
1/8 tsp. freshly grated nutmeg
Pinch of ground cloves
2/3 cup packed dark brown sugar (preferably muscovado)
1/3 cup granulated sugar
3 large eggs, at room temperature
1/2 tsp. pure vanilla extract
1/4 tsp. table salt
3-1/2 oz. crystallized ginger, finely chopped (1/2 cup)
More dark rum, for brushing

Put the rum, dried fruit, and orange zest in 2-quart saucepan, cover, and warm over medium heat for two to three minutes. Remove from the heat and let cool. Refrigerate – allowing the mixture to soak in the alcohol – for a minimum for at least a day and up to two days. Before making the cake, bring the fruit to room temperature and drain, reserving any of the rum liquid for basting.

To make the cake, position a rack in the center of the oven and heat the oven to 325°F. Butter or spray the inside of a 8-inch meatloaf pan. You can also line the pan with two strips of parchment in opposite directions, leaving an overhang for easy removal of the cake. In a medium bowl, whisk the flour with the cinnamon, allspice, cardamom, nutmeg, and cloves. In a stand mixer, beat the butter and both sugars on medium-high speed until fluffy and no lumps of brown sugar remain. Stop to scrape the bowl as needed. Beat in the eggs one at a time, scraping the bowl and mixing for up to one minute after each addition. Add in the vanilla and salt. Add 2 Tbs. of the flour mixture to the bowl and beat briefly. Reserve 2 Tbs. of the flour mixture and add the rest to the batter; beat on low speed for 10 seconds to incorporate the flour and then on medium-high for 1 minute. Combine the ginger with the fruit mixture. Scrape the batter into the center of the bowl. Put the marinated fruit on top of the batter and then sprinkle the reserved flour evenly over the fruit. Using a rubber spatula, fold the fruit into the batter until it's evenly distributed. Scrape the batter into the prepared pan, pressing it in to eliminate air pockets and smoothing the top to make it level. Bake for 15 minutes and then reduce the temperature to 300°F and bake until the center of the cake has risen slightly and a cake tester inserted in the middle comes out clean. Remove the cake and let it cool in its pan on a wire rack for 20 to 30 minutes. When cool, brush the cake with the reserved fruit-soaking liquid or fresh rum. Wrap tightly in plastic and then in foil; store the cake at room temperature before serving.

CHERRY MANGO FRUITCAKE

If you're going to call yourself fruitcake, at least have fruits people like to eat!

1/8 cup chopped dried cherries
1/8 cup chopped dried mango
1/4 cup dried cranberries
1/4 cup dried currants
1/2 cup butter

1/4 cup orange juice
1/4 cup packed brown sugar
2 eggs
1/2 cup all-purpose flour
1/8 tsp baking soda
1/4 tsp salt
1/4 tsp cinnamon
1/4 cup unsulfured molasses
2 tbsp milk
1/4 cup chopped pecans

Soak cherries, mango, cranberries, currants, and citron in 1/4 cup orange juice for at least 24 hours. Cover tightly, and store at room temperature. Preheat oven to 325 degrees F. Butter a 6x3-inch round pan or loaf pan and line it with parchment paper. In a large bowl, cream together butter and brown sugar until fluffy. Beat in egg. Whisk together flour, baking soda, salt, and cinnamon; mix into butter and sugar in three batches, alternating with molasses and milk. Stir in soaked fruit and chopped nuts. Scrape batter into prepared pan. Bake in preheated oven for 40 to 45 minutes. Cool in the pan for 10 minutes, then sprinkle with remaining juice. Once cool, place cake in an airtight container, douse with any remaining liquids and store until ready to serve.

Pfeffer Neuse

Or you could skip the fruitcake altogether and try this recipe. It's the traditional holiday treat in Germany. My cousins actually make this every year and it's become a tradition in their household.

1/2 cup molasses
1/4 cup honey
1/4 cup shortening
1/4 cup margarine
2 eggs
4 cups all-purpose flour
3/4 cup white sugar
1/2 cup brown sugar

1 1/2 tsp ground cardamom
1 tsp nutmeg
1 tsp cloves
1 tsp ginger
2 tsp anise extract
2 tsp cinnamon
1 1/2 tsp baking soda
1 tsp black pepper
1/2 tsp salt
1 cup confectioners' sugar for dusting

Stir together the molasses, honey, shortening, and margarine in a saucepan over medium heat; cook and stir until creamy. Remove from heat and allow to cool to room temperature. Stir in the eggs. Combine the flour, white sugar, brown sugar, cardamom, nutmeg, cloves, ginger, anise, cinnamon, baking soda, pepper, and salt in a large bowl. Add the molasses mixture and stir until thoroughly combines. Refrigerate at least 2 hours. Preheat oven to 325 degrees F. Roll the dough into acorn-sized balls. Arrange on baking sheets, spacing at least one inch apart. Bake in preheated oven 10 to 15 minutes. Move to a rack to cool. Dust cooled cookies with confectioners' sugar.

PUNCH BOWL FRUITCAKE

Have you ever heard of such a thing? That crystal punch bowl from the china cabinet can finally be used. And you can have some fun with this dish!

1 box instant vanilla pudding
1 box yellow cake mix
1 large can crushed pineapple with juice
1 can cherry pie filling (or strawberry)
2 cartons Cool Whip

Bake cake by directions. Mix pudding by directions. Take 1 layer cake and break into pieces in punch bowl. Add the following in order:

1/2 pudding over cake
1/2 pineapple over pudding
1/2 pie filling over pineapple
1 carton Cool Whip

Repeat with second layer of cake. Refrigerate to chill.

A "Hand-Made" Holiday

Giving the gift of food is always "in good taste."

When I was just getting started and baking and cooking professionally and living in California for the first few years, I used to make lemon pies and give them as Christmas gifts. I did this not because I thought I was some great baker and my pies were an amazing gift but because I simply could not afford to buy people store bought gifts. And so I made something handmade.

I was in California so lemons and lemon trees were easy to find. I would make these pies and give them to friends and family – people whose houses I would visit over the Christmas season and people who would come and visit me. I would spend days on end before the holidays making pies. People then, to my surprise, loved them and for the next few years, told me they looked forward to getting them each year. And so I made it my own tradition for 15 years living in and around Los Angeles, to make these pies at Christmas – sometimes I'd end up making 20 or 25 pies a month.

I know this recipe by heart because I have made it so much and so it took me a hot minute to stop and think about it and write it down. People often ask me "What is the secret to this recipe?" It's simple; that's my secret. And I have only shared it one other time before.

And so along with my own holiday lemon pie recipe, I thought it might be fun this holiday to include other recipes – for food as gifts. You honestly don't have to have or spend money to present a gift of love this holiday season. You can simply offer to cook or bake for someone, or present them the gift of any of the 12 suggestions you see here. The best gifts are handmade and homemade gifts – and the best part about giving someone food as a gift – they eat it and it's gone – nothing to pack away, nothing in the wrong size, and little chance of re-gifting.

Bill Hand's "Famous" Lemon Pie

Nine whole cinnamon graham crackers
¼ cup sugar
1/3 cup butter – melted
One egg
1 can sweetened condensed milk
1 tsp lemon peel – grated
½ cup fresh lemon juice

For the crust: Crush crackers until fine, mix in sugar and add melted butter. Press crust into pie pan. Bake at 325 degrees for five minutes or until the crust settles.

For pie mixture: Beat egg. Add lemon peel, lemon juice, and milk until thick. Pour mixture into pie pan. Refrigerate for up to two hours or overnight until firm. Garnish with a twist of lemon.

Chocolate Covered Cherries

1 1/2 cups confectioners' sugar, plus more for dusting
1 tbsp plus 1 tsp light corn syrup
1 tbsp unsalted butter, room temperature.
32 "Luxardo" cherries
1 cup Tempered Chocolate

In a bowl, stir together sugar, corn syrup, 1 tablespoon water, and butter until a dough forms. Transfer to a work surface lightly dusted with confectioners' sugar and knead until smooth, dusting dough with more sugar as necessary, until no longer sticky. Scoop 1 teaspoon of dough into your palm and flatten into a 1-inch round. Place a cherry in center of round and wrap dough around cherry, pressing with your fingers, if necessary, to enclose. Gently roll between your palms until smooth. Repeat process with remaining dough and cherries. Transfer to a parchment-lined sheet. Let stand, uncovered, until hard and dry, at least 2 hours and up to 1 day. Then... dip each cherry into chocolate, then lift and let excess chocolate drip back into bowl. Transfer to a parchment-lined sheet and let stand until chocolate is hard and dry, about 1 hour. Serve, or store in an airtight container at room temperature up to 1 month.

Bacon Jam

1 1/2 pounds sliced bacon, cut crosswise into 1-inch pieces
2 cups finely chopped shallots
4 small cloves garlic, chopped
1 tsp chili powder
1/2 tsp ginger
1/2 tsp mustard
1/4 cup maple syrup
1/3 cup sherry vinegar
1/3 cup packed light-brown sugar

Spread half of bacon in a single layer in a large skillet and cook over medium heat, stirring frequently, until browned, 20 to 23 minutes. Transfer to paper towels to drain. Remove fat; clean pan. Repeat with remaining bacon, reserving browned bits and 1 tablespoon fat in pan. Add shallots and garlic to pan and cook over medium heat, stirring, until translucent, about 5 minutes. Add chili powder, ginger, and mustard and cook, stirring, 1 minute. Increase heat to high; add maple syrup. Bring to a boil, scraping up browned bits. Add vinegar and brown sugar and return to a boil. Add reserved bacon; reduce heat to low. Simmer, stirring occasionally, until liquid reduces to a thick glaze, about 10 minutes. Transfer mixture to a food processor and pulse until it has the consistency of a chunky jam. Refrigerate in an airtight container at least 1 hour and up to 4 weeks. Place labels on jars for gifts.

Brownie Mix in a Jar

1 1/4 cups all-purpose flour
1 tsp baking powder
1 tsp salt
2/3 cup unsweetened cocoa powder

2 1/4 cups white sugar
1/2 cup chopped pecans

Mix together flour, baking powder, and salt in a quart jar. Layer remaining ingredients in the order listed. Press each layer firmly in place before adding the next layer. Make sure you wipe out the inside of the jar with a paper towel after adding the cocoa powder, so the other layers will show through the glass. Then simply attach a gift tag with the following directions:

"Preheat the oven to 350. Grease and flour a 9x13inch baking pan. Empty jar of brownie mix into a large mixing bowl, and stir to blend. Mix in 3/4 cup melted butter and 4 eggs. Mix thoroughly. Spread batter evenly into prepared baking pan. Bake for 25 to 30 minutes in preheated oven. Cool completely in pan before cutting into 2 inch squares."

GINGERBREAD CARAMEL SAUCE

3/4 cup unsulfured molasses
3 cups sugar
2 cups heavy cream
1 1/2 sticks cold unsalted butter, cut into small pieces
1 1/2 tsp salt
1 1/2 tsp cinnamon
1 1/2 tsp ground ginger

Combine molasses, 1/2 cup water, and sugar in a medium saucepan. Heat over medium-high, gently stirring, until sugar has dissolved. Bring to a boil; cook until foaming reduces and bubbles begin to slow, 4 to 5 minutes. Remove from heat and carefully whisk in cream, butter, salt, and spices, stirring until butter is melted and combined. Let cool completely. Transfer to 6 seven-ounce jars. Sauce can be refrigerated in jars up to 2 weeks; Attach with a gift tag to tell your recipient to gently reheat before serving.

Peppermint Fudge

Nonstick spray
16 ounces semisweet chocolate chips
1 cup round peppermint candies, plus 18 for garnish
3/4 cup heavy cream
3 1/2 cups mini marshmallows
5 tbsp unsalted butter
1 1/4 cups sugar
1 tsp salt

Lightly coat a 9-inch square baking pan with nonstick spray. Line pan with two pieces parchment paper in both directions, leaving 2 inches of overhang on all sides; spray parchment. Place chocolate in a bowl. In a food processor, pulse candies until finely chopped. In a medium saucepan, combine candies, cream, marshmallows, butter, sugar, and salt over medium-high. Whisk until smooth, 5 minutes. Then, pour mixture through a strainer into bowl with chocolate; let stand 1 minute, then stir until smooth. Pour into baking pan and refrigerate until set, 3 hours. Cut fudge into 1 1/2-inch squares. With a sharp knife, cut 18 candies in half; press a candy half into each square before serving or packing.

Classic Christmas Caramels

Vegetable oil, for baking sheet
2 cups heavy cream
2 1/4 cups sugar
6 tbsp unsalted butter, cut into pieces
1 1/4 cups light corn syrup
1/2 tsp salt
1/2 tsp pure vanilla extract

Lightly brush bottom and sides of a 9-by-13-inch rimmed baking sheet with oil. Line with parchment, leaving a 2-inch overhang on long sides; lightly brush parchment with oil. Bring cream, sugar, butter, and corn syrup to a boil in a large saucepan over high heat, stirring until sugar dissolves. Reduce heat to medium-high; cook, stirring occasionally, until caramel reaches 248 degrees on a candy thermometer, about 15 minutes. Immediately remove caramel from heat, and stir in salt and vanilla. Pour caramel onto baking sheet, and let stand, uncovered, at room temperature at least 8 hours and up to 1 day. Lifting by parchment overhang, transfer caramel to a large cutting board. Cut into 3/4-by-1 1/4-inch pieces; wrap each piece in waxed paper or cellophane.

Snowflake Snack Mix

3 cups bite-size rice square cereal
3 cups bite-size corn square cereal
1 cup small pretzel twists or pretzel sticks
1 cup honey-roasted peanuts
2 12 - ounce packages white baking pieces
1 12 - ounce package mint-flavored candy-coated milk chocolate pieces

In a very large bowl combine cereals, pretzels and peanuts; set aside. Melt baking pieces according to package directions. Pour melted chocolate over cereal mixture. Stir gently to coat. Spread on a large piece of waxed paper or parchment paper. Sprinkle with chocolate pieces. Cool and break into pieces. Store in an airtight container. Present in gift bags or foil lines decorative boxes.

Vegan Truffles

8 ounces dark chocolate, chopped
1/4 cup organic unrefined coconut oil
3 tbsp water
1 tsp pure vanilla extract
Pinch of sea salt
1/4 cup unsweetened cocoa powder, for rolling

Assorted toppings: cocoa powder, finely chopped nuts (pistachios, almonds, hazelnuts), and toasted unsweetened shredded coconut

Melt chocolate with oil and the water. Stir in vanilla and sea salt. Transfer to an 8-inch square baking dish, and refrigerate until mixture is set but still pliable, about 2 hours. With a 1-inch ice-cream scoop, make 28 balls, transferring each one to a parchment-lined baking sheet. Coat hands in cocoa, and roll balls to make smooth. Refrigerate on sheet 10 minutes. (Truffles can be refrigerated in an airtight container up to 2 weeks; let stand at room temperature 30 minutes before coating.) To serve, roll in cocoa or pat with nuts or coconut.

Shortbread Pinwheels

Using any pie crust that has remained from any recipe for pies, roll dough out flat. Slather generously with butter. Sprinkle to taste with sugar, brown sugar, and cinnamon. Roll dough now into a "log." Cut log in ¼ inch or ½ inch slices. Place on greased cookie sheet. Bake at 350 degrees for 15 minutes.

Spirit-Soaked Gifts

Fruitcake doesn't need to be the only spirit-soaked holiday gift. If someone loves martinis, prepare a jar of vermouth-soaked olives. Make some bourbon-drenched cherries for your friend who drinks Manhattans, and she'll never look at a store-bought maraschino the same way again. You can even make a bottle of flavored vodka – try tangerine peel, vanilla and cardamom, or pine and juniper). In pretty Mason jars with a hand written note or sticker, and you'll have a festive presentation.

On the First Day of Christmas my true love gave to me...

A Kuchan with fresh raspberries!
The 12 Desserts of Christmas

Ah, Christmas.

I used to not like the holiday. I'm serious. I wasn't a big fan. For someone who has spent his career in the culinary business and in several restaurants, to me, Christmas was another holiday I had to work when everyone was tucked in bed with visions of sugarplums.

It wasn't until 1999 that I started to enjoy this holiday again. I was actually involved in the publication of a holiday themed cookbook and even went on a short book tour with it – signing copies and giving baking advice over the winter season. And meeting people along the way gave me a renewed faith in the spirit of this season.

Christmas isn't about when you celebrate it. It's about who you celebrate the holiday with. I know for many people – restaurant workers, hospital personnel, safety forces – Christmas can be one of the busiest and even loneliest times of the year. But it doesn't have to be. You can celebrate the holiday on December 24 or December 26. I used to celebrate Thanksgiving the day after because I always worked that holiday. The beauty of that was that I could take leftovers home and the dinner was already prepared. The holidays are about family. And loved ones. The family who are born into and the family you choose. If you think about, the Christmas story itself is about a family.

And so this year, I thought I would give that gift to all of you. I have included in my column this month, my most requested holiday dessert recipes. These are the desserts everyone asks me about every holiday. Some of these dishes appeared in that cookbook I told you about and some have been passed down to me from a few of my favorite people and in my own family.

I also leave you with these thoughts – one of my favorite Irish blessings (also passed down in my family):

"The light of the Christmas star to you
The warmth of home and hearth to you
The joy of a thousand angels to you
Love and God's peace to you."

KEY LIME PIE

4 eggs
1 can sweetened condensed milk
1/3 cup key lime juice
1 tsp cream of tartar
3 tbsp sugar

Beat the yolks of the four eggs and the white of one egg until thick. Add milk. Beat again. Add key lime juice and mix until thick. Pour mixture into a pie shell and set aside. With remaining egg whites, start to beat at high speed with a mixer. Add the cream of tartar and sugar. Beat until fluffy peaks appear. Spoon on top of key lime mixture. Bake at 350 degrees until the top turns golden brown. Chill for several hours before serving.

FAYE'S HARD TACK CANDY

1 ½ cup of sugar
½ cup Karo syrup
¼ cup water

½ tsp flavoring
¼ tsp food coloring

Mix sugar, syrup and water in a medium sauce pan. Cook hard to crack stage. Add flavoring and coloring. Mix well and pour into buttered cast iron skillet. Let cool slightly and then roll into logs and cut into little "pillos" of candies. Sprinkle with powdered sugar to keep the pieces from sticking together.

RUTH'S CARROT PINEAPPLE BREAD

1 cup oil
1 cup sugar
1 cup brown sugar
1 tsp baking soda
1 tsp vanilla
1 tsp salt
2 cups grated carrots
1 cup crushed pineapple, drained
3 eggs
3 cups flour

Beat eggs until bubbly, add sugars and pineapple Beat well. Add carrots and oil. Add vanilla. Sift flour and soda and salt. Add flour mixture one cup at a time. Beat well. Pour into two greased and lightly floured loaf pans. Bake at 55 to 60 minutes at 325 degrees. Test with a tooth pick before allowing to cool slightly.

GRANDMA SHROYER'S COURTIN' FUDGE

Two cups white sugar
1 cup marshmallow cream
2/3 cups whole milk
1 cup peanut butter

Boil sugar and milk to form a soft ball. Remove from heat and add marshmallow cream and peanut butter. Beat until thoroughly blended and it begins to thicken. Pour into buttered or greased pan. Allow to set and then cut pieces into squares with a sharp knife.

KUCHAN

1 cup sugar
2 eggs
1 cup milk
2 cups flour
2 tsp. Baking powder
¼ tsp salt
1 tsp vanilla extract
1 cup whole raspberries or blueberries
1 tbsp butter

Mix sugar with eggs. In a separate bowl, mix together dry ingredients with vanilla. Blend with sugar mixture. Alternate flour mix with milk into a large bowl. Then blend in fruit. Melt butter and set aside. Place batter into an 8x12 inch glass baking dish. Drizzle melted butter over batter. Bake for 60 minutes at 350 degrees. Check with a toothpick at 45 minutes. If toothpick comes out dry (except perhaps for the wet fruit mixture) the cake is finished.

CARAMEL PECAN PIE

36 square caramels
¼ cup water
¼ cup butter
3 eggs
¾ cup sugar
1 tsp. Vanilla extract
1 1/3 cups chopped pecans
1 unbaked pastry pie shell

In a small saucepan, combine the caramels, water and butter. Cook and continue stirring over low heat until caramel squares have melted. Remove from heat. In a mixing bowl, beat eggs, sugar and vanilla. Add caramel mixture. Stir in chopped pecans. Pour into the pastry shell. Bake at 350 degrees for 35 minutes. Cool on a wire rack.

Marjorie's Dump Cake

1 can pie filling (apple, cherry, or peach)
1 can 20 oz. crushed pineapple (do not drain)
1 box yellow cake mix
1 cup crushed walnuts
1 stick butter (cut into pats)

Layer each ingredient as listed in an ungreased 9x14 inch cake pan. Bake at 350 for 55 minutes. Allow to cool just slightly. Serve to guests with whipped cream or ice cream. Offer up a cup of hot coffee and it makes the perfect dessert with friends on the back porn under a starry night.

Diane's Sugar Free Fruit Bars

For grown ups

1 envelope unflavored gelatin
¼ cup water
1 cup dried apricots
1 cup raisins
1 cup pecans or walnuts
1 tbsp flour
2 tbsp orange peel – grated
1 tsp rum extract

Sprinkle gelatin over water. Wait five minutes. Heat and stir until gelatin is dissolved. Combine the other ingredients. Add rum extract and stir until completely blended. Line an 8-inch square pan with waxed or parchment paper. Spread mixture evenly on paper and set aside to cool until candy is fir. Cut into squares or break into pieces and serve.

CRAN-ORANGE NUT PIE

12 ounces fresh cranberries
1 cup water
1 cup sugar
1 tsp orange rind
¼ cup orange juice concentrate
¼ cup walnuts
cinnamon and nutmeg to taste
2 tbsp cornstarch
1 ½ tbsp water

Pastry pie shell – baked according to directions

Boil cranberries, cup of water and sugar until cranberries pop. Add orange rind and orange juice to mixture. On the side, mix cornstarch with 1 ½ tbs of water until runny and then add to cranberry mixture until thick and binding. Pour mixture into pie shell. Refrigerate 2 hour or overnight until mixture firms. Serve with an orange twist garnish

The 20 Cookies of Christmas

*The Best of Grandma's Christmas
Cookies Volumes One and Two*

The year marks my 20th anniversary as a food writer. Back in 2000, a newspaper in Ohio asked me if I would be interested in being a food columnist for them. I said yes. That same year, that same newspaper then thought it would be a great idea to publish a cookbook full of reader submitted holiday recipes and they enlisted my help as a sort-of culinary editor, double checking all the entries. That little publication – later developed into a book called Grandma's Christmas Cookies. Volume One was released as a collection in 2000 and a second volume was published independently of that newspaper in 2002. To celebrate my 20th anniversary as a culinary contributor, and the 20th anniversary of my very first cookbook being released, I thought it was more than fitting to present 20 cookie recipes, some which were first featured in the Grandma's Christmas Cookies cookbooks and some that are just favorites of mine. Happy Baking and Happy Holidays!

CHOCOLATE MACAROONS

½ cup vegetable oil
4 squares unsweetened chocolate melted
2 cups sugar
4 eggs
2 tsp vanilla
2 cups flour
2 tsp baking powder
Powdered sugar for dusting

Combine oil, chocolate and sugar. Stir. Mix in one egg at a time, blending well after each egg. Add vanilla, flour and baking powder. Chill overnight for best results. Roll into balls and then roll in powdered sugar. Do not press or flatten. Bale at 350 degrees for 10 minutes.

ANNA K'S PEANUT BUTTER COOKIES

½ cup shortening
½ cup creamy peanut butter
1 cup brown sugar
1 egg well beaten
1 ¼ cup flour
½ tsp salt
½ tsp baking soda
½ tsp vanilla

Mix peanut butter, shortening, sugar and egg. Beat well. Sift flour, salt and soda together. Add vanilla. Then add to peanut butter mixture and stir until creamy. Pinch off small amounts, roll into balls, place on greased cookie sheet and score with a fork. Bake in preheated oven at 350 degrees for 10 minutes.

Teri's No Bake Cookies

1 cup sugar
2 heaping teaspoons of powdered cocoa
1/3 cup milk
1/3 cup butter

Place all the ingredients in a sauce pan, bring to boil, stirring frequently. Boil for two minutes then remove from heat and quickly add the following:

¼ cup peanut butter
1 ½ cup quick Oats

Stir well. Drop on wax paper with tablespoons. Allow to cool.

Aunt Ruth's Oatmeal Crunchies

1 cup butter or margarine
1 cup brown sugar (firmly packed)
2 eggs
2 tsp vanilla
1 ½ cup flour
1 tsp baking soda
1 tbsp baking powder
1 cup granulated sugar
Pinch of salt
½ cup chopped nuts
1 cup uncooked oatmeal

Cream first four ingredients. With the exception of the cup of sugar, add in dry ingredients in the order they are listed. Mix well. Roll into balls. Dip in sugar then press tops slightly with a fork. Back at 350 degrees for 10 to 12 minutes.

Nutty Diamond Cookies

1 cup flour
½ cup sugar
½ cup cold butter (divided)
½ cup packed brown sugar
2 tbsp honey
¼ cup whipped cream
2/3 cup each of crushed almonds, walnuts, and pecans

Line a greased 9 inch square baking dish with foil. Grease the foil and set aside. In a bowl combine the flour and sugar. Cut in ¼ cup butter until mixture is crumbly. Press into prepared baking dish. Bake at 350 degrees for 10 minutes. While this is baking, in a saucepan, heat the brown sugar, honey, and remaining butter until bubbly. Boil for one minute. Remove from heat and stir in whipped cream and nuts. Remove cookies from oven. Pour separate mixture over cookies. Bake at 350 degrees for 15 minutes or until surface appears to bubble. Allow to completely cool on a wire rack. Refrigerate overnight. Using the foil, lift the bars from the pan and cut into the shape of diamonds

Christmas Angel Cookies

1 ½ cup shortening
½ tsp baking soda
½ cup cream cheese, softened
½ tsp salt
1 cup light brown sugar, firmly packed
1 tbsp vanilla
½ cup granulated sugar
2 cups candied fruit, mixed
2 eggs
2 cups broken or crushed pecans or almonds
3 cups flour

Preheat oven to 350 degrees. In a large bowl, cream shortening and cream cheese until smooth and fluffy. Add sugar and eggs, mixing well. In a separate bowl, sift flour, baking soda and salt. Add flour mixture to egg and sugar mixture. Ad in vanilla. Mix well. Add candied fruit and nuts. Drop by rounded spoonfuls onto lightly greased cookie sheet and bake for 10 to 12 minutes.

BUTTER COOKIES

8 cups flour
12 egg yolks
2 cups sugar
1 lb. butter
½ lb. margarine
Rind of 2 lemons
½ tsp lemon juice

Mix all ingredients in order. Roll on floured cutting board. Cut with cookie cutters into desired shapes. Bake at 350 degrees or until edges become golden brown. Decorate with sprinkles and icing.

LEMON CHEESECAKE COOKIES

1 cup butter, softened
3 ounces cream cheese, softened
1 cup sugar
1 egg
1 tsp grated lemon peel
1 tbsp lemon juice
1 ½ cups flour
1 tsp baking powder

Cream butter, cheese and sugar until fluffy. Blend in remaining ingredients. Cover and chill for one hour. Preheat oven to 375 degrees. Fill cookie press with ¼ of dough at aa time. Form desired shapes on ungreased cookie sheet. Bake for 8-10 minutes or until edges are slightly browned.

Perfect Sugar Cookies

For the Cookie Dough:

3 cups. all-purpose flour, plus more for surface
1 tsp. baking powder
1/2 tsp. salt
1 cup butter, softened
1 cup granulated sugar
1 large egg
1 tsp. pure vanilla extract
1 tbsp. milk

For the frosting:

1 cup butter, softened
5 cups powdered sugar
1/4 cup heavy cream
1/2 tsp. pure almond extract
1/4 tsp. salt
Food coloring

In a large bowl, whisk together flour, baking powder, and salt and set aside.

In another large bowl, beat butter and sugar until fluffy and pale in color. Add egg, milk, and vanilla and beat until combined, then add flour mixture gradually until totally combined.

Shape into a disk and wrap in plastic. Refrigerate 1 hour. When ready to roll, preheat oven to 350º and line two baking sheets with parchment paper. Lightly flour a clean work surface and roll out dough until 1/8" thick. Cut out shapes and transfer to prepared baking sheets. Freeze 10 minutes. Meanwhile, make frosting: In a large bowl using a hand mixer, beat butter until smooth, then add powdered sugar and beat until no lumps remain. Add cream, almond extract, and salt and beat until combined. Bake cookies until edges are lightly golden, 8 to 10 minutes. Allow to cool and then frost and decorate.

Pumpkin Bars

2 cups flour
2 cups sugar
2 tsp baking powder
1 tsp baking soda
1 tsp cinnamon
1 tsp nutmeg
½ tsp salt
1 cup vegetable or olive oil
1 (16 oz) can pumpkin filling
4 eggs

In a bowl, combine all the ingredients. Mix well. Bake in a greased 12x18 pan at 35 degrees for 25 to 30 minutes. Cool to room temperature and cut into bars.

Oatmeal Raisin Cookies

1 cup butter, softened
1 cup firmly packed brown sugar
½ cup granulated sugar
2 eggs
1 tsp vanilla
1 ½ cups all purpose flour
1 tsp baking soda
1 tsp cinnamon
½ tsp salt
3 cups quick oats, uncooked
1 cup raisins

Preheat oven to 350 degrees. Beat together butter and sugars until creamy. Add eggs and vanilla and blend together. Add flour, baking soda, cinnamon and salt. Mix well. Stir in oats and raisins. Drop by rounded teaspoons onto ungreased cookie sheet. Bake 10-12 minutes or until golden brown. Cool for at least one minute.

Nutter Butter Snowmen

1 package Nutter Butter cookies
1 ¼ pounds white chocolate
16 ounces miniature chocolate chips
16 ounces M&M candies
Small pretzel sticks

Melt but do not boil white chocolate on a stovetop. Using tongs, dip cookies in melted white chocolate. Place on waxed paper. Place two chocolate chips on one end of cookies for eyes. Place M&Ms on center to resemble buttons. Stick broken pieces into the sides of the cookies to resemble arms. Allow to cool and harden.

Potato Candy

2 tbsp cooked and mashed potatoes
1 tbsp butter
1 tsp milk
½ cup confectioners sugar
½ tsp vanilla extract
1 cup peanut butter

Mix together potatoes, butter, milk and vanilla. Add enough powdered or confectioners sugar to make dough stiff. Roll out on a flat surface sprinkled with more powdered sugar. Spread on peanut butter and roll. Chill and slice.

Crème Brulee Cookies

3/4 cup butter, softened
1/2 cup packed brown sugar
1/2 cup granulated sugar
1 large egg
1 tbsp pure vanilla extract
2 cup all-purpose flour

2 tsp cornstarch
1 tsp baking soda
1/4 tsp salt

For the Frosting:

1 (8-oz.) block cream cheese, softened
1 1/4 cup. powdered sugar
1 tsp. pure vanilla extract
1/4 cup granulated sugar

Preheat oven to 350° and line two cookie sheets with parchment. Cream butter and sugars until light and fluffy, 3 to 4 minutes. Mix in egg and vanilla.

In another bowl, whisk together flour, cornstarch, baking soda, and salt, then add mixture to wet ingredients and mix until smooth. Dough will be thick.

Using a small cookie scoop, place tablespoon balls of dough onto parchment-lined cookie sheets. Press down lightly on each cookie to flatten slightly. Bake until edges are just starting to brown, 9 to 10 minutes.

Remove from oven and let cool 2 to 3 minutes, then transfer to a cooling rack to cool completely.

Make frosting: Beat cream cheese until smooth. Add powdered sugar and vanilla and mix until smooth.

Put sugar into a small bowl. Spread about a tablespoon of frosting onto tops of each cookie, then press into granulated sugar, coating frosting with sugar.

Just before serving, use a kitchen torch to caramelize sugar on top, then set aside to cool.

RED AND WHITE CHRISTMAS COOKIES

1 jar maraschino cherries, drained and chopped
½ cup shortening
1 cup sugar
2 eggs
2 tbsp milk
1 tsp vanilla
2 ½ cups flour
¼ tsp baking soda
½ tsp salt

Mix ingredients 2-6. Then add in ingredients 7-9. Then add cherries. Fold and drop mixture by rounded teaspoons onto a greased cookie sheet. Bake for 8-10 minutes at 350 degrees. Do not allow cookies to brown. When cookies have cooled, dust with powdered sugar.

CHRISTMAS TEA COOKIES

1 cup butter, softened
½ cup powdered sugar
1 ½ tsp vanilla extract
2 cups flour
1 dash of salt
1 dash of baking powder
¾ cups pecans, finely chopped
Powdered sugar for dusting

In a large bowl, beat together butter and powdered ½ cup powdered sugar, until smooth and creamy. Add vanilla. Blend together flour, salt and baking powder. Add flour mix to butter mix and blend together. Add the nuts and combine well. Roll out dough into balls. Wrap in plastic wrap and chill for at least one hour. Flatten dough and cut into equal pieces. Bake at 375 degrees for 1-12 minutes or until golden. While still warm, dust with powdered sugar. Let cool.

Traditional Ginger Bread Men

1 cup shortening
1 cup granulated sugar
½ tsp salt
1 egg
1 cup molasses
2 tbsp vinegar
5 cups all purpose flour
1 ½ tsp baking soda
1 tsp ground ginger
1 tsp cinnamon
1 tsp ground cloves

Cream shortening, sugar and salt. Stir in egg, molasses and vinegar. Beat well. Stir together with the remainder of the dry ingredients. Then add the molasses mixture and stir well. Chill for at least two hours. Then roll rough onto lightly floured surface to a thickness of about 1/8th of an inch. Cut with cookie cutters. Place cookies 1 inch apart on greased cookie sheet. Preheat oven to 375 degrees. Make eyes and buttons with raisins. Bake for 6 minutes. Allow to cool.

Holiday Rum Balls

1 cup powdered sugar
2 tbsp cocoa
2 ½ crushed vanilla wafers
1 cup finely chopped pecans
2 tsp vanilla
3 tbsp light corn syrup
3 tbsp dark rum
¼ tsp almond extract

Sift cocoa and sugar together and combine with cookie crumbs and pecans. Add corn syrup, rum and extract. Roll into 1 inch balls then roll in powdered sugar. Store in a tightly sealed container and refrigerate until ready to serve.

JEWEL FUDGE

3 (6 oz) packages of white chocolate chips
1 (14 oz) can of sweetened condensed milk (not evaporated)
1 ½ tsp vanilla
1/8 tsp salt
½ cup chopped green candied cherries
½ cup chopped red candied cherries

Over low heat, melt white chocolate with milk, vanilla and salt. Remove from heat once chocolate is melted. Stir in cherries. Spread mixture into a foil lined 8x9 inch square baking pan. Chill for two hours or until candy is firm. Turn fudge onto cutting board, peel from foil and cut into squares

SNEEBALLE

This is a very easy to make treat that actually originated, I am told, in the city of Rottenberg, Germany. Bakers did not believe in wasting any scraps of food when this recipe is said to have originated more than 300 years ago. So, when bakers baked pies they would take all the scraps from the pie dough, roll them into small softball shapes (hence, sneeballe) and then cut them into thin strips. Bake the strips until golden brown, brush lightly with melted butter and roll in powdered sugar. You can also dip them in melted chocolate and then roll them in crushed nuts.

Talk to the Hand

Some of my most popular Q&As

Q Dear Chef Hand

How do you cook liver without getting it so tough?

Kathy Gaines

A Dear Kathy

I am going to assume you are talking about beef liver – and not some weird Silence of the Lambs with Fava Beans scenario. You need to sauté slowly over medium heat in butter or bacon fat. If bacon fat is used, serve the liver with bacon. Do not cook well done. Cook medium to medium well depending on the thickness of the liver. 2 to 2 ½ minutes per side. Layer with grilled onions and serve. For a liver recipe that veers a little from the ordinary, consider the following recipe and let me know how it turns out for you.

LIVER SHANG HAI STYLE

1 lb. calf's liver, thinly sliced
½ tsp salt
2 tsp brown sugar
2 tsp corn starch
2 tsp cooking sherry
2 tbsp soy sauce
3 tbsp oil

4 scallions with tops (chopped)
1 tsp chopped ginger root
¼ cup chicken stock

Directions: Place liver in a bowl. Sprinkle with salt., sugar, corn starch, sherry, and soy sauce. Heat oil in a skillet. Fry scallions, stirring rapidly for one minute. Add ginger and stir fry for one minute more, taking care not to burn. Next, add the liver and fry for two minutes, stirring constantly. Gradually add stock and lower flame. Simmer over gentle heat for one to two minutes, or until the sauce in the pan has thickened. Serve at once.

Q Dear Chef Hand

How can I cook white boneless chicken breast or the white meat of chicken so the meat doesn't end up dry when it's done? I like it tender and juicy

M. Dyar

A Dearest M

What I tend to do is marinate the boneless chicken breast in olive oil and spices, orange juice, lemon juice or white wine. Marinate in a dish in your refrigerator overnight. Place in a casserole dish the next day and bake at 350 degrees for about 35 minutes – covered. Take the cover off and allow the sauce to reduce the flavors and blend for about 10 to 15 minutes until the chicken is done but not overdone. Pick meat with a knife. If the liquid runs clear, the meat is done and ready to serve. Since you like chicken, try this dish. It's mmmm mmmm good, M.

PABLONA CHICKEN WITH PEPPERCORNS

4 boneless chicken breasts cut
2 Pablona peppers or mild peppers – diced
2 ounces of crushed, cracked peppercorns
¼ cup white wine

1 bunch of cilantro
2 cups heavy cream
4 tbsp of butter
Pinch of salt
Half red onion – diced
1 lime
¼ cup grated parmesan cheese
Enough pasta for four hungry people

Heat skillet and melt butter in it. Sauté chicken in the butter. Cook for four to five minutes until chicken starts firming. Add peppers and red onion and sauté until they wilt. Add peppercorns and wine to mixture. Cook for one more minute. Serve over pasta.

Q Dear William

My good friend, Dan, had a birthday last week and I missed it. What sort of dish would I make for him that would be "special" enough to make up for my forgetfulness?

S. Smith

A S Smith,

First, shame on you. Personally, myself, I tend to believe that oysters can make a romantic dish – if this is what you mean by "special" and Dan would probably forget for the moment how old he turned this year. Plus, there's the common belief that oysters are good for the libido and could have a different effect – but I am not making any medical claims or promises. Good luck making it up to your "friend." Try this recipe and email me again with the results. And happy belated birthday to Dan.

OYSTERS ROCKEFELLER

24 oysters on the half shell
½ package washed spinach, minced
½ cup bread crumbs
½ cup grated Parmesan cheese
½ cup butter melted
1 dash Worcestershire sauce
2 tbsp cooking sherry
¼ cup chopped onion
4 sprigs parsley, minced
Salt and pepper to taste
Rock salt

Mix ¾ cups of the spinach, crumbs and cheese. Pour mixture over melted butter, Add seasonings, onion and parsley and mix well. Spread mixture over oysters. Lay oysters into rock salt and bake in oven at 500 degrees for about eight minutes or until brown on top. Serve at once.

Note: The oysters broil in less than six minutes but the rock salt has to be hot before you put the shells on it. So allow 10 minutes to get salt hot in the oven in a shallow pan.

Q Dear Chef Hand

What is the best way to prepare pork chops?

Donna Andrews

A Oh Donna...oh Donna

I tend to soak my pork chops in olive oil, garlic and either teriyaki or balsamic vinegar. Soak overnight. I like to grill pork chops but pork chops can also be baked. Try 35 minutes at 350 degrees. Be sure to bake in the marinade. By the way, I hear pork chops were a favorite dish of Richie Valens, who sang "Oh Donna." Any connection?

Q Dear Bill

Do you happen to have a recipe for something called Hot Bacon Dressing?

Mary David

A Dear Mary

Oh yes. Yes I do. And I get asked for this recipe quite often. When I got your email, I thought for my old job at the World War II themed restaurant in Ohio where the dressing was made by the gallons. Gallons! I spoke with the owner and he was kind enough to grant me permission to share the recipe with you and readers. We tended to make the dressing in six gallon increments and I am assuming you don't need that much so I had to put my math skills to use to pare it down a bit for you.

HOT BACON DRESSING

Courtesy Bob Scofield/356th Fighter Group

1 pound bacon
1 tsp garlic
¼ lb onions
1 1/3 cup red wine vinegar
¼ lb. brown sugar
1/8 tsp salt
1/6 tsp oregano
1/8 tsp basil
1 1/3 cup water
¼ cup corn starch

Grind and cook bacon until nearly crisp. Drain excess fat. Add garlic and onions. Sauté until onions become translucent. Add vinegar, brown sugar, oregano, basil and one cup of the water. Reserve the last 1/3 cup of water to dilute the corn starch that will slightly thicken the dressing when added.

Bring mixture to a boil and add the corn starch and water solution. Whip briskly to avoid lumping. Serve while hot over greens or garden salad.

Q Dear William

My Mom helps me cook dinner once every week. This week, I don't know what to cook. I am 11 years old. So I can't cook anything too fancy. Do you have any ideas?

Samantha Brown

A: Dear Samantha

Allow me to quote the Beatles when I say "Mrs. Brown, you have a lovely daughter." I am sure you are much too young to understand that reference but I am sure your Mother will. This is a nice dish you could try – chicken caccatori. It is very simple to make but has a fancy name. All you need is a casserole dish and a sauté pan to cook it in and some minimal help from your mother. She will need to julienne (cut) the vegetables in this but I think you can do it. You family should enjoy it and you will enjoy that time in the kitchen with Mom.

CHICKEN CACCATORI

2 chickens – cut into serving pieces
1 pound fresh mushroom caps
1 red pepper
3 to 4 cloves of garlic
1 14 oz. cans of stewed tomatoes
2 cups flour
1 tsp basil
1 tsp oregano
Salt and pepper
1 cup vegetable oil

Wash and dry the chicken pieces. Season the chicken with salt and pepper and set aside. Heat skillet with the oil. Next, dredge the chicken through the flour and lightly brown the chicken in the skillet on both sides. Heat your Mom's oven to 350. While waiting for the oven to heat, you go set a lovely table and ask your mom to julienne the peppers, mince the garlic and slice the mushrooms for you with the sharpest knife she has. When your Moms is finished and calls you back into the kitchen, combine all the ingredients together with the tomatoes and put in a covered casserole dish and bake at 350 degrees for one hour. Serve with a side of rice and green beans for dinner.

Q Dear Chef Hand

I am due for a raise at work next week. Would you please provide me with a recipe to help me "butter" up the boss? By the way, I think your columns every week are great.

H Jaber

A Thanks, H.

H is one of my favorite letters of the alphabet. Add an And to it and you got my last name. At any rate, try these simple Buttery Scotch Shortbread Cookies. They just might do the trick. Present them in a nice box that is lined with letters of recommendation on your behalf and see if you get your just….desserts.

BUTTERY SCOTCH SHORTBREAD COOKIES

1 cup sweet butter
1/3 cup powdered sugar
2 cups flour
¼ tsp baking powder
¼ tsp salt

Soften butter. Add sugar gradually. Add flour sifted with baking powder and salt. Roll shape and decorate with icing or sprinkles. Or both. Bake 20 to 25 minutes at 350 or until delicate and brown.

Q Chef Bill

What is the best way to prepare squid?

J. Lynn

A: Dear J

Ahoy Matey….a real challenge. The best way to prepare squid is not something I get asked with much frequency since fresh squid is not something I just have lying around in my refrigerator. I usually save my suction cups to hold up my holiday decorations on my patio door. But, I was able to wrap my tentacles around this recipe that has worked for me before.

SQUID

2 pounds very small squid, cleaned
5 tbsp olive oil
4 tbsp butter
Salt
Freshly ground black pepper
Cayenne pepper to taste
¼ cup Brandy
3 shallots minced
1 onion minced
3 carrots minced
1 sweet pepper peeled and minced
1 clove garlic minced
6 tomatoes, peeled seeded and chopped
1 bouquet of garni (bay leaf, thyme and parsley tied together at the stems like a floral bouquet)

3 cups hot cooked rice
Pimento strips

In a casserole, heat together 3 tablespoons of the oil and 2 tablespoons of the butter and cook the pieces of squid in it until golden brown. Season lightly with the brandy and then ignite. Pour the squid and the pain juice into a bowl and reserve.

Put the remaining oil and butter into the casserole with the shallots, onions, carrots, sweet peppers and garlic. Cook the vegetables over the lowest possible heat until they are so tender as to almost a puree. Add the tomatoes, the garni and the squid with the pan juices. Cover and simmer over low heat for 20 minutes. Butter a ring mold and fill it with hot rice. Unmold the rice on a serving dish and fill the empty center with the squid. Garnish with pimento strips.

Q Dear Bill

I am looking for ways to change regular recipes into sugar free recipes. I have not been able to figure out when to tell if the sugar is part of the "bulk" of the recipe or if changing it would be okay. Are there any "rules" to follow?

Diana Parker

A Dear Diana

Thanks very much for the question. And to answer it, you can always substitute fruit juices in your recipes – like white grape or apple juice and some citrus juices – in sauces, for instance. You can also use honey but keep in mind that you are still using a form of sugar if you use honey. As a rule of thumb, ¾ cup of honey can replace one cup of sugar in a recipe. You can also use sugar substitutes – like Sweet N'Low or Equal – both of which are available at local supermarkets in bulk amounts. And the last alternative – simply cut back on the sugar called for in the "bulk" recipe. In most recipes that call for sugar, you can reduce the amount 1/3 or even ½. You might be surprised how good some baked items taste with half the sugar content. By the way, Diana, not only does the sugar add the sweetness, it also adds most of the calories.

Q Dear Chef Hand

A few health related questions for you…I love muffins but I can't seem to find a good recipe for low fat low-cal muffins. Any tips or suggestions? Is it acceptable to replace vegetable oil with apple sauce? Can you offer any guidance?

Dan C.

A Dear Dan

Usually, it is acceptable to substitute applesauce for oil in muffin recipes. But I would actually suggest adding some oil to muffins because you do need the moisture. I would advise that instead of a vegetable oil, use a non saturated oil like safflower or canola. I would not recommend olive oil, however, in any kind of baking because the taste is too heavy.

Low calories usually means low sugar content. I think the body does need some forms of sugar. Like most things you enjoy, however, too much of a good thing can lead to trouble.

With that said, I am a professional in the kitchen and not in the medical field, so talk to your doctor about any health related issues your diet is causing you. You could have allergies to think I am recommending. But in the meantime, here is a tasty low cal and low sugar recipe that might take the edge off.

Banana Yogurt Pancakes

2 cups sifted flour
1 tsp sugar substitute

1 tbsp baking soda
A large banana, mashed (the more brown spots the better)
½ cup skim milk
½ tbsp safflower or canola oil
1 tsp vanilla extract
4 egg whites, beaten
8 ounces fat free plain yogurt

Combine the flour, sugar substitute, and soda in a large bowl. Add yogurt, banana, milk, oil, and vanilla. Stir until moist. Gently fold in egg whites. Use batter as you normally would to make pancakes on a griddle or skillet. Cook one side until bubbles come to the top of the cakes. Flip and cook the other side until the cake edges are browned.

Q Chef Hand

What exactly is an egg plant? Do you peel the skin off when you cook it? And do you have a good recipe for it?

Shelly L

A Dear Shelly,

Eggplant is more plant than egg. It is simply a garden variety fruit. Yes, since it grows on a vine it is a member of the fruit family – in the same way that a tomato is a fruit. However, the egg plant can be the most colorful attraction in your garden because when it is healthy and ripe, it is has the most distinct color of purple. It got its name, however, because it is shaped like an egg on the vine when it grows.

BAKED EGG PLANT

One large egg plant
Dash of salt
2 onions – diced

3 cloves of garlic
½ cup olive oil
½ cup butter
½ tomato sauce
½ cup white wine
½ cup parsley
1 pound grated Fontina cheese
2 cups white sauce (see companion recipe that follows)
4 eggs beaten
1 cup grated Parmesan cheese

Cut egg plant in ½ inch slices. Sprinkle with salt. Let stand for 20 minutes. Drain liquid. Bake eggplant on greased cookie sheet for 10 minutes at 350 degrees. Sauté onions and garlic in some oil and butter. Add parsley, tomato sauce and wine. When heated, remove from stove and gradually add Fontina cheese. Grease casserole dish. Brush layers of eggplant with oil and sandwich filling between the layers of eggplant. Pour basic white sauce over eggplant. Sprinkle with parmesan and bake for an additional 350 degrees for one hour.

Basic White Sauce

2 tbsp butter
2 tbsp flour
1 cup heated milk
Salt and pepper

Melt butter. Add flour. Cook mixture in pan over stove top for a few minutes so the flour is not "raw tasting." Add milk to mixture ¼ cup at a time. Stir constantly to prevent burning. Season with salt and pepper.

Q Dear Bill

Do you happen to have a good recipe for Crab Imperial sauce? I have tried several recipes and none of them seem to turn out with the "restaurant quality." Is it something I am doing or just something I could do better? Is there an easy recipe for this dish and do you have any "short cuts?"

Wendy B

A Dear Wendy

The reason you probably have not had a good "Crab Imperial" and you can't get yours to match the "restaurant quality" may be an arithmetic problem. When restaurants make it, they make a lot of it so trying to get a recipe of that quality may be a matter of narrowing down the quantity of it and reducing the recipe one ingredient at a time to fit the number of people around your dinner table. The following is a restaurant recipe for the dish, already fragmented and ready to make at home. Let me know how it turns out!

CRAB IMPERIAL

½ tsp thyme
1 bay leaf
1/8 tsp dry mustard
1 ½ tbl dry sherry
2 tsp lemon juice
1/8 tsp Tabasco
1/8 tsp Worcester sauce
¼ cup clam juice

Add all of those ingredients one at a time to a basic white sauce…. The recipe for that is a page of two back.

The sauté the following:

½ medium onion minced
5 button mushrooms sliced
3 cloves of garlic – minced
½ sweet red pepper

After sauté, add to sauce mixture and then add:
¼ tsp pepper
2/3 cup Parmesan cheese – grated
Salt and pepper to taste

Have crab meat ready and prepared according to specifications in individual casserole dishes and then pour the sauce over the crab meat. Top with Julienne red pepper and red onion. Bake in the oven at 350 for 10 minutes and then to give the dishes a browning touch, put them in the broiler for just a few minutes to create a crust.

Q Dear Chef Hand

Every time I make pecan pie, the bottom of the crust in the pie pan forms a huge bubble. When I use a glass pan, I can see the bubble from the bottom. What causes this and how can I prevent it?

Theresa P

A Dear T.P.

The "bubble" in the pan is probably caused by moisture that gathers in the pan and gets "stuck" under the crust during baking. Because that air pocket has no place to go, it forms that bubble in your crust. To prevent this, you will need to vent the crust with a fork by poking a few holes in the bottom – not so much that your filling will seep out, however. But enough that it will allow your crust to "breathe" during baking. Or you could prebake the crust slightly before you put in the pecan filling. That should do the trick. Or you could simply keep the bubble in and show your guests before serving. A bubble always makes for an interesting conversation starter.

Since you seem to be a fan of pecans, I have enclosed a recipe for you to try. Best of all, this suggestion comes with no unsightly bulges—in the bottom of your pie pan, that is.

No "Bubble" Pecan Nut Balls

3 cups sugar
1 cup cream
1 cup chopped pecans
¼ cup corn syrup

Mix all of the above ingredients (with the exception of the pecans) in a pan and stir. Cook on high heat and continue to stir, keeping the side of the pan wet with a pastry brush. When mixture begins to boil, cease stirring and turn the heat to medium. Cook until the mixture begins to thicken. Remove from heat. Pour into a platter and let cool. Remove mixture from platter and shape into "balls" for serving.

Sugar and Spice Pecans

1/4 cup butter
3 cups pecan halves
½ cup sugar
3 tbsp sugar
1 tsp cinnamon
½ tsp ginger
½ tsp nutmeg

In a 10 inch skillet, melt the butter. Stir in the pecans and ½ cup of the sugar. Stir mixture until the sugar melts and the pecans begin to brown (about eight minutes). Combine all the ingredients and coat pecans with it. Spread our wax paper and empty contents of skillet onto it. Allow to cool and serve.

Q Dear William

Your "What's Cooking" newspaper column is great. I love those recipes as they are simple and that is for me. Any more than five steps or ingredients and I lose interest. Your recipes could become favorites that everyone can follow and make. Keep up the great work and the interesting information.

Carla Z.

A Thanks Carla

What I find interesting about your email to me is that it didn't contain a question. But I was so honored and humbled by your kind words that I am giving you a couple of recipes anyway. Since I noticed from your message to me that you live in Pennsylvania, I thought you might find it interesting (or even amusing) that your state is home to many interesting firsts in history. For instance, did you know Pennsylvania shaped not only the nation itself but it is also home to the circus, number two pencils, cable cars, libraries, Little League baseball, motion picture theatres, Mr. Rogers, commercial radio and interestingly enough – weekly newspapers.

Culinarily speaking (if that is a phrase – if it's not, I just invented it), Pennsylvania is the home of root beer, ice cream sodas and the pretzel. And since you said you like recipes short on ingredients, I have a couple of easy ideas for you – items that started in your own backyard.

ORIGINAL ROOT BEER FLOAT

Two scoops vanilla ice cream
Your favorite brand of root beer

Large mouth 16 oz glass mug, chilled overnight in the freeze. Place two scoops of ice cream in the chilled mug. Pour root beer over top of ice cream until mug is full and ice cream "stands" at the top forming a mound. Place two spoons and two straws in the mug and invite a favorite someone over to the stool next to you at the counter. Play some oldies in the background.

Old Fashioned Homemade Pretzels

1 packet active dry yeast
1 tbsp honey or sugar
1 ½ cups warm water
1 tbsp oil
1 tsp salt
2 cups whole wheat flour
2 cups unbleached flour
½ cup butter melted

In a large bowl, mix the yeast and honey with the warm water. Let the mixture sit for about five minutes. Stir in the oil, salt, whole wheat flour and unbleached flour. Mix with hands and turn out dough onto a lightly floured cutting board and knead the dough for about 10 minutes, or until dough is smooth but just a little tacky to the touch.

Grease a cookie sheet. Preheat oven to 425 degrees. Form dough into "ropes" and shape into pretzel forms. Keep pretzels about 1 inch apart when placing on the baking sheet.

Coat or brush with butter. Sprinkle with pretzel salt and bake in oven for 15 to 20 minutes or until pretzels appear browned to your liking and well done.

Q Dear William

I love your column. Kudos. I also have a copy of your book "Grandma's Christmas Cookies." It has been truly inspirational. I am one of those people who reads cookbooks for pleasure and I am sure I am not the only person who can curl up with a good cookbook. I would like to see you put out a cookbook sometime full of romantic meals. But, on to my questions – I am the busy mother of teenagers, also employed outside the home. I need ideas for fast meals that even picky teenaged girls will eat. Next question – other than good pots and pans – what is your favorite kitchen "gadget?"

Beth R.

A Dear Beth

Let me answer your questions in reverse order. The favorite gadget in my kitchen is my commercial sized mixture. I can't really say the name here but let me just say in the room where I use it most it has become quite the "Aid." I actually have two – a yellow one and a red one. The yellow one burned out and it was the best looking paperwork I had until a former student said he could fit and got it up and running again. With proper attachments and a handy splash guard, you can do a multitude of things from elaborate cakes, dressings, cookies, and restaurant style cheesecakes. With other accessories added on, you can make fluffy meringues, grind meats, shred carrots, and even make your own ice cream.

Now, on to your second question, every teenager is picky. Remember, you were one of them once. Did you ever, for instance, refuse to eat a sandwich unless your mother cut off the crust? This suggested Orange Roughie may work, depending on whether your girls have other plans for dinner. (Don't let the boy just honk the horn. Make him come in…and invite him to dinner – the fish won't be the other item grilled that night!_

Best of luck. Now go take this book and curl up somewhere cozy with it. Send me a picture.

Easy Orange Roughie

4 nice pieces Orange Roughie Fish Filets
(But to be honest, any nice piece of white fish will do)
2 to 3 tbsp olive oil
Lemon pepper to taste
Black pepper to taste
Four cloves of garlic – minced fine
Fresh lemon juice

Season fish with garlic and peppers. While heating skillet on high heat, go ahead and place the fish in the pain and allow the spices to soak. Cover pan for about two minutes. Reduce heat to medium. Cook fish about three minutes per side or until done. Fish will flake with a fork when done.

Squeeze lemon juice over the fish when it is finished but still in the pan. I would suggest topping this with the following "Hand" Marinara sauce – my very own recipe.

"Hand" Marinara

4 cloves garlic – minced
10 to 12 Roma tomatoes – diced
½ stick of butter
Salt and pepper to taste
Fresh basil – four leaves – minced

Melt butter in sauce pan over medium heat. Add garlic, tomatoes, salt and pepper. Stir well. Cook until tomatoes begin to "juice" (about 8 minutes). Add basil. Serve on top of fish, pasta, or chicken.

Q Dear Chef Hand

Do you have any good recipes for Chicken Quesadillas that wouldn't be too spicy?

S. Andrews

Q Dear Bill

Would you happen to have any good recipes for hot to mild salsa?

Wendy P.

A Dear S. and P (ha-ha),

Your questions arrived at the same time – oddly and so I thought I would answer them at the same time. Yes…yes I do. And here you go. Let me know how these work out for you. And invite me over next Cinco De Mayo, will ya?

QUICK QUESADILLAS

Package of prepared flour tortillas
Jack and Cheddar cheese – shredded
Sautéed or grilled chicken – cut into pieces
Green onion – chopped or cut into pieces
Cilantro – a bunch
Banana peppers
Tomatoes – diced
Maria's salsa (see following recipe)

I like to prepare my quesadillas in a cast iron skillet for an authentic taste. Heat skillet dry. Place tortilla in skillet. Place all ingredients inside flat tortilla. As cheese begins to melt, flip one side of the tortilla over. Remove from heat. Garnish with sour cream or Guacamole.

MARIA'S SALSA

Tomatoes – diced
Onions
Cilantro
Lemon juice
Lime juice
Jalapeno peppers
Salt

Cut peppers in half. You might wish to wear rubber gloves because pepper oil can burn and anything you touch will also burn. It's worse than cooking bacon naked, trust me on that. De-seed the peppers. Mince peppers. Set aside, separately. Mince onions. Set aside, separately. Add tomatoes to onions. Sprinkle with salt. The salt will draw the juices out. Add cilantro to taste. Squeeze juice into mixture to taste. Add peppers a little at a time until you like it. Chill and serve.

Q Dear Chef Hand

I just found your column in my local newspaper and I love it. Will you be doing this question and answer format all the time? I do have a few quick questions for you – how do you keep a Bundt cake from sticking to the bottom of the pan? Also, besides hamburgers and hot dogs, what's your favorite item for the grill? While I have your attention, is there a substitute for vinegar in a recipe? And finally – I know I have asked a lot of questions but how can I clean my good cooking pans without scratching off the protective coating? Thanks. Keep up the great work!

Joyce F.

A Dear Joyce

Whew. Let me catch my breath after reading your note. You know you can send me any question at any time. Thanks for "discovering" the column. I was at a dinner a couple of weeks ago and a very nice lady named Phyllis approached me and said "Hey, you're that newspaper cooking guy!" It's nice to get recognized for well…being nice.

At any rate, on to answering your questions….

1) To keep your Bundt cake from sticking, lightly grease the pan with shortening and then dust with flour. Shake off any excess. That should do the trick.
2) I have included two of my favorite grill suggestions – other than the usual hamburgers and hot dogs – but I do love a good burger on the grill too.
3) As far as vinegar substitutes, there are none that I know of. Maybe some readers out there can help me out if they have heard of any but I have done a little research in my day and I can't find a replacement. Usually, vinegar is added for a "tangy" flavor in a recipe. I would recommend if you are not a big fan of vinegar, just use less of it.

By the way, did you know that raw vinegar is good for you? If you can stomach it (pun intended), when you are a little under the weather, drink some raw apple vinegar mixed with honey. It's a holistic treatment that reportedly helps to restore your body's pH balance.

4)   Finally, to keep your pans from scratching, I would recommend using a common dish cloth, or non abrasive cleaner like those green and yellow scrub cloths. If it's hard to get some of that baked on gunk off the pan, just soak it in warm water with dish detergent for at least an hour. Good pans can be a lifelong investment and you don't want to ruin them. I totally get that.

GRILLED SWORDFISH

My favorite dish for the grill is swordfish. Any novice can prepare burgers and dogs. But to impress, go a little exotic. Swordfish is very good when fixed on the grill and retains it flavor. It is a firm fish and holds up well on the grill. It won't fall apart while cooking.

Marinate one or more nice filets of sword fish overnight in olive oil, lemon juice and black pepper. Grill both sides until fish become white and flaky. Serve with an avocado butter and your guests will melt.

SHRIMP ON THE BILLY

Seafood is a good grill item if you find the right recipe. Shrimp fixed on skewers – shrimp kabobs – is not only easy, it's fun to piece together. You can get your guests involved and it looks pretty good sitting on that grill too.

On long skewers, alternate jumbo shrimp, cherry tomatoes, peppers, pearl onions, and even small potatoes. Place on grill and turn skewers until shrimp turns orange or red. Serve with cocktail sauce.

Q Dear Bill

What is that squiggly white thing attached to the egg yolk? I always pick it off my eggs before I use eggs in food. Is that safe to eat? Do restaurants pull that out?

Lou C.

A Dear Lou C

One, does everyone love Lou C?

That said, that "squiggly white thing" is called the "chalaza" of the egg. It is the membrane that holds the yolk inside of the shell. That's all it is. When you crack or break or egg, you have jarred that membrane loose from the shell. I don't know what the membrane is made of because I'm not a biology teacher but I do not it is not harmful if ingested. Some restaurants where I have worked have removed it. Other have not. I think it is a chef's preference.

Most times, when an egg is separated – for an omelet for instance, that part of the egg will be removed anyway. If an egg is run through a china cap or sieve, it will most likely also be removed.

I know some people prefer to remove it in a recipe that calls for egg and you can simply remove it with a fork if it grosses you out.

CRÈME BRULEE

(Squiggly removed)

Four egg yolks
1 ¼ cup sugar
1 tbsp corn starch
2 cups heavy cream
½ tsp cinnamon

Grated rind of 1 lemon

1 tbsp minced or crushed pistachios

¼ cup water

Blend the egg yolks with ¼ cups of the sugar and the cornstarch in a saucepan over low heat and consistently stirring with a wooden spoon, immediately add the heavy cream, a little at a time.

Flavor the mixture with the cinnamon, lemon rind, and pistachios. Cook over low heat, stirring constantly, for about 10 minutes or until the mixture is smooth, thickened and resembles a custard.

Pour into an eight inch shallow glass serving dish, allow to cool – chill in the refrigerator overnight is recommended.

Meanwhile, put the remaining sugar and water in a saucepan over medium heat, stir until the sugar is dissolved, and then boil until the mixture becomes caramelized.

Pour this mixture immediately and evenly over the surface of the set custard and serve.

Q Dear William

I have trouble when I make cakes with them coming out too dry. Any helpful kitchen tips for making a cake more moist?

Norma C.

A Hi Norma

Sure…let's end this cookbook the way it began. With eggs. Why not? It will bring all of these tips full circle.

To answer your question, add an extra egg. Putting another egg into your cake recipe should not only make your cakes more moist, it will make them fluffier. You can also add another add to a brownie recipe to make them more like cake. Actually, you can add an egg to almost any baking recipe that calls for an egg. I have included a cake recipe for you and already added the extra egg to this so when you follow this recipe you should be all right. Let me know how it turns out, will you? Or save me a slice!

MOIST CHOCOLATE CAKE

With an added egg for Norma

½ cup butter
1 cup sugar
3 eggs
½ cup milk
1 ½ cups flour
¼ tsp salt
2 ½ tsp baking powder
2 squares chocolate, melted
½ tsp vanilla

Cream butter, gradually add half the sugar and chocolate. Separately, beat egg whites until stiff. Add remaining sugar and set aside. Beat yolks until thick and add to butter and sugar mixture. Mix and sift dry ingredients and add alternately with milk. Now, combine all ingredients into a large mixing bowl. Add vanilla. Mix well. Bake in shallow baking pan 350 degrees for 40 minutes

COFFEE COCOA FROSTING

1 cup confectioner's sugar
2 tbsp cocoa
1 tbsp melted butter
1 tsp vanilla
Hot steaming cup of strong coffee

Mix sugar, cocoa and butter. Moisten with hot coffee until of proper icing or frosting consistency. Dip knife in cup of coffee while spreading on cake or cookies.

One for the Road

Because I promised I would include this if I ever published my own cookbook… and to thank him for the introduction, among other things.

SHANE'S PB & J BARS

3 cups flour
1 ½ tsp salt
2 tsp baking powder
2 sticks butter
1 ½ cups sugar
2 eggs
1 tsp vanilla
2 ½ cups peanut butter (Crunchy or Smooth)
1 ½ cups jam (flavor of your choice)

Directions: Mix first three ingredients and set aside. In a separate bowl, combine butter and sugar. Add eggs, one egg at a time. Mix well. Add vanilla and blend ingredients. Add to flour mixture and mix together. Add peanut butter to mixture and blend well. Evenly place 2/3 of the mixture in a greased baking pan. Spread jam of choice evenly on top of mixture with spatula. Break up leftover dough and sprinkle on top. Bake at 350 for 35 minutes or until golden brown. Allow to cool to room temperature for at least one hour but this is also best when refrigerated overnight. Cut into bars.

Author's Note

I sincerely hope you have enjoyed this cookbook – the best of the columns I have written over the last two decades. I look forward to providing you with even more in the years and articles to come! If you'd like to see my future tips in your favorite local publication, reach out and we can talk about it. Find me on social media, look up my Facebook page, and we will chat. Stop by a signing event when I am in your area. I would love to talk about cooking with you. Please let me know if you have any questions or comments – I really would love to hear from you about how some of these recipes turned out in your own kitchen.

Until next time.
Keep on cookin'!

Bill

Lightning Source UK Ltd.
Milton Keynes UK
UKHW011118120121
376872UK00009B/1107/J